Dissensuous Modernism

UNIVERSITY PRESS OF FLORIDA

Florida A&M University, Tallahassee
Florida Atlantic University, Boca Raton
Florida Gulf Coast University, Ft. Myers
Florida International University, Miami
Florida State University, Tallahassee
New College of Florida, Sarasota
University of Central Florida, Orlando
University of Florida, Gainesville
University of North Florida, Jacksonville
University of South Florida, Tampa
University of West Florida, Pensacola

Dissensuous Modernism

Women Writers, the Senses, and Technology

Allyson C. DeMaagd

UNIVERSITY PRESS OF FLORIDA

Gainesville / Tallahassee / Tampa / Boca Raton

Pensacola / Orlando / Miami / Jacksonville / Ft. Myers / Sarasota

Library of Congress Control Number: 2021951063
ISBN 978-0-8130-6916-6 (cloth)

The University Press of Florida is the scholarly publishing agency for the State University System of Florida, comprising Florida A&M University, Florida Atlantic University, Florida Gulf Coast University, Florida International University, Florida State University, New College of Florida, University of Central Florida, University of Florida, University of North Florida, University of South Florida, and University of West Florida.

University Press of Florida
2046 NE Waldo Road
Suite 2100
Gainesville, FL 32609
http://upress.ufl.edu

Contents

Acknowledgments

Writing this book has been a privilege and a pleasure made possible by so many. I would be remiss not to begin by thanking Hilda, Mina, Virginia, and Elizabeth (if I may) for their brilliance and bravery. Your spellbinding sentences continue to mystify and delight me, and your books remain some of my most treasured companions: I hope I did them justice.

This book would not exist without Lara Farina, whose imaginative and inspiring sensory studies class led me to see, touch, and taste the world and words anew. Julia Daniel, a magical unicorn of a being, gave so much to me and this project. Lisa Weihman has been my unrelenting cheerleader and champion. Dennis Allen kept my spirits high with his humor, wit, and wisdom. Pamela L. Caughie's generosity, goodness, and pioneering scholarship helped shape this from a crumb of an idea into a fully baked book. Thank you all for your constancy and compassion: you top my list of all-time favorite humans.

My gracious reviewers' enthusiasm and expertise made working on this project a delight—I wish your kindness on every aspiring author. My stalwart editor, Stephanye Hunter, was warmer and more wonderful than I could have imagined. Thank you for believing in me. Thank you to West Virginia University and the Jackson Family Fellowship for affording me this opportunity.

Thank you to the Ball State University English Department and to the Talbot Mentors/Mid-Shore Scholars organization for your ardent support.

So many friends and colleagues helped me find and use my voice throughout the years. I am grateful to Katherine and Hannah Richards and Rachel Hoag for their collective love, righteous rage, and unwavering encouragement. Thank you for long talks over tea, cathartic family dinners, and hilarious text threads. To my oldest and best friends, Marta Dulaney and Erin VanderHenst, who have a special slice of my heart, thank you for all the love and all the years. To Evan, for his bright, unbreakable spirit. To the strong, inspiring women in my life, who lift, ground, and always surround me: Katy, Kristina, Christina, Linda, Amber, Kaye, Angela, Emily, Jennifer, Kathryn, and Amanda. I am so grateful for your friendship. Special gratitude goes to my cousin, Erin, for belly laughs and fierce love—thank you for having me, Gupsh.

Growing up, my brother, Brad, loved reading and writing, and because he did, I did, too. Thank you, brother, for "letting" me join your detective agency and "borrow" your dinosaur books. You'll always be my hero. When we were children, our parents showed us that books were gifts. I still remember the excitement of visiting the bookstore; the smell of new books remains one of my most beloved scent memories. For taking me to the library, buying me the umpteenth Baby-Sitters Club book, spending nights at Young Authors events, and supporting me in countless other ways, thank you, Mom and Dad. I love you more than you can know. Thank you to my stepfather, Rodney, for his endless support and one-of-a-kind sense of humor—they broke the mold when they made you. Thank you to Chris for her big heart and to the Cliffords for their unconditional love. Thank you to my Aunt Corrine, whose jokes and tenderness carried me here and sustain me still. Because of my family, I dreamed, and still dream, big dreams.

Finally, my thanks go to my team captain, Hatley Clifford, the smartest scholar and most dedicated teacher I know. Your love, patience, and encouragement are in every page of this book. Thank you for picking me up, putting up with me, and standing by my side. I'd do it all again if I could do it with you. To my feline spirit animal, York, a constant companion who telepathically sent me words when I had none left. And to my sister, Ashley, who I carry always in my heart. You were the greatest gift. This and every brave thing I do is for you, Ash.

Abbreviations

BM *Becoming Modern: The Life of Mina Loy*, by Carolyn Burke

BA *Between the Acts*, by Virginia Woolf

CA *The Color of Angels: Cosmology, Gender and the Aesthetic Imagination*, by Constance Classen

CW *Critical Writings*, by F. T. Marinetti

ET *Eva Trout, or Changing Scenes*, by Elizabeth Bowen

H *HERmione*, by H.D.

I *Insel*, by Mina Loy

MTB *Modernism, Technology, and the Body*, by Tim Armstrong

WS *Ways of Sensing: Understanding the Senses in Society*, by David Howes and Constance Classen

Introduction

> The flux of life is pouring its aesthetic aspect into your eyes, your ears—
> and you ignore it because you are looking for your canons of beauty
> in some sort of frame or glass case or tradition. Modernism says: Why
> not each one of us, scholar or bricklayer, pleasurably realize all that is
> impressing itself upon our subconscious, the thousand odds and ends
> which make up your sensery [*sic*] every day life?
>
> Loy, "Gertrude Stein" 437

> War and the slow recovery have been in all fields threatening us with a
> loss of standard: isolation, restrictions, substitutes and make-do's bred
> a resignation, or thankfulness for anything in any form, which could
> affect art badly if we were not pulled clear. Aesthetically our senses
> need resharpening.
>
> Bowen, "Third Programme" 204

In 1924, Mina Loy called for a sensory awakening. In the essay "Gertrude Stein," Loy beckoned fellow modernists to look to oft-ignored sensory impressions as a means of reinvigorating art and redefining notions of beauty.

More than two decades later, in 1947, fellow writer Elizabeth Bowen issued a similar call, but with a stronger sense of urgency. Bowen emphasizes that, in the wake of WW2, art and the senses are more dramatically in need of "resharpening." Despite the years that separate Loy and Bowen, both women exhibit a mutual investment in the senses. They share a concern that their fellow modernists do not value or engage sensory experience to its fullest potential and that the senses are being overlooked as important avenues to artistic creation. Their investment in the senses begs the question, how did these writers respond to their own prompts? How did they take stock, as Loy says, of "the thousand odds and ends which make up [one's] sensery [sic] every day life" ("Gertrude Stein" 437)? What did they, and other modernist women writers, do to make the senses new? *Dissensuous Modernism: Women Writers, the Senses, and Technology* foregrounds these questions as it joins the effort to recover modernist women writers' radical subversion of literary forms and ideas through the senses and technology.

Dissensuous Modernism examines how H.D., Mina Loy, Virginia Woolf, and Elizabeth Bowen respond to and revise traditional conceptualizations of the senses and the role technology plays in that reconceptualization. As Sara Danius observes in *The Senses of Modernism: Technology, Perception, and Aesthetics*, the modernist period was "an age where technological devices increasingly claim sovereignty over and against the sensorium" (23). However, in a paradox common to modernism, technology also inspired individuals to reclaim that sovereignty. This book places modernist women writers at the center of this sensory reclamation. Danius notes that "the relation of gender and technology in literary modernism is a crucial yet strangely undertheorized topic," and *Dissensuous Modernism* attempts to fill this void (11). It examines women's everyday encounters with technology and demonstrates how those encounters affect the way modernist women think and write about the senses. In so doing, *Dissensuous Modernism* shifts the scholarly conversation away from the masculine senses of sight and sound, which have historically been privileged in modernist scholarship, and toward the so-called lesser, feminine senses of smell, taste, and touch. In addition to shifting the critical discourse toward the so-called lower senses, it also expands the conversation to address the subversive potential of sensory integration. By examining the confluence among the senses, technology, and gender, I hope to contribute a synthesis that revises our understanding of modernist women writers' lived experience and illuminates the important role they play in defining the senses.

The women writers featured in this book wage dissent by questioning and complicating what constitutes "common sense." Common sense or "consensus," a term coined by Jacques Rancière, refers to those sensory practices that, over time, become common to and accepted by a given society—those sensory practices that society values, as opposed to those that it marginalizes, ignores, or deems deviant. These values are upheld within "consensual communities," "in which the spiritual *sense* of being-in-common is embedded in the material *sensorium* of everyday experience" (Rancière 81). Through repetition, these everyday experiences become naturalized and normalized. However, when individuals or groups of individuals expose this process of naturalization and question these norms, they engage in "dissensus." Dissensus, according to Rancière, "breaks with the sensory self-evidence of the natural order that destines specific individuals and groups to occupy positions of rule or of being ruled, assigning them to private or public lives, [and] pinning them down to . . . specific 'bodies,' that is to specific ways of being, seeing, and saying" (139).[1] The dissensuous women highlighted herein make it their mission to offer alternatives to these norms: to articulate new ways of being, seeing, and saying.

Sensory Hierarchies, Privilege, and Power

To appreciate how H.D., Loy, Woolf, and Bowen trouble sensory norms, we must first understand those norms and their social implications. According to anthropologist and sensory scholar David Howes, "sensory rankings are always allied with social rankings and employed to order society" ("Scent" 164). Societies develop sensory hierarchies that divide the senses into higher and lower orders and connect those senses with so-called superior and inferior groups of people. These hierarchies associate members of dominant groups with the more valued, higher senses, and they associate marginalized groups—those people deemed inferior due to their gender, sexuality, class, race, religion, or physical ability—with the less valued, lower senses. In Western sensory hierarchies, sight and sound earn praise as high or superior senses because of their supposed association with reason and the mind, whereas smell, taste, and touch earn the label low or inferior because of their supposed association with the body. Such distinctions reify harmful sensory narratives and stereotypes that equate certain bodies with certain sensory capacities. Namely, they perpetuate the belief that white, wealthy men are governed by the higher senses and their minds, and that women, the lower classes, and minorities are enslaved by the lower senses and their bodies. Howes and Constance Classen (a cultural historian who specializes in the senses) remind us that "the sensory typing of social groups was not thought simply to be a matter of associations and markers. . . . People were believed to be *made* for their social roles" (*Ways of Sensing* 68).[2]

Sensory narratives maintain these identarian categories and uphold unequal power structures. One of the most obvious sensory divisions occurs along gendered lines. In *A History of the Senses: From Antiquity to Cyberspace*, Robert Jütte cites Henri Foquet's 1765 article on sensibility as one of the first instances where philosophers and physicians acknowledged significant differences between men's and women's sensory capabilities (137). According to Jütte, men and women have long been positioned as "paired opposites. Where man is a person of reason, woman is a creature of the senses" (139). The telling use of "person" when referring to man and "creature" when referring to woman underscores the sensory othering inherent in sensory hierarchies.[3] These gendered, sensory categories are mutually exclusive and mutually constitutive, so that the lower women descend on the sensory totem pole, the higher men ascend. For example, men's assumed access to the higher senses has long granted them access to opportunities in the public sphere. Scientists believed that the hard, male body was evidence of a firm "masculine mind," which, in turn, was thought to "resemble the eye and the ear" (Jütte 140). Because of their perceived powers of vision, hearing, and subsequent intellectual prowess, men ventured into the world with confidence and social support. Accepted logic maintained that men's (assumed) ability to see and hear clearly made them more suited for mental work and "made intellectual endeavors such as the arts and sciences the prerogative of men" (*CA* 66).

Sight, in particular, has long been theorized as an activity of the brain not the body and, as such, has been labeled a masculine sense. Descartes went so far as to assert that it is "the mind that sees, not the eye" (qtd. in

Conor 21). Because men were considered the more logical and reasonable of the sexes, they were, therefore, better equipped to see. In contrast, popular thinking maintained that women were governed by their bodies, which interfered with their ability to see clearly. This dichotomy is prevalent in narratives about the Enlightenment, an age known for its "ocular obsession," when scientific discovery was "heralded as a triumph of clear-sighted masculine vision over the murky 'feminine brew' of superstitions and myths that had previously dominated Western thought" (Classen, "The Witch's Senses" 361). Because masculine vision is associated with discernment and good judgment, men have, historically, been labeled visionaries and decision-makers. They determine who and what are worth seeing and who and what are not.

Men's association with sight gave (and continues to give) them power over women and women's bodies. A figure of masculine vision common to the modernist period is the flâneur. For the flâneur, seeing is an exercise of ownership: the flâneur is a man about town whose mobility and privilege grant him unmitigated access to public spaces. While he strolls, he surveys those spaces, and the people who inhabit them, as one would property. Women are especially susceptible to the proprietary gaze of the flâneur, which posits women as objects for male consumption. In *The Spectacular Modern Woman: Feminine Visibility in the 1920s*, Liz Conor suggests that gendered thinking about vision, "excluded [women] from the privileged standing of spectator" and reinforced the belief that "men look and women appear" (18). Women did "appear" more frequently in public spaces during the modernist period—a result of women's suffrage, the proliferation of optic technologies like film and photography, and visual marketing campaigns that commodified women's bodies. According to Conor, these "altered conditions of feminine visibility . . . compounded the traditional status of Western women as objects" (L. Conor 18).[4] Though women often used these "altered visual conditions" to their advantage, such conditions continued to disproportionately benefit men.

Men enacted further sensuous control over women through "disciplinary surveillance" (Conor 18) and narratives that dictated how and where women used their bodies and senses. Such narratives associated women with the lower senses and discouraged them from exercising the higher senses. Women "were expected to eschew mental labour for 'body work'"—

work to which their bodies, senses, and minds (or lack thereof) were better suited (*WS* 68). Popular thought promoted (and continues to promote) the idea that women were designed for domestic work—indeed, that their very organic makeup demanded it—because their bodies and senses were uniquely equipped for such activities. In the late eighteenth century, the French gastronomer Jean Anthelme Brillat-Savarin commented that women better enjoyed "the pleasures of the table . . . [because] gourmandism . . . agrees with the delicacy of their organs" (qtd. in Jütte 140). Similar logic viewed women's bodies as "half-baked" and "doughy" and suggested that women enjoyed baking because of their bodily affinity with baked goods (Classen, *The Color of Angels*).[5] Sensory narratives also suggested that women possessed a keener sense of smell, taste, and touch, which made them perfect candidates for the kitchen. Lower-class women, in particular, were assumed to be natural cooks and caretakers, whereas upper-class women often performed "a refined version of . . . 'women's work,' embroidering, arranging flowers and 'tastefully' adorning themselves and their homes" (*WS* 68).

Regardless of class, common belief maintained that women's bodies were so sensitive and their minds so dull—their lower senses so overripe and their higher senses so unrefined—that they were subject to a sort of sensory "tyranny" from which they needed sheltering (Jütte 138). Jütte notes that because patriarchal societies doubted women's ability to see and hear clearly, they also doubted their ability to reason and make sense of the world. As such, they considered women to be ill-equipped for converting sensory experiences into higher knowledge and, as a result, to be destined to suffer from constant sensory bombardment. Such sensory narratives, in casting women as overly sensuous, vulnerable, and defenseless, justified assigning women to the private sphere and limiting their social access.

Gender was, and continues to be, only one means of establishing sensory hierarchies. Race is another indicator of sensory privilege and oppression. In the nineteenth century, the historian Lorenz Oken went so far as to "imagin[e] a sensory hierarchy of racial types, with the European 'eye-man' at the top, followed by the Asian 'ear-man,' the Native American 'nose-man,' the Melanesian 'tongue-man,' and the African 'skin-man'" (*CA* 67). According to Howes, "workers, 'primitives,' and 'idiots,'" as well as religious and sexual minorities, have also historically been associated with the lower senses ("Charting" 120). Smell, in particular, has long been one of the strongest indicators of social inferiority and was often featured in divisive sensory rhetoric. The twentieth-century writer George Orwell proposed that "the real secret of class distinction in the West . . . [can be] summed up in four frightful words which people nowadays are chary of uttering, but which were bandied about quite freely in my childhood. The words were: *The lower classes smell*" (127). Such distinctions perpetuated the belief that "[e]ven 'lower-class' people who you knew to be quite clean—servants, for instance—were faintly unappetizing. The smell of their sweat, the very texture of their skins, were mysteriously different from yours" (Orwell 128).[6]

In each of the above instances, the dominant social group uses the senses to dictate norms and establish dichotomies. Consensual communities maintain these dichotomies and perpetuate the belief that there are desirable and undesirable ways of sensing and being sensed. While, in some instances, sensory perversion can be "corrected" or overcome, typically, a person's sensory status was understood as biologically unchangeable. According to Classen, "This biopolitics of the senses—conferring social values on sensory (or pseudo-sensory) traits for political ends—emphasized the futility of rebelling against one's lot in life" (*WS* 68). Ultimately, sensory categories function to keep people in their so-called proper places, and those who stray from these sensory identifications, or who misuse their sensory faculties, threaten the larger social order.

Modernist Sensescapes

The threat to the socio-sensory order was particularly prevalent in the modernist period, when bodies refused to stay in place. The twentieth century was a period of social mobility and fluctuating identity categories. Women's suffrage, the Great Migration, and increased immigration transformed the social landscape. Such flux incited a sort of frenzy, what Michael Trask calls a "crisis of modernity" (35). This crisis was brought on by "the terminal evasiveness of status fixity—as notable in the tendency of the affluent to lose caste as in the ability of the lowborn to pass for affluent" (Trask 35). Here, "lowborn" designates not only the working class but also other so-called slippery individuals, including immigrants, women, and "sexual subjects whose desires were likewise unsettled and roaming, divorced from conventions"

(Trask 35). While the conventions of which Trask speaks are not sensory, the marginalized groups to which Trask refers—in their "restless craving and instability, [their] endless striving and motion"—also disrupt easy sensory categorization (2).

However, as sensory historian Mark M. Smith asserts, the senses are not as easily or naturally categorizable as dominant sensory narratives suggest. Though traditional, twentieth-century sensory hierarchies maintain that there are five, separate senses, Smith suggests that the senses are not isolated but intersensorial (12). Intersensoriality "allows us to think in terms of how the senses are combined in a given society, how they work together" (M. Smith 12). Sensory experience is seldom isolated to a single sense but is, instead, relational and multiple—sound is often accompanied by touch, for instance, just as taste is often accompanied by smell. Eating is one example of the intersensory in that when we consume food, we not only taste it but also see its colors, smell its aromas, and hear and feel its various textures as we chew. Smith points out that the intersensory is a fairly recent phenomenon, which, as of 2007, historians were only just beginning to take seriously (12). As *Dissensuous Modernism* will illustrate, the impulse to dismiss the intersensory significantly impacts modern bodies.

Instead of embracing the muddled, often messy, intersensorial body, dominant sensory narratives subscribe to a phenomenon known as sensory segmentation. Sensory segmentation conceives of the senses, and the people who use them, as separate and divisible. In *Eyesight Alone: Clement Greenberg's Modernism and the Bureaucratization of the Senses*, Caroline A. Jones examines how, by segmenting the body and its senses, the powers that be managed populations and directed ever-moving modern bodies. "Segmentation," Jones asserts, "was key to being 'modern'" (390). She goes on to explain that, during the modernist period, "the body's place as undifferentiated corpus was nowhere. The body's limbs, portals, products, and pathways, as separated functions and administrative units, were everywhere" (Jones 391). The era Jones describes is one that increasingly monitors, marketizes, and regulates the sensuous body. Consumerist culture promoted the newest technologies, fitness programs, and dietary regiments, with the goal of perfecting and, in some extremes, purifying the body and its senses.

In an effort to keep the body and its senses separate, dominant sensory narratives deny not only the intersensory but also the synesthetic. The term "synesthesia" derives from the Greek συναίσθησις, meaning joint perception ("synaesthesis"). The *Oxford English Dictionary* defines it as "a sensation in one part of the body produced by a stimulus applied to another part" ("synaesthesia"). Synesthesia can be biological (as when letters of the alphabet or musical notes appear as colors) or cultural (as when artists feature synesthesia or cross-modal sensory experience in their work). Historically, synesthesia has been viewed as a neurological phenomenon and labeled either a "pathology or a gift" (*WS* 153).[7] In the centuries leading up to the modernist period, scientists and psychologists leaned toward the former. They viewed synesthesia as evidence of a disturbed mind that forged irrational associations among the senses. In the eighteenth century, there was a general feeling that "the senses have been *confused* and mingled; what is needed is further purification and segmentation: the nose alone should smell, the eyes should only look, and taste should be reserved for the tongue" (Jones 395). At the end of the nineteenth century, the German physician Max Nordau echoed these claims. Nordau was a key figure in the vilification of synesthesia in the arts. He asserted that the intentional use of synesthesia by the Symbolists and other fin de siècle writers was a sign of "degeneracy," which he describes in his monograph of the same name. Such sensuous degeneracy could be found in all corners of the art world, and, in the following, Nordau describes one such moment in Symbolist theater:

> A hose is set up in the theatre, by which the spectators are sprayed with perfumes. On the stage a poem in approximately dramatic form is recited. In every division, act, scene, or however the thing is called, a different vowel-sound is made to preponderate; during each the theater is illuminated with a differently tinted light, the orchestra discourses music in a different key, and the jet gives out a different perfume. (14–15)

For Nordau, synesthetic productions like these were a danger to the art world, and the negative impact of artists who experimented with synesthesia could not be overstated. Of such artists, Nordau cautioned, "They corrupt and delude; they do, alas! frequently exercise a deep influence, but this is always a baneful one. . . . They, likewise, are leading men along the paths they themselves have found to new goals; but these goals are abysses or waste places" (24). While Nordau feared the corruptive and corrosive powers of synesthetic art, he also believed that, as the twentieth century progressed, so, too, would the human race, and synesthesia would become a thing of the past. "Degenerates must succumb," he proclaimed (541).

Histories of the senses suggest that synesthesia, and those "degenerates" who practiced it, did succumb. According to Howes and Classen, modern societies viewed synesthesia as "the product of soft, fuzzy thinking in an age that demanded clear minds and cold, hard fact" (*WS* 173). By the end of WW1, Classen explains, "the theory of a unity of the senses had lost much of its artistic and public favor" and "the ideal of a sensory interplay, if not entirely forgotten, was nonetheless deemed to be out of date" (*CA* 112).[8] When artists did experiment with sensory interplay, especially when that experimentation privileged the lower senses, they found their work maligned and marginalized or "shorn of their unusual sensory dimensions" (*WS* 28).[9] Because of a general consensus that synesthesia and intersensoriality were outmoded and unconventional, Classen suggests that "[t]he multisensory aesthetics of the late nineteenth century, consequently, provide us with a compelling last glimpse at a shared vision of a world in which 'sounds, fragrance, and colours correspond'" (*CA* 113).

Dissensuous Modernism suggests differently. I identify a shared vision among modernist women writers, one that spans several decades of the twentieth century. I work from a culturally inflected definition of synesthesia to examine how it "function[s] as a fundamental vehicle for the production of cultural meaning" (*WS* 11). Twentieth-century efforts at sensory segmentation and purification encouraged some modernists, like those women writers *Dissensuous Modernism* foregrounds, to undertake sensory unification projects. In his study of modernist sensation, Steven Connor submits that "[t]he very separation of the senses into different channels encouraged efforts to put them back together or amalgamate them in new and unexpected ways. From the mid-nineteenth century onwards, there was a growing cult of synaesthesia" (Connor, "Literature" 187). He goes on to say that sensory unification projects "were validated by a romantic view that the senses were by nature a fluid continuum that was violently and illegitimately broken apart by social forces" (Connor, "Literature" 187). Though Connor acknowledges the presence of synesthesia in modernist art, his use of "cult" implies that synesthetic writing was limited to a relatively small, perhaps misguided group of individuals who bought into a "romantic" or naive view of sensory perception. His comments provide insight into why synesthesia, as a literary phenomenon, has not been widely explored among modernist scholars.

First, scholars are sometimes unwilling to divorce cultural synesthesia from biological synesthesia, and, second, sensory narratives often code synesthesia as feminine. In 1938, psychologist and self-proclaimed Nazi E. R. Jaensch identified synesthetes as the "Gegentypus or Anti-Type" who is prone to "a kind of perceptual slovenliness, [where] the qualities of one sense [are] carelessly mixed with those of another" (38). The Anti-Type, Jaensch implies, is womanly—"characterized by ambiguous and indefinite judgments and lacking in perseverance" (38). Her antithesis was "the tough, masculine, firm . . . man you could rely on" (38).[10] Disparaging rhetoric about synesthesia and women align: both were considered soft, messy, imbalanced, and irrational. However, like those modernist women writers to which this project turns, synesthesia also surpasses boundaries and refuses limitations. *Dissensuous Modernism* centers these qualities of synesthetic and intersensory writing to recover women's sensory experimentation.

Modernist writers played a central role in rethinking sensory paradigms and reimagining the senses. In *Modernism: A Cultural History*, Tim Armstrong acknowledges the work of H.D. and Virginia Woolf as evidence that "a heightened sensitivity to sensation is central to modern experience" (90). Likewise, Ralf Hertel, who studies literary depictions of the senses, notes, "In the modern period, with its technical extensions of the senses and its overflow of stimuli, perception itself becomes the focus of literary investigation" (176). Such literary investigations have, in turn, become the subject of modernist scholarship, much of which fruitfully attends to literary depictions of the senses. However, modernist scholarship also reflects traditional sensory hierarchies by privileging sight and sound. Monographs like Karen Jacobs's *The Eye's Mind: Literary Modernism and Visual Culture* and Sam Halliday's *Sonic Modernity: Representing Sound in Literature, Culture, and the Arts* valuably examine modernist sight and soundscapes by focusing on the eye and the ear. This is not to say that such studies proclaim the superiority of sight or sound. For instance, among those works devoted to sight, Martin Jay's *Downcast Eyes: The Denigration of Vision in Twentieth-Century French Thought* challenges the supposed hegemony of vision that was once synonymous with the modernist period. He offers a more nuanced view of the relationship between modernism and sight, identifying "a palpable loss of confidence in the eye" during and following WW1 (212), as well as later attempts at "visionary redemption" (236). While modernist scholarship about the higher senses continues to be valuable, recent scholarship that turns to the less-studied, lower senses helps to more fully shape our understanding of modern sensory experience. Abbie Garrington's *Haptic Modernism: Touch and the Tactile in Modernist Writing* is a noteworthy example of this lower-sensory turn. In *Haptic Modernism*, Garrington examines the way "modernist texts—literary, scientific, philosophical and journalistic—return with unprecedented alacrity to the haptic experiences of the human body" (50). Touch, Garrington claims, is central to the modernist experience and integral to how modernist subjects came to know themselves and their worlds. In reclaiming touch's centrality, Garrington refashions what Aristotle called the "base sense" as a foundational sensory modality, "a scaffold on which the other senses are built" (18). "To study touch," Garrington proclaims, "is to study the whole body in its carnal, fleshly reality" (19).

It is to this "whole body" experience that my project turns. *Dissensuous Modernism* continues the ongoing recovery of the lower senses in modernist literature, but it does so in the broader context of the larger sensorium. Although modernist scholarship has not ignored the roles of the senses entirely, it has, at times, overlooked their holistic representation. Because of this, most current studies on the senses have been single-sense projects. My project removes the senses from the limited framework of the single-sense study, places them in the context of the broader sensorium, and underscores their connectivity in order to more fully articulate their role in modernism. I consider the senses within the larger sensorium—with its intersensory relationships and synesthetic connections—in order to more fully account for the complex ways that senses shape society. Unlike previous studies that focus on one or two senses, *Dissensuous Modernism* transcends the single-sense paradigm to address the subversive potential of sensory integration. I attend to this intersensory experience by demonstrating how H.D., Mina Loy, Virginia Woolf, and Elizabeth Bowen's willingness to integrate the senses inspires them to breach other sensory borders, namely, those borders societies erect between men and women, nature and technology, queer and heterosexual, abled and disabled, and human and nonhuman.

Modernism, Technology, and the Senses

The borders H.D., Loy, Woolf, and Bowen cross inspired me to breach scholarly borders and extend modernist time past its usual stopping place. For my purposes, the modernist period ranges from the high modernism of the 1920s to a late modernism of the 1960s. I see in Bowen's 1967 novel, *Eva Trout, or Changing Scenes*, a distinctly modernist preoccupation with technology and a continuation of the dissensuous work started by her peers. In so doing, I follow Emily Bloom, who asserts that *Eva Trout* is best "understood as a late modernist novel" in its "striving for presence through the extensive use of hypermediation" (126). The particular technologies that mediate the lives of Bowen's characters, and Bowen herself, reflect the cultural moment of the 1960s, and the same can be said of each writer in this book, who encountered different emerging or predominating technologies in her lifetime, as well as changing societal attitudes toward technology. I discuss these changes and the specific technologies that informed each writer's work in a later section of the introduction. In this section, I examine the various ways technology shaped, and was shaped by, sensory experience.

As new technologies emerged in the modernist period—or as existing technologies became more mainstream and accessible—humans began to reconsider the bounds of their senses. Technologies like the telephone, X-ray, and hearing aid extended the range of the eye and ear.[11] With the help of technologies like these, humans could see and hear farther than before, which was an exciting prospect. However, at the same time technology expanded sensory capacities, it also underscored the limits of the naked human sensorium. As Tim Armstrong observes in *Modernism, Technology, and the Body*, "modernity brings both a fragmentation and augmentation of the body in relation to technology; it offers the body as lack, at the same time as it offers technological compensation" (3). Modern subjects began to realize that without the aid of technology, they could sense only so far and so deeply. For instance, human vision paled in comparison to microscopic vision, which could reveal sights otherwise invisible to the naked human eye. Likewise, camera vision could freeze sight, thereby capturing myriad visual details that the everyday human eye might overlook.

Such technologies challenged the superiority and reliability of the senses and the sensing body, inciting what Sara Danius calls a "technologically mediated crisis of the senses" (1). While this crisis was debilitating for some modern subjects, many responded as they did to other crises of the time: they sought to channel its disruptive energy for productive ends. Scientists, sociologists, artists, and writers used this moment of technological disturbance to experiment with the senses. The following paragraphs outline how modern subjects come to redefine the senses through technologies that both outline sensory limits and illuminate sensory possibility.

Understanding the senses in a new, technological context often meant confronting how little power people had over their senses. This was especially true in urban spaces, where city-goers felt unable to regulate their exposure to technology's sensuous impressions—the choking smell of automobile exhaust, the visual assault of electric streetlights, and the hum of the radio. Such impressions became more invasive and more difficult to pinpoint as technologies became more sophisticated. With each passing decade, advances in radio, electronic, atomic, and nuclear innovation meant that modern subjects were increasingly surrounded by technology's invisible energies. The impact of these energies on the human psyche, body, and senses was troubling. In his 1924 manifesto, *Broadcast Over Britain*, the director general of the BBC addressed "fears and concerns about what the medium of radio—with its invisible, speed-of-light electromagnetic pulses traveling through bodies and buildings—might be doing to humans" (Guida 306).

In other instances, technology's influence on the senses was more visible (or as the following example illustrates, more audible) but no less concerning. In *The Soundscape of Modernity: Architectural Acoustics and the Culture of Listening in America 1900–1933*, Emily Thompson examines how twentieth-century cities became saturated with technological sounds. In the following excerpt from a 1925 article in the *Saturday Review of Literature* titled "Noise," a New Yorker explains how inescapable such sounds were: "The air belongs to the steady burr of the motor, to the regular clank clank of the elevated, to the chitter of the steel drill. Underneath is the rhythmic roll over clattering ties of the subway; above the drone of the airplane . . ." (qtd. in Thompson 117). Thompson points out that 30 years before this, New Yorkers primarily complained of "traditional sounds: horse-drawn vehicles, peddlers, musicians, animals, and bells" and that the onslaught of technological sounds is a distinctly twentieth-century phenomenon (117).[12] This technological onslaught not only changes modern subjects' relationship with sound but also shapes their understanding of the senses more broadly.

Modern people did not always occupy a passive role in their relationships with technology, however. While technologies sometimes produced sounds, sights, and smells that were overwhelming and intrusive, they also evoked new sensations and inspired sensory exploration. When F. T. Marinetti asserted in 1923 that there are "senses not yet defined" (*CW* 379), he appealed to a modern imagination continually transformed by technological encounters. Flying was one such encounter and a source of sensuous inspiration for Marinetti. He argued, "The sense of orientation when airborne was beginning to emerge with the development of aviation. There are airmen who are able to pinpoint their whereabouts without a compass, and even in the thickest of fogs" (*CW* 379). Airplanes uncovered not only new senses, like the sense of direction Marinetti describes, but also new sensory combinations, such as those he scrupulously outlines in *The Futurist Cookbook.* At the "First Futurist Aerobanquet" in 1931, the layout was designed to resemble an airplane's cabin, replete with motorcycle cylinders emulating the sound of airplane engines (*The Futurist Cookbook* 95). The sensory-rich environment and experimental menu—featuring dishes like "The Roar of Ascent" and "Sculpted Meat with Veal Fuselage" (*The Futurist Cookbook* 96)—reflect the influence of this particular technology on the sensuous act of eating.

Just as technology gave rise to new sensations and sensory combinations, so, too, did it prompt new ways of thinking about everyday sensations. The telephone, for instance, changed not only the way people communicated but also how they listened and conceived of listening. Danius notes that when the narrator of Proust's *Remembrance of Things Past* first encounters the telephone, he realizes how much seeing has impacted (and perhaps diluted) his sense of hearing. When he speaks to his grandmother over the phone without the ability to see her, he feels as if he was hearing "her voice itself . . . for the first time" (qtd. in Danius 12). In this moment, the telephone renders hearing anew. Pamela L. Caughie aptly explains technology's role in reimagining sensation, observing that "human perception . . . is organized differently by new media so that how we see and hear, even what we see and hear, changes" (introduction xxi). By troubling previous understandings of the senses and drawing attention to the interconnectedness of sensation, technology invites new definitions of what it means to see, hear, smell, taste, and touch.

Modern technologies not only helped redefine the senses but also helped shape sensory communities. Acoustic technologies often played an important role in this process. In *Modernist Soundscapes: Auditory Technology and the Novel*, Angela Frattarola observes that many modernist literary characters, like their creators, "strive to create intimacy, connectivity, and community through music, voice, and shared listening experiences" (6). Such experiences include "tuning into radio stations, making and buying phonograph recordings, talking over distance through telephones, and hearing sound become synchronized with film" (Frattarola 6). Shared listening experiences were especially important during times of crisis, as when the BBC designed programming to build and maintain morale during WW2. One particular program featured the ornithologist Ludwig Koch, a Jew who fled Germany for London in 1936. Koch's wildlife "sound pictures" unified British citizens who "reaffirm[ed] their social and national identities" through communal listening (Guida 298; 302).[13] In addition to uniting listening communities, radio programming also expanded those communities. Around the same time the BBC aired Koch's birdsongs, it also began multicultural programming, featuring theretofore largely unheard voices of writers from former British colonies. Among them was the Jamaican poet Una Marson, who later began the popular broadcast *Caribbean Voices* (Bloom 178–79). Programs like these helped listeners envision a more diverse community. Though acoustic technologies did not always promote inclusivity—a point I discuss later in the introduction—the above examples illustrate how definitions of self and community were entangled with the senses and technology.

In thinking through the various ways technology mediates sensation, it is important to note that much of the above discussion focuses on vision and hearing. One reason for this is that technologies often readily correspond to a particular sense organ and are labeled as such: optic technologies appeal to the eye; acoustic technologies appeal to the ear. However, even if a technology is not explicitly designed to engage multiple senses—even though the telephone is primarily designed to amplify hearing, for instance—the larger sensorium still figures in one's experience of that technology. We see this in the above example of the New York City sensescape, where technologies of speed like the automobile, subway, and airplane leave a large acoustic footprint. It is to these less obvious, often overlooked relationships between technology and the larger sensorium that this book turns.

Many important studies examine how technology influences modernist writers and writing about the senses. Some scholars view this question through the lens of a specific technology or group of technologies. Angela Frattarola engages with a range of acoustic technologies—from telephones to headphones—in *Modernist Soundscapes: Auditory Technology and the Novel. Broadcasting Modernism*, edited by Debra Rae Cohen, Michael Coyle, and Jane Lewty, locates the radio at the center of modernist thinking and writing. Other works, such as Pamela L. Caughie's edited collection, *Virginia Woolf in the Age of Mechanical Reproduction*, explore technology's impact on specific writers. Still other scholars, like Sara Danius, examine technology's impact on specific senses. Importantly, though Danius focuses on the eye and ear, she acknowledges that modernist literature "may appeal to all the senses," remarking that "[i]n the age of sensory dissociation and reification, such a synaesthetic ideal is no coincidence" (4).

Dissensuous Modernism's approach to the senses and technology takes this synesthetic ideal as its premise. This study illustrates how H.D., Loy, Woolf, and Bowen challenge the assumption that "[t]he spread of new technologies in sensory transmission and reproduction, such as the telephone, the phonograph, the radio and the movie camera, called attention to the divisibility of sensory reality, not to its unity" (*CA* 112). The writers *Dissensuous Modernism* examines take issue with the idea that technologies were often associated with a single sense—that the telephone and gramophone favored the ear, for instance, just as the fluoroscope and X-ray favored the eye. While this book details how single-sense ideology persists, it also questions how technology impacts the lower senses and interactions among the senses. How, for instance, does the microscope invite questions about the power dynamics of seeing? And how do those questions prompt modernist women writers, in particular, to mingle sight with other sensations or to illuminate the sensory experiences of other species? How might a visual technology, like the X-ray, impart a gendered sense of touch? How do acoustic technologies, like the gramophone, welcome not only new sounds but also new sensory combinations, both technological and naturally occurring?

Modernist Women Writers, Technology, and the Senses

Though many male modernists asked and sought to answer these questions, my choice to focus on women writers is purposeful. Technology aided women in their fight for civil rights, but it also hindered them. Throughout the modernist period, men continued to control technology and narratives about technology, often to women's detriment. Patriarchal narratives attempted to prevent women from gaining power through technology while also limiting women's sensory experiences. In the case of artists and writers, such narratives also attempted to curb sensuous experimentation. However, as this book aims to show, women persisted. The women this book foregrounds write against male-centric modernist narratives. Their perspectives are vital to a fuller understanding of what technology and the senses mean in modernism. In the following paragraphs, I examine how the gendering of technology during the modernist period inspires women's dissensuous writing.

While technological changes arguably impacted all modern subjects, they were especially meaningful for women, whose newfound freedoms emerged alongside, and in part because of, popular modern technologies. Suffragists used many of these technologies to their advantage. Within homes, the popularization of technologies like the electric washing machine helped to unburden middle-class women, freeing them to lend their bodies, minds, and voices to the women's movement. The National American Woman Suffrage Association utilized film technology to advocate for the cause in *Votes for Women* (1911) and *Your Girl and Mine* (1914) (Finnegan 101–2). In suffragette novels, characters use "the telephone, typewriter, telegraph, newspaper 'wire' service, and linotype" to spread democracy and diversify public discourse (Chapman 25). Through acoustic technologies like the megaphone and (less modern) hurdy-gurdy, suffragists "create[d] 'sound out of place' in the modern cityscape" (Chapman 40–41). Women's hypervisibility and commitment to "making noise"—through "'loud fonts,' hectoring editorial personae, acoustically noisy barrel organs, and barking suffrage 'newsies'" (Chapman 23)—drastically altered the public sensescape. Women's personal sensescapes also expanded during this period. As they entered cities and other public spaces men had long inhabited, women were confronted with new technologies and the unfamiliar sights, sounds, and smells they produced. In this way, women's liberation was entwined with the discovery not only of new spaces but also of new sensory experiences.

However, despite technology's role in women's political and sensuous liberation, women's relationships with technology continued to be shaped and stifled by patriarchal societies seeking to limit women's power and influence. Manufacturers and advertising companies often used women to promote and sell their products while reinforcing sexist stereotypes about women and technology. The airplane, for instance, gained popularity during the 1920s and 1930s due, in part, to female pilots. Because much of the public was fearful of flying, the aviation industry began enlisting female pilots, hoping to prove that flying was safe. Earlier rhetoric suggested that the skyways were the purview of elite "birdmen": to fly a plane, one needed "an extraordinary combination of active energy, courage, decision of purpose, a quick eye, clearness of judgment, the utmost presence of mind, and great physical dexterity" (qtd. in Corn 558). Such a description excluded women, who were seen as anything but mentally and physically strong. Even when women began flying, stereotypes persisted. The new narrative argued that piloting a plane was so foolproof, as one male pilot asserted, that even unskilled women with no "air sense" could manage it (qtd. in Corn 560).

The 1920s also saw the mass marketing and domestication of the radio. Domesticating radio, Richard Butsch explains, required "softening" what had theretofore been seen as a masculine technology that only garnered the interest of boys and men (562). In America, publications like *Wireless Age* and *Radio News* previously catered to a male audience who were interested in radio mechanics, as opposed to radio programming. However, in the early 1920s, the same publications began running advertisements that depicted radio as domestic and familial, a technology that women could bring into the home for their family's sake. In such advertisements, the mechanical components of radio were "tamed" (Butsch 562)—the wires, cords, and batteries were neatly tucked away so as not to seem invasive or intimidating. Despite the notion that radio needed domesticating to interest women, other publications noted that women were not just radio listeners but also radio hobbyists. The 1922 column "Radio and the Woman" printed stories about women purchasing, building, and repairing radios and often exceeding men in their mechanical abilities. Such acknowledgments were short-lived, however, and by the mid-1920s, stories of women as capable radio mechanics were replaced by advertisements of women in bathing suits, passively listening to the radio while lounging on the beach (Butsch 567).

Behind sexualized images of women are optic technologies, which significantly contributed to the objectification of women throughout the modernist period. During this time, vision and visual technologies continued to be primarily associated with and controlled by men. Take, for instance, the X-ray, which deepened the power imbalance between male physicians and female patients. While men, too, were subject to the penetrative gaze of the X-ray, it doubly impacted women, who were also subject to the male gaze of their doctors. Abbie Garrington casts the X-ray in sexualized terms, saying that it "was culturally received as an extreme form of striptease" (96). Like the male gaze, the X-ray held "promise of access to previously impenetrable layers" (Garrington 96) and further underscored the vulnerability of women's bodies. Women were also subject to dehumanizing optic technologies in other male-dominated fields. In the sciences, the microscope perpetuated a detached and dehumanizing gaze; in Surrealist art, the camera enabled the voyeuristic and violent dismemberment of women's bodies.[14] Because women were subject to harmful visual technologies, they had a vested interest in exposing and correcting that harm. Frattarola identifies "a story of modernism in which writers revel in the destabilization of vision . . . [and] perhaps even aid in compromising the dominance of the eye" (23). I suggest that this destabilization was especially important and empowering for women. Troubling sight and sound and turning to the lower senses, as the writers in this book do, allowed women to reclaim power over their bodies and rewrite limiting narratives.

This is not to say that male modernists do not contribute to re-thinking the body, the senses, or technology; but it is to say that they often lack perspective when it comes to women and women's issues. Bonnie Kime Scott notes that, for the "men of 1914," technology often figures as a masculine corrective to nature, which was coded as sensuous and feminine.[15] James Joyce appears more willing to revel in these so-called feminine realms, but his treatment of women is still problematic. *Ulysses*, for instance, has been praised for its embodied prose and attention to the lower senses but also criticized for perpetuating sensory stereotypes about, and technological violence against, women.[16] Maud Ellmann argues, "Women are restricted to the sidelines of male discourse in *Ulysses*, where they figure as objects of exchange—like the soiled photographs in 'Eumaeus'—rather than participants" ("Endings" 104).[17] The camera—one of the most popular technologies of the early twentieth century—aids in this objectification, and Ellmann describes Bloom's sharing of Molly's photographs as almost equivalent to "pimping his wife" ("Endings" 101). Writing from a male-centered position of privilege, Joyce may not have found his treatment of women problematic, but his inability to decenter himself was not lost on his female colleagues. Woolf points out Joyce's limitations, comparing *Ulysses* to "being in a bright yet narrow room, confined and shut in, rather than enlarged and set free" (*The Common Reader* 156). She goes on to wonder if Joyce's mind and method are to blame for the novel's limitations, for leaving readers "centered in a self which, in spite of its tremor of susceptibility, never embraces or creates what is outside of itself and beyond?" (Woolf, *The Common Reader* 156). "Did not," Woolf asks, "the reading of *Ulysses* suggest how much of life is excluded or ignored?" (Woolf, *The Common Reader* 156).

H.D., Loy, Woolf, and Bowen understood what it meant to be "excluded and ignored." They each were marginalized not only because of their gender but also because of their sexuality, nationality, or ethnicity. H.D. and Woolf were queer, and Bowen was queer and Anglo-Irish. Loy was Anglo-Jewish and, although heterosexual, was often censured for speaking openly about sexuality. As such, they have personal and political stakes in centering women and other marginalized groups in their writing. Their novels reflect women's firsthand experience of technological and sensory subjugation and seek to dismantle the systems that diminish those experiences. This dismantling occurs, largely, through form.

Many, if not all, of the novels in this book are lesser known works, in large part because of their experimental and difficult prose. The formal innovation of each writer reflects and heightens their sensuous innovation. For instance, in *HERmione*, H.D.'s protagonist embraces an expansive sensorium and, in so doing, develops a more expansive consciousness. This is mirrored in H.D.'s stream of consciousness prose: her words overflow syntactic borders, just as Hermione's senses breach social boundaries. *Insel* is equally, though differently, radical in form. In *Insel*, Loy works to revalue multisensuous experience by combining the senses. In the same way that she unexpectedly mixes the senses, so, too, does her prose contain unexpected formal mixtures. Loy often moves from flowery to technical to prosaic language, all within the course of a single sentence. As such, her prose, like the sensuous female body she elevates, refuses stasis and easy categorization.

In *Between the Acts*, Woolf's formal innovation is somewhat easier to categorize because she draws on recognizable genres. However, her blending of generic forms—namely, those found in plays, poetry, and novels—disrupts readerly expectations. Through this generic amalgam, Woolf also disrupts sensuous expectations and discourages habitual sensory responses. While *Between the Acts* purposely disorients in order to undiscipline the senses, *Eva Trout* reflects a society that is disoriented to the point of detachment. Overwhelmed by visual and aural technologies, the characters in Bowen's novel are distanced from the lower senses, as is Bowen's prose. The lush, embodied writing of H.D., Loy, and Woolf is notably absent from *Eva Trout*. Likewise, *Eva Trout*'s form is frenetic and floundering, symbolic of a society unsuccessfully seeking sensuous fulfillment.

Because they are so formally difficult, readers are encouraged, if not forced, to read these novels differently. There are times when the cognitive meaning of a sentence, littered with adjectives and absent of punctuation, may escape us, or when a character or plot point does not make sense in traditional ways. In these moments, readers must grasp the material in new ways, through our bodies and senses. We taste words alongside H.D. and look through the Surrealist eyes of Mina Loy; we feel the cadence of Virginia Woolf's rhythmic sentences and smell the streets of *Eva Trout*'s overwhelming cityscapes. Through form as much as content, the novels I profile offer meaningful sensory experiences, not only for their characters but also for their readers.

I move through H.D., Loy, Woolf, and Bowen's novels chronologically to illustrate how they challenge biases about women, the senses, and technology across decades. I also link them thematically. The first two novels, by H.D. and Loy, are autobiographical and more overtly feminist than the others. Controlling men feature in both these texts, which take up issues of women's exclusion in the fields of art and science. The second two novels, by Woolf and Bowen, do not explicitly feature controlling men but instead point to aggressive masculine forces that threaten not only individual characters but also entire communities. There is a pessimistic bent to *Dissensu-*

ous Modernism: it begins with the redemption of the lower senses through technology in *HERmione* but ends with their erasure in *Eva Trout*.

Each novel herein examines personal or societal sensory practices, as well as the technologies that enable and impede them. I loosely categorize those technologies into three groups: technologies of science and medicine, such as the microscope and X-ray; technologies of transmission, such as the gramophone, radio, and telephone; and technologies of transportation, such as the automobile and airplane. Some of the technologies are twentieth-century inventions, others date to an earlier era but became more sophisticated and/ or popular during the modernist period. In the following section, I provide technological context before each chapter summary to better situate H.D., Loy, Woolf, and Bowen in the various cultural climates in which they wrote. I also discuss the different political and personal stakes that influenced each writers' project and illustrate how their distinct approaches contribute to a shared dissensuous aesthetic.

Dissensuous Women

H.D., Loy, Woolf, and Bowen variously expose patriarchal or authoritarian powers who use technology to standardize minds, bodies, and senses or to amplify some voices and sensory experiences and silence others. For H.D., this begins at home. Living in a household of scientists and growing up on the grounds of an observatory, H.D. was surrounded by "lensmen" engaged in various forms of visual study (Morris 202). H.D.'s grandfather, the Reverend Francis Wolle, was an amateur turned internationally known microbiologist, who published several books on botany at the end of the nineteenth century. H.D.'s father, Professor Charles Leander Doolittle, was a respected astronomist who directed the University of Pennsylvania Flower Observatory. Optic technologies like the microscope and telescope enable the scientific pursuits of the patriarchs in H.D.'s family and were common objects in her home. It is unsurprising, then, that optic technologies, scientific and otherwise, influence much of H.D.'s work.[18] The same year H.D. began writing *HERmione*, she also collaborated with Bryher and Macpherson to publish *Close Up*, a little magazine devoted to the study of cinema.[19] Cinema changed forever when, also that year, the first sound film was released. It is significant that H.D. undertakes *HERmione* at a time when the merging of sight with other senses was made possible through technology. It is in this milieu of multisensuous experimentation that I ground my reading of her novel.

Chapter 1, "H.D., Synesthete," examines how the titular character of *HERmione* forges connections among the seemingly divergent senses of sight, sound, and touch. I argue that she does this through optic technologies, first by exposing how such technologies reinforce gendered, sensory hierarchies and then by repurposing those technologies for more feminist, sensuously inclusive ends. *HERmione*'s setting resembles that of H.D.'s childhood home, replete with her father and brother busy at their microscopes. Through these microscopes, Hermione recovers the so-called feminine, lower senses, which the misogynistic, ocularcentric milieu of male science buries. Hermione is aided in her work through a romantic relationship with a woman, Fayne Rabb. Their relationship challenges sexual and societal norms and fosters sensory investigation. As Hermione conducts her own scientific study of the senses, she challenges masculine science and alters understandings of human perception and sensation. Importantly, she uses the microscope to illuminate the sensorium of sea animals, thereby expanding sensuous thinking beyond human strictures. In her willingness to inhabit animal perspectives and learn from animal sensations, H.D.'s project aligns with Virginia Woolf's, a convergence I explain further in the overview for chapter 3.

Just as H.D. deconstructs male scientific technologies and exposes misogynist sensory practices, so, too, does Mina Loy. Like *HERmione*, *Insel* is also a roman à clef. It depicts the period from 1933 to 1936, when Loy was curating art in Paris for her son-in-law's American gallery. During this time, Loy befriended Surrealists such as Man Ray, Eugene Atet, and Richard Oelze, the latter of whom inspired the titular character in Loy's *Insel*. Among the Surrealists, Loy was something of a celebrity-by-association: her former husband, Arthur Cravan, was considered a proto-Surrealist (Kinnahan 77). Just as H.D. was surrounded by men attached to optic technologies, so, too, was Loy. The Surrealists were quite enamored with the camera.[20] While touting the camera's ability to reinvigorate sight, the Surrealists used the camera to exploit women's bodies, a practice I discuss in detail in chapter 2. The violence against women's bodies that Loy witnessed was amplified by technological violence on a larger scale. As Hitler assumed power in Germany and threatened to invade other countries, he enlisted various technologies—from the megaphone to the crematorium—to commit violence against marginalized bodies en masse. As an Anglo-Jewish woman, Loy writes *Insel* at a time of personal and global precarity, when technology enabled bodily and sensuous violence.

In chapter 2, "'choked by a robot!': Technology, Gender, and the Battle of the Senses in Mina Loy's *Insel*," I read the sex war as a sense war—a battle modernist women fought (and contemporary women continue to fight) for sensory access and affirmation of their embodied experiences. Like *HERmione*, Insel examines how vision and visual technologies were often coded as masculine and used to alienate and objectify women. Ultimately though, just as the microscope inspires H.D. to explore intersensory experience, the technologies Loy encounters inspire her to conjoin (rather than unjoin) the senses. In *Insel*, Loy juxtaposes two artists, Insel, a character based on the German painter Richard Oelze, and Mrs. Jones, a character based on Loy herself. Through this juxtaposition, Loy outlines two distinct artistic approaches to the body, senses, and technology. The first she associates with the misogynist work of Futurists and Surrealists who, like Insel, use technology to discipline the senses and commit violence against the sensuous female body. Though the Surrealist camera itself does not feature in *Insel*, similarly objectifying and penetrating visual technologies, like the X-ray and fluoroscope, do. Through medical technologies that intervene on the body in unwanted and corrective ways, Loy alludes to the toxic misogynist and eugenicist ideologies that plagued this period. She illustrates how men use technology to perpetuate violence against women's bodies and senses, through the dehumanizing process of segmenting and suppressing sensation. To combat this sensory violence, Loy offers an alternative, integrationist approach that combines the body, the senses, and technology. Mrs. Jones, who adopts this approach, elevates the female body and the so-called lower senses at a time when they were increasingly denigrated, especially in the sciences. Repurposing misogynistic rhetoric, Mrs. Jones imagines the female body itself as a sensory technology, one that registers sensations machines cannot. Thus, she posits the so-called feminine senses of smell, taste, and touch as valuable sources of knowledge and creativity that contribute positively to science and literature.

While Fascist technologies inform Loy's work and linger in the background of *Insel*, they take center stage in Woolf's *Between the Acts*. As Woolf wrote her final novel, from 1938 to 1941, the war in Britain intensified. Hitler's architect, Albert Speer, credits Hitler's success with his technological prowess. "[Hitler's] was the first dictatorship," Speer asserted, ". . . which made the complete use of all technical means for domination of its own country. Through technical devices like the radio and loudspeaker, 80 million people were deprived of independent thought" (qtd. in Wiesner et al. 335). Radio is widely recognized as one of the most effective technological means Hitler had of conveying his message and amassing followers, and he fought to control the airwaves much like he fought for geographic territory. To reach more listeners, German propaganda minister Joseph Goebbels tasked engineers with developing a more affordable radio (Bergerson 95). The Volksempfänger, or "people's receiver," enabled Hitler to broadcast his messages to the working class, thereby dominating Germany's soundscape. Across Europe, Hitler further dominated the soundscape through the airplane—both through the roar of its engine, which filled the skies, and through the shrieking air raid sirens that announced its presence (Holman 248). Such techno-acoustic invasions incited fear of authorial oppression and sensory control, which Woolf captures in her final novel.

In chapter 3, "'. . . A zoom severed it': Sensory Interruption in Virginia Woolf's *Between the Acts*," I argue that Woolf extends Loy's repurposing of technology to combat sensory violence not only against women but also against nations. Woolf invokes threatening technologies associated with WW2, such as the gramophone, megaphone, and airplane, to wage her own war on sensory habituation. Sensory habituation refers to those sensory practices that, over time, become sensory habits that humans enact automatically, without much thought or consideration. Woolf, however, asks her readers to sense anew. Combining affect theory, animal studies, and cultural accounts of technology, I demonstrate how Woolf promotes nonnormative sensory practices and advocates for diverse sensory communities. In *Between the Acts*, lower-class characters, environmental interjections from trees and birds, and various rogue technologies serve as models for how to interrupt sensory habituation and challenge sensory normativity. Animals and nature play an important role in Woolf's subversion. At a time when eugenicist thinking was rampant and Hitler was proclaiming groups of people subhuman, Woolf's esteem for "lowly" animal perspectives was all the more defiant.

I would like to pause here to provide brief context on modernist animal studies, which link my readings of Woolf's *Between the Acts* and H.D.'s *HERmione*. H.D. and Woolf join other artists, biologists, and philosophers of their time in showing an interest in animal subjectivities. During the first half of the twentieth century, when comparative psychology was in vogue, modernist thinkers "were exploring animal perspectives to reconsider the nature of knowledge" (Hovanec 159). This specific kind of exploration, Caroline Hovanec argues, is uniquely modernist (162–63). Unlike previous generations, modernists viewed animals as "sentient subjects rather than Cartesian automatons," which led to increased research in animal consciousness and embodiment (Hovanec 3). Modernist writers showed a willingness to decenter themselves, explore unfamiliar perspectives, and experiment with literary form, thereby enabling what Carrie Rohman calls "a linguistic becoming-animal" (27). For H.D. and Woolf, this "becoming" is highly sensuous. By imagining how animals see, hear, touch, taste, and smell—and how they transcend these sensory definitions and divisions— H.D. and Woolf disrupt anthropocentric sensory paradigms. They rewrite the sensorium to encompass both human and nonhuman animals. Technology aids them in this reimagining as they question who controls it and how that control delineates subjects from objects. As they explore technological and sensuous power dynamics, they illustrate how technology can not only reify but also subvert sensory norms.

The animal and natural worlds that appear in H.D.'s and Woolf's novels are virtually absent from the last novel this book examines, Elizabeth Bowen's *Eva Trout*. While the other novels illustrate how technology can be repurposed to challenge harmful sensory narratives and defy sensory standardization, *Eva Trout* is less optimistic. In its skepticism, Bowen's novel reflects the technological thinking of late 1960s societies, which she likely encountered in her transatlantic travels.[21]

Though people had long feared the devastating impacts of technology on human and environmental biology, their trepidation intensified during the 1960s.[22] Citizens across the globe became increasingly suspicious of technology and fearful of technological domination. If Woolf's final novel speaks to a cultural moment when people feared Fascism and its technologies of mass social and sensuous control, Bowen's final novel reflects a period when technology itself became an authoritarian threat. Sungook Hong, associate professor at the Institute for the History and Philosophy of Science and Technology at the University of Toronto, attributes this fear to a confluence of technological events. To begin, the development of "cybernetics, systems theory, and intelligent computers," Hong maintains, "blurred the strict boundary between machine and organism" (Hong 50), provoking anxiety about human identity and exceptionalism. Meanwhile, the Vietnam Conflict and counterculture movements drew attention to the havoc technology wreaked on humans, animals, and the environment. As Hong notes, "manmade machines—chemical pollutants, defoliants, the electronic battlefield, and the hydrogen bomb in particular—began to threaten the very existence of humans" (Hong 50). At the same time, the 1960s saw the birth of fully autonomous technologies, or technologies that operated without human intervention, making people's place and purpose in the world less certain. These threats—of computerized, lethal, and automated technology—combined so that people began to feel outnumbered and overpowered by technology.[23] Much of this overpowering and confusion was sensory, and Bowen's novel depicts how technological progress results in sensory stagnation.

Chapter 4, "Sensory Dystopia: Stifling Sounds, Sights, and Technologies in Elizabeth Bowen's *Eva Trout*" works from a popular view of technology as threatening and examines how a proliferation of visual and audio technologies impedes broader sensory experience. In *Eva Trout*, Bowen expresses anxiety about technology and sensory impairment by crafting a limited, dystopian sensorium that excludes the lower senses. She does this, in part, through depictions of all-consuming visual and acoustic technologies that demonstrate and encourage society's unhealthy fixation on seeing and hearing. Bowen further illustrates this fixation through depictions of a character who is deaf and whose disability underscores bodily and sensuous lack. In my reading of this chapter, I draw on disability theory, modernist radio studies, and historical accounts of 1960s technologies to demonstrate how Bowen argues for a more expansive sensorium by illustrating the harmful effects of ocular- and auralcentrism. Though less overtly feminist than the other novels I examine, *Eva Trout* still lends itself to a feminist reading. The novel's aggressive technologies and its absence of the lower senses gesture toward harmful, patriarchal ideologies that dehumanize and disconnect people. As its titular character moves from England, to America, to France, *Eva Trout* illustrates the modernist "crisis of the senses" on a global scale (Danius 1).

This sensory crisis incites a crisis of self that resounds on both sides of the Atlantic.

In true modernist fashion, the writers this book celebrates find possibility in crisis. Chaos inspires them to question tradition; upheaval generates opportunity for them to create anew. *Dissensuous Modernism* locates itself in a cultural moment where uncertainties about technology, autonomy, gender, and sensory experience converge. Together, H.D., Mina Loy, Virginia Woolf, and Elizabeth Bowen seize this cultural moment as an occasion to dismantle and expand. Their writing shows a refusal to adhere to gendered sensory strictures or sexist narratives about technology. They invite us to reconsider what we thought we knew about technology, the senses, and the sensing body in modernity. They bring us the senses in surprising configurations, with broader definitions, and from unexpected people, places, and beings. In so doing, they engage in a feminist modernism that celebrates sensuous and bodily diversity and liberation. This book hopes to draw attention to their dissensuous work as an essential and underexplored facet of modernism.

1

H.D., Synesthete

In 1895, German physician Max Nordau published *Degeneration*, a book containing scathing remarks about the prevalence of smell, taste, and touch in literature. These senses, Nordau proclaimed, belonged to an "epoch anterior to man" and were the purview of beasts, not of respectable writers (503). Nordau found synesthesia, or "joint perception," equally worthy of condemnation ("synaesthesis"). Writing that featured synesthesia—such as plays where lines were paired with perfumes, colored lights, or musical notes—was evidence of social decline, in Nordau's opinion, and he accused those artists and audience members who enjoyed synesthesia of "moral insanity, imbecility, and dementia" (Nordau viii). While *Degeneration* predicts that the valorization of synesthesia and the lower senses will end with the advent of the twentieth century, sensory experimentation in writing persisted.[1] This chapter concerns itself with one such sensory-rich, twentieth-century novel, H.D.'s roman à clef *HERmione*. In *HERmione*, H.D. confronts and contests the sensory norms upon which Nordau, and society at large, rest their biases and aversions. H.D. posits synesthesia not as reductive but as productive: through it, she destabilizes distinctions between high and low, normal and abnormal, human and nonhuman. The nonhuman is especially important to H.D.'s sensuous experimentation, as it is to Virginia

Woolf's, which I discuss in chapter 3. Where Nordau declares the nonhuman sensuously inferior, H.D. (and later, Woolf) finds the nonhuman a source of sensory inspiration. She draws upon nonhuman sensory modes to challenge anthropocentric sensory paradigms. Similarly, where Nordau conceives of the lower senses as degenerate, H.D. sees them as generative: they offer new ways of sensing and new modes of being through which H.D. subverts the sensory status quo.

To understand how *HERmione* troubles sensory norms, we must first unpack traditional sensory classifications and what it means to "make sense." Political theorist Davide Panagia explains, "We always already know what it means to sense, what seeing, touching, and hearing are" (7). In other words, we take perception for granted and assume that sensory practices are natural as opposed to socially constructed.[2] Panagia suggests that "sensory regimes" or "regimes of perception" (what Rancière calls the "distribution of the sensible") "confer what counts as common sense" (7). These regimes are often controlled by social elites: wealthy, white, heterosexual men. There are moments, however, when these sensory regimes and their "common sense" practices are challenged—moments when sensory hierarchies are broken and when habitual sensory practices yield to personal sensory choices. Such is the case with H.D.'s *HERmione*. H.D.'s so-called failure to conform to sensory norms is a productive one, I argue, in that it offers an alternative sensorium that challenges normative sensory practices and divisions. I read *HERmione* as a dissensuous text—one that wages dissent through radical acts of sensing and radical reconfigurations of the senses. Through *HERmione*, H.D. resists male sensory imposition and sensory technologies that divide not only the senses but also the sexes. Though H.D. fails to meet sensory standards, to make "common sense," she succeeds in promoting sensory alternatives and challenging the damaging assumptions upon which traditional sensory narratives rest.

H.D.'s alternative sensorium has particular implications for women, especially queer women. Feminist scholars and cultural historians have long discussed the gendering of the senses, which affords men privileges that women are denied.[3] Traditional sensory narratives commonly associate men with the privileged senses of sight and sound, which are, in turn, associated with reason. These "distance" senses enable men to engage in "'distance activities,' such as traveling and governing" (Classen, *CA* 66). In contrast, smell, taste, and touch, the proximity senses, have been imagined to confine women to the home, since these so-called lower senses are inherent in household duties. Smell, taste, and touch are often conceived of as being more embodied than sight or sound and, in this way, more befitting women, whose minds have long been considered less developed than men's. Heteronormative narratives, by reinforcing gender binaries, also reinforce these so-called sensory norms. Such narratives suggest that coupling men with women results in the perfect balance of reason and emotion, pragmatism and sensuousness. Like other gendered binaries, sensory binaries are mutually exclusive and mutually constitutive so that, the lower women sink on the sensory scale, the higher men rise. In the twentieth century, women's increasing social mobility and political agency put pressure on these narratives. Once-contained female bodies—with their smells and sounds and the threat of their touch—were more public, more visible, and more contaminating.[4] As twentieth-century women transgressed traditional sensory categories, they demanded new sensory identifications. H.D. plays an integral role in rewriting sensory narratives for women and for modernist literature, more broadly.

H.D.'s feminist sensory writing starkly contrasts, and was undoubtedly influenced by, that of her once-lover and self-proclaimed mentor, Ezra Pound. Pound sought to establish modernist literary philosophies, aims, and techniques, many of which reflect his limited view of the senses. Several scholars note the influence of visual arts on Pound's literary aesthetic and examine the relationship between the poet's increasing ocularcentrism and his antidemocratic political views.[5] To understand Pound's sensory ideology, we can look to his forebear, Remy de Gourmont, whose work Pound greatly admired.[6] Gourmont valued sight above all other senses. He considered it ordering and elite—a tool of the intelligentsia. In contrast, Gourmont considered sound disordering and democratic—"emblem and medium of the undistinguished, undistinguishing masses" (Sherry 71). According to Gourmont, the ability to distinguish among the senses—to divide and classify sensory impressions—was evidence of a superior mind and higher art. He finds this in Homer's writing: "The sensations are sequential so the language is sequential [. . .] impressions strike [Homer] one by one; he describes them one by one, without confusion" (qtd. in Sherry 70). Instead of celebrating sensory multiplicity—what Gourmont refers to as "confusion"—he applauds sensory division. The result is an artistic representation that feels artificial in its sensory mastery, where embodied experiences are stripped of sensuous fluidity and spontaneity.

Similar ideals are at work in Pound's *Cantos*, which reflect the rigidly engineered, single-sense aesthetic that Gourmont lauds. Vincent Sherry cogently traces Pound's transition from privileging sound to privileging sight. In Pound's early cantos, Sherry observes a "new (visual) métier [that] entails a forsaking of 'sounds' altogether" (68). By suggesting that sight and sound cannot coexist, Pound divides and hierarchizes the senses, creating false sensory oppositions. Not only does he needlessly pit sight and sound against each other, but Pound also fails to account for the lower senses altogether. In so doing, he reenacts a literary inheritance of sensuous restraint and impossibility. The work of Pound and Gourmont reflects a wider trend among some modernist writers and their French forebears. They favor a unisensory, visual hegemony; a contrived sense of bodily control; and an exclusionary sensory elitism—all of which H.D., and the other writers this book centers, emphatically opposes.

Because of H.D.'s association with Imagism and cinema, and because of modernism's links to the visual, it is not surprising that scholarship on H.D. often attends to the optic aspects of her oeuvre.[7] H.D., however, can be numbered among those modernist writers who, Karen Jacobs proposes, share "a diminished faith . . . regarding the capacity of vision to deliver reliable knowledge" (3). Rachel Connor similarly notes that "H.D.'s writing resists the dominant scopic economy" (61). I suggest that part of this resistance involves undercutting the divisiveness of the scopic economy and challenging the "forms of violence that vision inevitably seems to entail" (Jacobs 3). Extending the visual work done by earlier critics, I articulate how H.D. provides an alternative to visual dominance not only by creating new ways of looking but also by imbricating the senses in unexpected junctions. She disrupts attempts to stabilize or reinforce traditional ways of classifying both the senses and sensing bodies. By foregrounding women, queer women, and animals, *HERmione* revalues marginalized sensory experiences and promotes sensory inclusivity.

In this chapter, I also emphasize the importance of touch in the larger sensorium, thereby continuing the ongoing recovery of the lower senses in modernist literature. However, unlike previous studies that focus on one or two senses, I transcend the single-sense paradigm to address the subversive potential of sensory integration. As historian Mark M. Smith reminds us, the senses do not operate in isolation but are intersensorial—they "work together," often in unexpected and productive ways (12). I view synesthesia—an intersensory experience where one sense activates another—as equally productive. Herein, I examine the role touch plays in producing intersensory and synesthetic experiences that transcend male and human-centered paradigms.

Using sensory theory and queer phenomenology, I argue that the novel's heterosexual relationships discourage sensory integration and experimentation, while its lesbian relationship encourages them. Throughout the novel, male figures uphold traditional sensory hierarchies, privilege vision, and enact sensory violence against women. I implicate the microscope, an ocularcentric technology, in this violence and illustrate how it prompts Hermione, the novel's eponymous protagonist, to reenvision the senses. Hermione's queer relationship further counteracts male sensory imposition by encouraging her to explore nontraditional sensory practices and to reconfigure her understanding of not only sexual relationships but also sensory relationships. While doing this revisionary work, Hermione crafts a synesthetic sensorium, one that features sensory interplay. Specifically, she emphasizes the redemptive qualities of multisensuality by coupling touch with sight through hapticity and with sound through vibration. Hermione's exploration of sensory connections inspires her to explore and connect the human and the nonhuman. Like Virginia Woolf, H.D. uses nonhuman senses and sensations to circumvent constraining human sensory norms. In her quest for sensuous possibility, she turns to sea life as a model for sensory integration.

Written in 1927 but not published until 1981, *HERmione* revisits events that occurred in H.D.'s life between 1905 and 1911. Set in the author's childhood home of Bethlehem, Pennsylvania, *HERmione* follows its protagonist through her dismissal from Bryn Mawr, her unexpected engagement to George Lowndes (the novel's figure for Ezra Pound, to whom H.D. was briefly engaged), and her controversial relationship with Fayne Rabb (the novel's figure for H.D.'s lover Frances Josepha Gregg). Hermione's complicated relationships with her lovers, her parents, and, ultimately, herself, exacerbate her feelings of difference and un-belonging. Anxious and uncertain, her mental state deteriorates until she becomes physically ill and bedridden for three months. H.D. recounts Hermione's struggle in wandering, stream-of-consciousness prose that often leaves the reader, like Hermione herself, unaware of where she stands in the greater narrative. However, the disorienting quality of *HERmione* allows reader and protagonist alike to reorient themselves in a fresh sensorium.

The Microscope and Male Imposition: Denying Sensory Agency

While many technologies of the modernist period called into question previous assumptions about the senses, their associations, and their limits, other technologies were rooted in tradition and reinforced gender and sensory divisions. Technologies of science, for example, often belonged to an antiquated social and sensory order and remained under the purview of men. Though women played active and important roles in scientific discovery, the media and male scientists often framed women's contributions as maternalistic. As part of a scientific family, whose father and paternal grandfather were well-respected in the fields of astronomy and botany, H.D. would have been familiar with such rhetoric and discrimination. Even the most renowned female scientists were subject to public dismantling. When Marie Curie won the Noble Prize in 1903, she was treated as "a maternal martyr who had used science for womanly ends" (Des Jardins 43). During Curie's 1921 tour of America, scientific associations and universities posited Curie's discovery of radium "as a gesture of humanitarianism rather than as evidence of scientific acumen" (Des Jardins 40).

The minimization of women's work also occurred in Charles Doolittle's field, astronomy. Of the award-winning astronomical physicist and Harvard University professor Annie Cannon, one journalist wrote in 1931: "'Oh those untidy men folks,' we can hear Miss Cannon say as she took up astronomy. 'Let's get some order in this kitchen, I mean heaven'" (qtd. in Des Jardins 89). Despite their obvious skill, women were denied access to scientific technologies, both due to the perception that women were incapable of operating such so-called masculine machines and as a way to limit women's power and influence within scientific communities. National observatories, for instance, did not grant women access to telescopes until the 1960s (Des Jardins 90). Optic technologies like these were doubly contested due to long-standing myths about women's underdeveloped sense of sight. Ultimately, women were deemed intellectually and sensuously deficient and, therefore, technologically inept.

The microscope that features in *HERmione* not only draws attention to technology's gendering but also underscores sensory segmentation. In so doing, it resembles other so-called single-sense, optic technologies that proliferated at the beginning of the twentieth century. Film was one such technology. In 1910, the editor of *Licht-Bühne*, a German film journal, had this to say of cinema: "We are no longer looking for things like personality and individuality, insights into the emotional lives of others, the contact between stage and audience, the vibration of sounds through the ears and into the heart, the language of poets. No. We just want to indulge our eyes" (qtd. in Jütte 300). In this description, sight subsumes the other senses, so much so that everything "smells of film" (qtd. in Jütte 300). Optic technologies figure as an infliction, a "see-sickness [that] will spare no one" (qtd. in Jütte 301). In *HERmione*, many of the male characters succumb to this "see-sickness." Hermione's brother Bertram, and father, Carl are both botanists, often glued to their microscopes. Their association with the microscope underscores it as predominantly male, a technology of the mind and not the body. Of the microscope, the German physician Max Nordau gushed, "What saintly legend is as beautiful as the life of an inquirer who spends his existence bending over a microscope, almost without bodily wants . . . without any other ambition than that perhaps one little new fact may be firmly established?" (110). Responding to this comment, Constance Classen observes that "the intense visualism of the scientist at his microscope 'almost without bodily wants,' provides a contrast to the artistic celebration of multisensory experience" (119). Such single-sense, male-oriented technologies are antithetical to H.D.'s intersensory aims.

Through the microscope, H.D. conveys masculine and visual dominance, the male-centric and ocularcentric sensory hierarchies against which Hermione rebels. For Hermione, the microscope functions as a sort of panopticon, looming in the background of the novel, amplifying her failures and unconventionalities, and serving as a constant reminder of how, as Rachel Connor puts it, "the economy of the scopic works to reinforce heterosexual privilege, as well as gender binaries" (67). The microscope, and the scopic regime it represents, depends, in part, on granting sensory access to some and limiting sensory access for others. Carl

Gart enforces the sensory regime in his household and attempts to control which senses are used where, when, and by whom. This is most visible in Carl's relationship to his wife and the limited sensory agency he grants her. When Hermione asks her mother, "Why are you always knitting? Only old ladies knit and knit like you do," Eugenia answers, "I can knit in the dark. I can't sew in the dark. Your father likes the light concentrated in a corner. He can work better if I'm sitting in the dark" (*H* 79). Here, Carl hoards light and, along with it, the ability to see, leaving his wife in darkness. With an emphasis on what Eugenia "can" and "can't" do, this moment emblematizes the division of sensory work common to the traditional, gendered sensorium: Carl employs vision to do public work, while Eugenia employs touch to do domestic work. H.D., however, is critical of these binaries and positions Carl as a sort of sensory oligarch: "Father, your father. Eugenia sitting in the darkness, the green shade, fixed now here, now there over the just one blazing electric light, just one concentrated circle of light across the half of a desk, strewn with papers, only Gart's papers were always piled in little heaps, folded up in little bundles" (79). The repetition of "one" underscores Carl's dominance—his way is the only way—and he uses his power to maneuver not only the light but also his wife's sensory faculties. The space allotted for light/sight is painfully reduced—"just one" small circle on only half of a desk—and the more Carl sees, the less Eugenia can. Unable to do her own work, Eugenia tends to her husband's. She keeps his papers, folding them into little bundles, since this is the only sighted work she can do freely.[8]

Male-imposed ocularcentricity limits and dehumanizes women throughout the novel. H.D. further illustrates this ocularcentricity through awkward encounters between Hermione and her father. In one, Hermione walks into her father's laboratory and announces, "Father. I am going to marry George Lowndes." Carl responds to his daughter's announcement as if emerging from a haze. He "pulled away his eye from the microscopic lens and with an effort jolted himself back, with a jolt brought himself back to—'Eugenia.' 'I'm not Eugenia,'" Hermione corrects him, "'I'm Hermione'": "Carl Gart saw a tall creature, his own daughter, with odd unholy eyes. Eyes shone odd and unholy in a white face. . . . Carl Gart brought his mind by a superhuman effort to readjustment to the thing before him. He saw an odd fury-ridden creature with white face and flame-lipped face and a face where two lips were drawn tight almost like dead lips across a skeleton. He saw ridges in the face, fine bones beneath the face" (*H* 99). Seeming not to hear Hermione, Carl stares at his daughter as if seeing her for the first time. "Face" repeats obsessively, suggestive of Carl's scientific fixation on the "thing" before him, of which he tries, but fails, to make sense. Similarly, he tries and fails to enact an empathetic gaze. Though he searches his daughter's expression for signs of humanity, he sees only fury and rage. Hermione remains "odd" and unidentifiable, a "creature" more akin to a scientific specimen than a human being. Carl's X-ray vision does not see Hermione as much as it sees *through* her, rendering her "dead" and skeletal, the "bones" not of his daughter but of a mere "thing." This kind of seeing dehumanizes both Hermione and her father. Hereafter, Hermione obsesses over being seen by others. She repeats to Eugenia, "Don't you see?" in a desperate attempt to validate both herself and her way of seeing (97). Ironically, by investing all his faith in sight, Carl is blinded: with one eye always open to the microscope, his other eye remains shut to alternative identities and their subsequent alternative sensory practices. Under the eye and in the hands of men, the microscope represents single-sense engagement and a rigid worldview—a literally shrunken perspective—that shrinks and otherwise limits not only their own sensory capacities but also those of the women around them.

Through the microcosm of Hermione's home, H.D. represents the larger social opposition Hermione faces as a woman and a writer. Within the home space, Carl and Bertrand restrict women's bodies and contain their sensuous output. Such containment is apparent in Hermione's angry avowal that "God, some sort of Uncle Sam, Carl-Bertrand-Gart God, shut [Hermione and Eugenia] up in a box, with temps too high and too low to breed new specimens like Bertrand Gart, like Carl Gart in their aquariums" (*H* 96). Hermione implicates Carl and Bertrand in the larger patriarchal structures of nationalism and religion, all of which, she suggests, restrict women. Hermione and her mother do not have rooms of their own; they have little room at all—they are boxed in and denied use of their bodies and their senses. Carl and Bertrand, perhaps fearful of women's bodies and bodily capabilities, divest women of the ability to breed and, instead, appropriate that power, as seen in father and son's laboratory-based breeding experiments. This regulation of breeding and bodies, along with Eugenia's very name, bring to mind eugenicist projects common to the modernist period, which waged "broadly based attempts to control gender, sexuality, and reproduction" (Armstrong, *Modernism, Technology, and the Body* 155). Hermione resents this attempt at control and decries "Gart and the formula," which invest in "conclusive things" and demand "the exact fitting to one type" (*H* 113, 17, 233). Such formulaic thinking, which Hermione sees as distinctly patriarchal (and American), relies on prescriptive sensory practices that foreclose not only the sensorium but also the possibility for more fluid and less prescriptive sensory identities like Hermione's, which, she proclaims, "was not conclusive" (17). H.D.'s declaration "Her Gart wanted a nobler affinity" speaks to the less conclusive, more inclusive quality of Hemione's feminist sensory project (17).

Hermione's sensory project, like H.D.'s, is often curtailed by male figures, and no one enacts this interference more obviously than George Lowndes, the novel's Ezra Pound figure. In the novel, Hermione and George are briefly engaged, but their relationship is contentious, and George is very controlling. Just as Carl robs Eugenia of sight, George, too, tries to direct Hermione's vision. Though Hermione longs to "see through reaches of sea-wall, to push through transparencies," George reduces her vision (*H* 7). He "puts everything out of focus," causing Hermione to wonder, "Why couldn't George ever let me alone to see things in my own way[. . .]?" (147, 133). George censors what Hermione sees when, for example, he, "tugging her at her elbow," pulls her away from the "old Academy" of artwork she admires and commands, "Don't look at those things" (134–35). George attempts to train Hermione's sight and ensure that she maintains her position as the unseeing woman so that he can maintain his mutually constitutive position as the seeing man. Notably, George directs Hermione's sight away from the art of her choosing. Such moments exemplify H.D.'s troubled relationship with the often-elitist Ezra Pound, who also notoriously attempted to curate, or otherwise appropriate, H.D.'s vision through Imagism.[9] H.D.'s artistic vision—her unique way of seeing and sensing the world—had particular stakes for Pound, who sought to maintain control over the literary world that modernist women writers, with their synesthetic sensory agendas, were increasingly infiltrating.

H.D. realizes her sensory aspirations, in part, by detailing sensory violence that exceeds the visual and impacts the entire sensorium. H.D. describes the pressure that George/Ezra exerts as not only emotionally and mentally inhibiting but also physically and sensorially damaging. H.D. thereby illustrates Sara Ahmed's contention that "the social pressure to follow a certain course, to live a certain kind of life, and even to reproduce that life" can manifest bodily, "like a physical press on the surface of the body" (555). This is most apparent in a disturbing physical encounter between Hermione and George: "Sound of chiffon ripping and the twist and turn of Hermione under the stalwart thin young torso of George Lowndes. Now more than ever thought made spiral, made concentric circle toward the darkened ceiling. The ceiling came down, down . . . Walls were coming close to suffocate, to crush her" (*H* 173). Panicked repetition and dark imagery charge this scene with fear—fear that Rachel Connor interprets as "Her's horror of the stifling nature of heterosexual sex" (58). This scene also illustrates the stifling pressure of heteronormativity as Ahmed describes it. By conflating the walls with George's body, H.D. magnifies the pressure to conform, socially and sexually, but also sensuously. George's touch "suffocates" and otherwise disables Hermione: she cannot move under his weight, and she loses bodily and, in turn, sensory agency. The encroaching walls increasingly reduce Hermione's scope of vision, boxing in and containing her sight. Although the scene begins with the violent sound of ripping, George's violent touch seems to block out all other sensations and (temporarily) reduces Hermione's sensory capabilities to ineffectual gawking. Her sensorium is flattened, just as the ceiling threatens to flatten her. Ultimately, the scene is one of sensory dominance, in which George attempts to divest Hermione of sensory agency and perceptual abilities.

George further enacts sensory violence through sound. When George speaks, Hermione hears "tin pan noises, little tin pan against my ear . . . striking, beating on it" (*H* 42). Sound, here, is painful, intrusive, and notably tactile. Hermione feels sound and uses the language of physical abuse to describe George's damaging aural touch. His is a sort of disciplinary aurality, and here again we can liken this to descriptions of Ezra Pound elsewhere in H.D.'s oeuvre. For instance, in H.D.'s memoir, *End to Torment*, she recalls that "[Ezra] seemed to beat with the ebony stick like a baton . . . there is a sense of his pounding, pounding (Pounding) with the stick against the wall" (8).[10] A noisy man, both in name and in practice, Ezra's aurality is imposing, as H.D.'s violent description attests. And while George's "pounding" may not be as overt, his use of sound is just as aggressive. George is a wordsmith, his cooed "bella, bella,

molta bella, bellisima" are sickly sweet words that work on and against Hermione (*H* 42). Aural pressure translates into symbolic social pressure, as George
uses sound to strike and beat Hermione out of shape, only to attempt to mold
her into his own beautiful feminine ideal. Unsettling at best and misogynistic
at worst, George's compliments and so-called praise further objectify and gender Hermione, simultaneously denying her sensory agency.

Queer Possibilities: Countering Sensory Tyranny

While Hermione's heteronormative relationships reify sensory norms, her
queer relationships provide a counter-space within which she responds to
sensory violence and reconfigures sensory standards. The myopia of the men
in her life encourages Hermione to envision new ways of sensing and being
sensed, and she finds the freedom for this exploration in queer commu-
nions. Queer relationships, both in the novel and in H.D.'s personal life, open
sensory possibility. Ahmed notes that, in contrast to heterosexual cultures
that aim to keep bodies "in line," "queer cultures . . . draw different kinds of
lines, which do not aim to keep things in their places" (557, 565). According
to Ahmed, queer cultures make room for different kinds of orientations—
socially, sexually, and sensuously. Sara E. Chinn makes a similar claim, suggesting that lesbian relationships serve as a "conduit" wherein women can
"readjust the balance among the senses" and rework sensory associations
that rely on strict gender binaries (196, 197). In Hermione's case, her queer relationship empowers her to make room for new sensory orientations. Queer
desire, Ahmed suggests, supports this kind of work, and "Lesbian desire can
be rethought as a space for action, a way to extend differently into space
through tending toward 'other women'" (564). Ahmed describes this tendency not only as a story of "coming-out" but also "as a story of 'coming to,'
of arriving near other bodies, as a contact that makes a story and opens up
other ways of facing the world" (565).

Hermione regains sensory space and agency through her relationship
with Fayne Rabb, the novel's Frances Josepha Gregg figure. Unlike George,
who shrinks and restricts Hermione spatially, leaving her feeling claustro-
phobic and "dehumanized," Fayne grants space (*H* 77). Hermione describes
Fayne as "This thing that made the floor sink beneath her feet and the wall
rise to infinity above her head" (52). The walls that closed down upon Herm-

ione in her earlier encounter with George, here, open with possibility. Direct touch, so prevalent in Hermione's encounters with George, is absent from this scene. Instead, Hermione associates Fayne with an *indirect* sense of touch—a touch that manifests through movement. Hermione feels the space around her widen as the floor "sinks" and the ceiling "rises." Within this space, Hermione is free to move as well, and this freedom has physical and sensuous consequences. Hermione's relationship with Fayne foils her relationship with George: while he entraps and attempts to stabilize, thereby limiting what Hermione can do with her body and her senses, Fayne offers and invites what Ahmed calls "alternative forms of world making" that have important sensory implications (565). Hermione acknowledges that with Fayne "[a] whole world was open"; within this world, she begins to chart new sensory territory (62).

H.D. begins this work by refashioning sight, the so-called sense par excellence. Rachel Connor comments that *HERmione's* "'realignment' of the gaze through an alternative paradigm of looking . . . is intrinsic to H.D.'s politics of the visual and her understanding of gender politics" (67). "Realignment" is key: *HERmione* challenges the gendered, hegemony of vision by transforming, not merely subjugating, sight. Sarah Chinn observes a trend, in some lesbian literature, toward an "eyes-free sexual vocabulary" (182). While *HERmione* does exhibit "an anxiety about visual access," she does not shy away from the eye but instead repurposes vision, making it more inclusive (Gallagher 411). The sighted relationship between Fayne and Hermione, specifically, serves as a model for reconfiguring sight in H.D.'s oeuvre. H.D. juxtaposes Fayne's vision with traditional ways of seeing, such as those emblematized by Nellie Thorpe, Hermione's former Bryn Mawr classmate. Nellie, like George, represents the societal norms Hermione shuns and the restrictive identity categories from which she turns. When first introducing Hermione to Fayne, Nellie coaxes, first "come to see me—to see a girl I want to see you" (*H* 34). The repetition of the word "see" underscores Nellie's insistence on the act of seeing and illuminates the importance of sight in the traditions she upholds. Nellie does not encourage any other sensory interaction; she asks only that each "girl" play the role of objective observer/ detached onlooker.

Hermione is accustomed to such objectifying modes of visual perception, but Fayne represents a different way of seeing, and a different way of sensing, that enables and encourages Hermione's sensory transformation. According to Georgina Johnston, when Hermione and Fayne first encounter one another, their mutual act of looking disrupts traditional modes of seeing, "their own desire queering patriarchal objectification by positing simultaneous subject and object" (67). When Hermione and Fayne first meet, Hermione's initial response to Fayne's gaze, "Don't look at the eyes that look at you," suggests her discomfort with the unusual offering of sighted exchange—an exchange wherein she is not only seen but also invited to see, not only looked upon but also encouraged to look (*H* 52). Hermione expresses surprise that Fayne "*was* seeing Her," the emphatic "*was*" suggesting that Hermione is not often seen—at least not in the way Fayne sees her (52). In contrast to Nellie's sister, Jessie, who "saw just around the corner," and Nellie herself, who "could see as far as the room wall," Fayne's sight is more far-reaching (49). Hermione comments that "seeing everything, Fayne Rabb saw nothing . . . Fayne Rabb saw as a bird, seeing nothing of importance" (143–44). "All the things that make the world important," Hermione tells Fayne, "all the things, I mean mama thinks important . . . you don't . . . you don't . . . recognize. I mean you don't see the things. It isn't as if you were destructive. Nellie said you were odd and so destructive. You just don't see them" (144). Notably, Fayne is not unable but unwilling to see: she chooses not to see in the same way as others. Her sensory choice is admirable and unexpected—indeed, Hermione seems almost puzzled by Fayne's willful assertion of sensory agency. Fayne's purposeful enactment of sensory difference is a threat to the sensory and social order and may explain why Nellie finds her "destructive." By not recognizing what others deem important, Fayne undercuts tradition and the principles on which it stands. In terms of offering sensory alternatives, however, Fayne's way of seeing, in its birdlike alterity, is productive. Her embrace of nonhuman sensory modes enables Fayne to challenge anthropocentric, patriarchal sensory norms. This serves as prelude to Hermione's own sensory and sexual experimentation. Because Fayne lacks a sighted agenda, she does not try to limit what or dictate how Hermione sees. Instead, Fayne draws attention to Hermione's sensory subjugation by telling her "You are yet repressed, unseeing, unseen . . ." and encourages her to exercise her sense of sight anew (146).

Hermione develops a new way of seeing that exceeds sensory categories by integrating sight and touch. She enacts what Cassandra Laity calls "an Imagism of different desires," one that "implant[s] alternative forms of . . . sensation in the Image" and posits seeing as a multisensory act (42). Sight, H.D. asserts, is haptic. According to Garrington, haptic is "an umbrella term denoting one or more of the following experiences: touch (the active or passive experience of the human skin, subcutaneous flesh, viscera and related nerve-endings); kinaesthesis (the body's sense of its own movement); proprioception (the body's sense of its orientation in space); and the vestibular sense (that of balance, reliant upon the inner ear)" (16). While sensory hierarchies position sight and touch at opposite ends of the spectrum, hapticity unites them. Mark Paterson, whose research interrogates the relationship between sight and touch, explains that the haptic "does not oppose the eyes with the hands, but acknowledges the sensory interdependence of the whole haptic (hand-eye-motion) system" (86).

H.D. illustrates this interdependence in the following exchange, as Hermione lulls Fayne to sleep: "Hands pressed against the swallow-blue that were now the swallow-black great-pupiled eyes of Fayne Rabb, were the long cold hands of Her Gart. Her Gart dropped book, dropped affectation of sanity, sank down to the floor, through the floor, above the earth [. . .] Prophetess to prophetess on some Delphic headland, Her Gart pressed cold hands against the eyelids of Fayne Rabb" (*H* 180). Here again, Fayne's avian eyes underscore nonhuman ways of sensing. For her and Hermione, as well as H.D., the nonhuman serves as a path to sexual and sensuous liberation. Fayne's birdlike embodiment enables her to breach not only human/nonhuman sensory boundaries but also sexual boundaries. Her nonhuman eyes serve as foundation for the queer, intersensory exchange that follows. Syntactically, the first sentence of the above passage creates sensory confusion, as "were" conflates Fayne's eyes and Hermione's hands. This confusion breaches the barrier between sensory organs, rendering them neither one thing nor the other, but both hands and eyes. As sensory organs merge, so, too, do sight and touch. Hermione's hands upon Fayne's eyes may seem to interfere with Fayne's ability to see, but this gesture expands, as opposed to impedes, sensation. Hermione's touch interrupts "eyesight alone" and emphasizes the intersensoriality of haptic vision (qtd. in Jones 411).[11] Through haptic vision, Hermione sees and feels her place in her surroundings, noting depths, movements, and surfaces. Haptic elements are at play in verbs that connote motion, such as "dropped" and "sank," as well as through prepositions that connote position, such as "above," "through," and "down." The sense of movement that infuses this passage also speaks of movement in the sensory order, as one sense moves or transforms from its previous position into a new, more nuanced one. Just as Fayne's eyes were once "swallow-blue" but "were now . . . swallow-black," so, too, were the senses of sight and touch once one thing and now another. In short, touch heals the rift sight creates between itself and the other senses. Fayne says as much about Hermione's hands: "Your hands are healing," she remarks. "They have dynamic white power . . . Your hands are white stars. Your hands are snowdrops" (180). The healing whiteness of this interaction between Hermione and Fayne starkly contrasts the threatening "darkened" and "black" tints of Hermione's physical encounters with George (173). The "dynamic white power" of Hermione's touch highlights the complexity of sensation and the redemptive qualities of intersensory experience.

Sound, Vibration, and Sensory Transformation

In addition to redeeming sight, touch redeems another characteristically masculine sense, sound. As H.D. writes sound anew, she underscores how she transforms sound, just as sound transforms her. She thereby highlights the transformative power sound holds for women, in particular. H.D. draws attention to sonic stifling at a time when women were often discouraged from making too much noise, especially in public and in politics. While the patriarchy seeks to silence women, H.D. suggests that communion among women can reverse this sensory damage. She marks this possibility with the opening of a new section in the novel, which signifies a new chapter in Hermione's life. Part 1 of *HERmione* ends with George dismissing Hermione's observations about art. He uses one of his favorite phrases—"Don't talk such rot, Hermione"—before pushing Hermione into a theater (137).[12] In contrast, part 2 opens with Hermione and Fayne freely discussing art and perception and Fayne urging Hermione to use her voice to read aloud.

H.D. links the sound of Hermione's voice with the touch of Fayne's hand, thereby illustrating the rehabilitating effect of their relationship. With a "[s] mall, heavy swift hand . . . hard dynamic forceful vibrant hand," Fayne's touch works to "dra[g] words out of the throat of Her Gart" (*H* 145). Where others silence Hermione—where George urges Hermione "Don't talk . . . don't talk," and Eugenia bids her "Hus-ssh"—Fayne coaxes her to speak (68, 45). Fayne's encouragement takes tactile form—her hand acts as metonym for the haptic and for sound's more-than-aural impact. In drawing attention to the throat, H.D. crafts a reverse eating moment, a moment of regurgitation. Where ideas and others' voices were once forced down Hermione's throat, Fayne "drags" or forces sound up from the depths. The ferocity of this interaction counteracts violent male imposition, and the description bears a striking resemblance to the forced feeding undergone by suffragists, the images of which were widely circulated in the years before H.D. wrote *HERmione*.[13] H.D. aligns herself and Hermione with such women, for whom asserting sensory agency—whether by making a sound or denying the touch of food— is a courageous act.

Touch and sound play important roles in Hermione's radical acts of self-definition. Early in the novel, as Hermione grapples with her "failure" and feelings of uselessness, she realizes that her former identity no longer fits: "clutching out toward some definition of herself, she found that, 'I am Her Gart' didn't let her hold on. Her fingers slipped off: she was no longer anything" (4). Touch features predominantly in Hermione's desire to define herself. She conceives of her identity as tangible, a self that she can grasp not mentally but sensuously. Her hand serves as a measure of understanding and authenticity—it will not let her hold what is not true. Hermione continues seeking knowledge through touch when she escapes to her bedroom and picks up two books, a translation of the *Mahabharata* and Shakespeare's *The Winter's Tale*. Holding the latter, Hermione acknowledges that her grandfather named her after the Shakspearian character, and she is, therefore, "out of this book" (32). When she picks up the *Mahabharata*, she feels a similar connection. However, Hermione appears moved less by the content of the books than by their sensuousness. She comments on the smell of the leather, which "wafted through and through innumerable compartments [of her mind] bringing dispersed elements and jaded edges together" (32). In this "healing" and "fluid" state, Hermione unexpectedly thinks, "I am the word AUM" (32). She finds this unfamiliar and disturbing. She reacts by trying to "forget the word AUM, said 'UM, EM, HEM,' clearing her throat, [and] wondered if she had offended something" (32). I suggest that "AUM" offends by disturbing sensory divisions and immersing Hermione—and H.D.'s readers—in the intersensory.

"AUM"'s intersensory power is rooted in vibration. In *Senses of Vibration: A History of the Pleasure and Pain of Sound*, Shelly Trower suggests, "Vibration provides a basis for thinking about relations between the senses . . . in so far as it can be simultaneously palpable and audible, visible and audible" (5). Ever-unsettled, vibration does not stay in place but "crosses sensory thresholds" (Trower 5). "AUM" crosses sensory thresholds through haptic vision and haptic sound. Written in capital letters, "AUM" asserts itself visually, especially in comparison to the words around it, but also tactilely, by demanding more space on the page. "AUM" also draws attention to position, by looming over other words, and to motion, by seeming to grow in size. Not only the sight but the sound of "AUM" is haptic. It enacts touch by vibrating the mouth, nasal cavity, lips, and chest. Because it is so vibratory, "Aum" (an alternative spelling of the Sanskrit "Om") is considered a sacred sound in many Eastern religions. In meditation, "AUM"'s vibrations enable transformation and connection to a higher self.

H.D. illustrates one such transformation when vibratory sound alters Hermione's sense of self. In his research on mobilities, affect, and bodies, David Bissell describes vibrations as "*becomings* that undermine stable forms and identities" (481). Through its vibrations, "AUM" shakes Hermione, physically and symbolically, alerting her to her own "becomings" (481). She admits, "I am the word AUM . . . frightened her" (32). Dropping the book she was holding, Hermione "hugged HER to Hermione Gart" and repeated "I am HER . . . The thing was necessary . . . It was a weight holding her down" (*H* 33). Against "AUM"'s disruptive vibrations, Hermione's name provides sensuous stability and reassurance. "HER" soothes sonically and tactilely—Hermione repeats "HER" as one might a mantra and holds "HER" as one might a pet. "HER" anchors Hermione to her former self—it weighs her down and acts as "ballast to her lightheadedness" caused by "AUM"'s disruptive vibrations (33).

Hermione, however, eventually accepts "AUM"'s transformative offering. Her act of redefinition, like the word that incites it, is intersensory. Hermione thinks, "God is in a word. God is in a word. God is in HER. She said, 'HER, HER, HER. I am Her, I am Hermione . . . I am the word AUM'" (*H* 32). Hermione's declaration that "God is in a word" resonates sonically and semantically. H.D. stresses this through the repetition and breathy assonance of "HER," "God," and "AUM." Here, again, the sound of language appears more impactful than its meaning. "AUM"'s sonic vibrations shake things up: they rattle the sensory structure by conjoining the senses, and they rattle the sensing subject by reverberating throughout her body. Such reverberations are common to "audible language," which, Michel Serres suggests, "tremble[s] from the multiple meanings contained within it" (118). "AUM" signals multiple meanings through its BIG, godlike capacity. By aligning herself with "AUM" and rewriting her name in an equally intersensory way, Hermione asserts her own limitlessness and ineffability. "God is in HER," and HER refuses to be contained.

Just as Fayne's radical act of seeing empowers Hermione to see differently, "AUM"'s radical vibrations empower her to listen differently. As Brian Massumi asserts, the human sensorium contains limitless bodily "potentials" through which we subconsciously sift until "only one . . . is 'selected'" (32, 32–33). Hermione "selects" sensation in the following, as she tries on sound for size: "Clear throat, Em, Um, Hem. Aum. It was AUM. I am the word AUM" (*H* 38). In this moment, Hermione sifts through sounds and enacts choice as opposed to automatic sensory habits. "AUM" is so new a sound that it initially gets stuck in Hermione's throat, but eventually it emerges as a powerful, synesthetic assertion. "AUM" becomes Hermione's tactile, rather phlegmy, articulation of her identity—a means through which she hears, sees, touches, and tastes herself anew.

Synesthesia and Sensory Rebirth

Hermione's, and H.D.'s, embrace of a more fluid, synesthetic sensorium had social and personal repercussions. Except for Fayne, the people surrounding Hermione do not understand or condone her ideas or perceptions. Hermione's difference eventually manifests as illness. Near the end of the novel, after breaking her engagement with George Lowndes (in part because she is in love with Fayne Rabb), Hermione takes to bed for three months. Though she does not name what causes her to be bedridden, she appears to suffer from a debilitating mental illness or trauma. A nurse watches over Hermione as she drifts in and out of consciousness, sometimes babbling incessantly, sometimes hallucinating. Often, Hermione sleeps, presumably a side effect of the medicine she takes, and her dreams are plagued by a sense of social and familial failure. She dreams of failing a math exam because she had "forgotten logarithm" and of failing a science exam because "she went on breaking test tubes and the hydrochloric acid was spilt and someone said 'She needn't take it. There's no use forcing these things'" (196). Hermione's dream highlights futility and her failure to follow in her father's scientific footsteps, let alone complete school. The compounding "and" speaks to the forces piling against her, under whose weight she eventually buckles.

Hermione's illness also shows evidence of sensory strain. When she first feels sick, Hermione tells George, "'There's something wrong here'—[. . .] 'I've got a—sore throat or something'" (*H* 193). The dashes signify the stops and starts of a distraught mind, and Hermione's sore throat suggests that her sickness extends to the body. She cannot clear her throat and sound "AUM"; she can no longer use the sound and texture of her voice to orient herself. Isolated from the larger sensorium, Hermione again turns her attention to sight. Distressed, she tells her nurse, "I can't see anything," and her battle with ocularcentrism seems to overshadow all other sensory considerations (210). In fact, the lack of attention Hermione pays to the other senses during her "crisis" seems to exacerbate, if not cause, the crisis itself. By positing single-sense perception and sensory segmentation as a cause, as opposed to a cure for mental illness, H.D. goes against the grain of popular opinion and challenges common thinking about the destructiveness of synesthesia. According to H.D.'s contemporaries in the medical and social sciences, synesthesia was symptomatic of insanity. In the tellingly titled *Degeneration* (1895), Nordau declared that synesthetic tendencies were "evidence of diseased and debilitated brain-activity" (142). This was true not only of neurological synesthetes, who were unable to control the sensory associations that arose in their minds, but also of artists, who purposely employed synesthesia in their work. However, while synesthesia and multisensualism were thought to incite mental unrest, in Hermione's case, single-sense engagement is the culprit. The "disease" of which Nordau speaks can be read as a disunity among the senses: a dis-ease that society reifies through sensory segmentation and one that Hermione must cure.

Hermione remedies this dis-ease by undercutting sensory individuation and reuniting the senses. Upon waking from her "crisis," Hermione's first request underscores her commitment to synesthetic and intersensory experimentation. She tells her nurse, "I see clearly" and bids her, "Open the window ever so little, just enough so that I may hear the sun rise" (*H* 211). Hermione's choice to listen to as opposed to look at the sunrise, and the rising sun itself, signify a sort of synesthetic awakening. She does not fall back on the single-sense orientation of the microscope; she refuses to use the senses as prescribed. Instead, Hermione's ability to see clearly entails a rejection of sight as the sense par excellence. Hermione's choice to listen to as opposed to look at the sunrise indicates sensory interchange and signifies H.D.'s contribution to an expanded sensorium that promotes sensory cross-pollination. In this way, Hermione's mental collapse—what Susan Stanford Friedman calls her "psychic death"—enables sensory re-scaffolding and "becomes the chrysalis of rebirth, the emergence of a healed Hermione" (115).[14] Hermione heals not only psychically but also sensorially, and her rebirth owes an unlikely debt to the sensorium of the sea.

Sensory DeRegeneration: Mining the Subterranean Sensorium

Hermione's break from George and her temporary break from reality are evidence of larger breaks from the social and sensory status quo, which H.D. further illustrates by including sensory others and marginalized modes of perception in her ideal sensorium. Thus, H.D. offers an alternative to what Peter Nichols identifies as a male modernist impulse "to defend the self against collapse into the other" (Armstrong, *Modernism: A Cultural History* 93). H.D., instead, enacts this collapse: she purposely plummets from the height of man into oceanic metaphor where she, in the words of Rachel DuPlessis, "claims Otherness . . . claims the uncontained self" (34). Hermione's ultimate claim is a self without borders: she will not be contained to the earth and the world of the human. Like Fayne, with her avian eyesight, Hermione aligns herself with nonhuman sensory modes. Though George's mother once called Hermione "Undine," Hermione declares that "Undine was not her name, would never be her name, for Undine (or was it the Little Mermaid?) sold her sea-inheritance, and Her would never, never sell this inheritance, this sea-inheritance of amoeba little jellyfish sort of living creature separating from another creature" (*H* 112; 120). Unlike Undine, who gives up her voice (sound) for human legs (touch), Hermione will not give up one sense for another, nor one sensory identification (merwoman) for another (human woman). Hesitating to name

Undine "(or was it the Little Mermaid?)," H.D. also hesitates to name and, therefore, limit herself. She proclaims her nebulousness and her malleability—her likeness to the "amoeba little jellyfish sort of living creature" that cannot be qualified. Through the fluidity of her "sea-inheritance," Hermione sheds a socially imprinted sensory skin in favor of the shape-shifting abilities of the nonhuman. Much like she refuses to choose between the senses, Hermione refuses to choose between sensoriums but draws on *both* the human *and* the nonhuman in refashioning her sensory self.

To understand the implications of Hermione's refusal, we must look more closely at the sensory makeup of sea creatures, specifically the mollusk, jellyfish, and amoeba, which feature in H.D.'s work, as well as in early-twentieth-century scientific discussions of sensation. Nordau, for instance, posited the mollusk as the least privileged of sensory beings, in part because of the lack of differentiation among its sensory faculties. In the mollusk, eyes, skin, mouth, ears, and nose are one and the same. Because of this, sensation is not segmented or consigned to a particular sensory faculty but registers across multiple faculties. That is to say, within the mollusk, synesthesia occurs naturally. Maurice Merleau-Ponty explains that "[the] distinction between touch and sight are unknown in primordial perception. It is only as a result of a science of the human body that we finally learn to distinguish between our senses" (15). Science, in other words, attempts to naturalize certain forms of embodiment while pathologizing others and to impose order onto what it deems disorderly. Nordau decries such disorder, proclaiming, "If consciousness relinquishes the advantage of the differentiated perceptions of phenomena, and carelessly confounds the reports conveyed by the particular sense . . . it is a descent from the height of human perfection to the low level of the mollusc [*sic*]" (142).[15] Science views the mollusk's sensory makeup as primitive and chaotic—qualities that many modernists drew upon to invigorate their art. Nordau was particularly condemning of such "art" and viewed "the synesthetic strivings of contemporary poets and artists [as] 'symptoms of degeneracy and cultural decline, an aesthetic effort to valorize a reversal of the progressive specialization of the human senses'" (qtd. in Howes and Classen, *WS* 173). When artists deny the one-to-one ratio between sensations and sensory organs and shun the unique ability to differentiate between sight, sound, smell, and so forth, they engage in subpar sensory acts, dishonor the elite sensory system, and abandon their position of human sensory privilege. This, of course, was just the sort of dissensuous abandon H.D. desired.

Defying warnings like Nordau's, H.D. willingly descends into the subhuman water world, which she further mines for sensory inspiration. Therein, she finds creatures who, like herself, eschew sensory standards. Through creatures like the mollusk, namely the amoeba and the jellyfish, H.D. embraces sensory failure—what Robert Michael Brain calls, the "fortunate failure of protoplasm to differentiate itself" (192). By failing to differentiate among the senses—to segment them and assign them different values—Hermione, like the protoplasm, gains the "extraordinary powers to perceive the world in its original condition of undifferentiated unity" (Brain 192).[16] While, in popular opinion, the perceptive apparatus of creatures like the mollusk signaled degeneration, H.D. posits such creatures as regenerative *because* of their devolution—because they have not been subjected to sensory ordering and are not bound by sensory mores.

Significantly, Hermione comes to this conclusion at a time when she feels unduly bound by heteronormative social mores. One night, shortly after Hermione agrees to marry George, the two of them are laying in the woods, George "pressing [Hermione's] head down into tufts of soft moss" (*H* 117). Though Hermione seems more interested in talking, George is intent on kissing her. She recalls that "like a sponge, [George] had smudged her smooth face with kisses, had somehow . . . smudged something out" (*H* 118). While she endures George's kisses,

> The back of her head prompted the front of her head, slid a fraction of a fraction (of a tiny measurement on a thermometer or a microscope) away from the front of her head, actually almost with a little click, separated from the front of her head like amoeba giving birth by separation to amoeba. (118)

Hermione then says aloud to George, "Some plants, some small water creatures give a sort of jellyfish sort of birth by breaking apart, by separating themselves from themselves" (118). George quickly dismisses Hermione, telling her to "forget all that rot" (*H* 118).

In this scene, H.D. talks back to the patriarchy through its own scientific rhetoric. Her technical language undoes scientific thought, which proclaims some species and sensory experiences less valuable than others.

Hermione is silenced and "smudged out" by George in the same way that creatures like the amoeba are smooshed under the microscope slides of Carl and Bertrand Gart. Hermione feels a kinship with these creatures, who her father and brother breed and objectify. This kinship involves not only a shared experience of erasure but also a shared sensory makeup. Serres suggests, "The body remembers its previous aquatic life," and Hermione values that lineage (141). The "amoeba" and aquatic creatures she invokes have an ability to separate from their former selves that H.D. admires and enacts. Through them, she underscores themes of separation and rebirth, of parting—the back of her head sliding away from the front—in order to impart. We can read this as a metaphor for H.D.'s artistic evolution: H.D. gives birth to creation by separating herself from social constraints and rhetoric that inhibit her.

In the single-celled organism, unhampered by social codes, H.D. finds a structure-less sensory model ripe for the building, and upon which she did build her artistic manifesto. In "Notes on Thought and Vision," which, like *HERmione*, was unpublished in her lifetime, H.D. challenges the marginalization upon which sensory hierarchies stand by lauding what she terms the "jelly-fish experience." The jellyfish experience is a form of perception characterized by the "abnormal consciousness" of "the over-mind" ("Notes" 19). The over-mind, quite aptly, fits over the standard mind. H.D. writes that it "seems like a cap, like water, transparent, fluid yet with definite body, contained in a definite space. It is like a closed sea-plant, jelly-fish, or anemone" ("Notes" 18–19). Though the over-mind is "contained," "closed," and somewhat self-protective, its transparency and fluidity are plastic and permeable. It is not only a state of mind but also a state of body. Despite the essay's title, the over-mind is not solely visual. Instead, it evokes multisensuality through "a set of super-feelings [that] extend out and about us; as the long, floating tentacles of the jelly-fish reach out and about him" ("Notes" 19). H.D. conceives of the jellyfish as an empath, eager to commune with and explore the world around it. Notably, the jellyfish explores by feeling through tentacles or oral arms where touch and taste—two stereotypically feminine senses—are not segmented but one and the same. Not only are touch and taste concurrent, they—not vision, the sense typically associated with knowledge—provide a means of comprehending the world. By elevating the feminine sensorium, H.D. combats male sensory elitism; by taking the jellyfish as a model,

H.D. suggests that there are different ways of conceiving sensation and of knowing the world through our senses.

HERmione is an ode to this sensory difference. Declared "H.D., Imagiste" by Ezra Pound and consigned to the realm of the visual, H.D. reacts to that limitation. *HERmione* is a declaration of H.D.'s multisensuality: a dissensuous assertion that she is more than a conjurer of images, just as she is more than an image herself. The resulting sensory revolution renegotiates the gendered, heteronormative, segmented sensorium that H.D. refuses to adopt. Her refusal begins by recognizing the sensory regime of the microscope and all it signifies. The microscope makes material an abstract, often invisible, sensory hierarchy that is complicit with other normative practices, and it sheds light on the compactness of sensory experience under normative dictates. Its prescriptive ways of seeing encourage Hermione to see as well as to hear, smell, taste, and touch differently. This difference is rooted in uprooting, in challenging sensory norms, and in committing dissensuous acts that shake the sensory establishment. Hermione positions her mother and father within this establishment, although at opposite ends of the sensory spectrum, and her question "what am I between them?" underscores her struggle to navigate the gender and sensory divides that confront her (*H* 81). H.D. chooses, however, to break the binary: she remains in-between— "swing-swing between worlds" (25)—wherein her sensorium flourishes, and she claims her protean, sensory self.

2

"choked by a robot!"

Technology, Gender, and the Battle
of the Senses in Mina Loy's *Insel*

As discussed in the previous chapter, H.D.'s sensory experimentation challenges limiting, patriarchal ideas about women and sensation. Specifically,
H.D. counters an ocularcentric, unisensory worldview through queer and
nonhuman sensory modes, which enable the integration of the senses. In
this subversive experimentation, she is not alone. Like H.D., Mina Loy exposes how masculinized vision and visual technologies malign the female
body and the so-called feminine senses. To counter this trend, Loy evokes a
multisensuous prose that is at once technologized (masculinized) and embodied (feminine). In so doing, she argues for an integrated, expansive, and
decidedly feminist sensory worldview. For Loy, the body—in its messy sensuousness—is something to be celebrated, not denigrated.

Writing to her friend Carl Van Vechten, Mina Loy proffers a surprisingly
cheerful description of her experience as a Red Cross volunteer in WW1.
"You have no idea," Loy professes,

what fallow fields of psychological inspiration there are in human
shrieks and screams . . . I'm so wildly happy among the blood & mess

for a change & I stink of idioform—& all my nails are cut off for op-
erations—& my hands have been washed in iodine—& isn't this all a
change . . . I will write a poem about it—& you should hear what a tramp
calls the Madonna when he's having his abdomen cut open without
anesthetic. (qtd. in Burke, *Becoming Modern* 187)[1]

Loy's gleeful response to the horrors she witnessed is unexpected, even disturbing. However, as readers, we have to question if we are conditioned to
see Loy's comments as disturbing because of her gender. Should a woman
celebrate such horrifying sights and smells? What kind of woman would do
such a thing? The average woman, Loy might answer, whose sensory experience was too often limited to hearth and home. For this woman, as for Loy,
the sensory-rich environment of war is a welcome "change" to an otherwise
sterile, everyday environment. Loy finds the sensuous "mess" of the surgical
hospital a source of artistic inspiration. She conceives of the smells, sounds,
and sights associated with the human body as fodder for her embodied
aesthetic: an aesthetic that, as a woman, she was often prevented from or
criticized for realizing. Carolyn Burke suggests that Loy's war poems often
say less about the war men fight—"the machine war"—than about the war
women fight—the "sex war"—and the same can be said of Loy's less-popular
prose (*BM* 188). In her posthumously published novel, *Insel*, Loy situates the
sex war on sensuous grounds, uncovering and critiquing sensory violence
done to women through technology.

Insel charts the relationship between Mrs. Jones, a writer who narrates the
story, and Insel, a Surrealist painter with an eccentric personality. Loy's novel
is loosely based on her three-year relationship with the German painter
Richard Oelze, whom she met and befriended in Paris while curating art
for her son-in-law's gallery. Just as Loy encouraged Oelze and supported his
work, so, too, does Mrs. Jones encourage and support Insel. Acknowledging
his talent, as well as his aimlessness, Mrs. Jones gives Insel a key to her Paris
apartment to use as a studio space when she travels. So begins the story
of their strange and intense relationship. Insel/Oelze epitomizes the ragtag,
underbelly of society that Jones/Loy finds so alluring. Elizabeth Arnold refers to Insel as an "ethereal bum [who] belongs to a long line of materially
destitute characters in whom Loy located spiritual riches" (*Insel* 169).[2] When
Mrs. Jones first meets Insel, he has taken the persona of starving artist to an

extreme. A "clochard" and "wastrel" who seems both deprecatory of and dependent on women, Insel nevertheless emits a magnetism that appeals to Mrs. Jones (*I* 28, 40). She is drawn to his rays or "Strahlen"—the "kind of radioactivity [he] gives off"—and asks permission to write Insel's biography, of which *Insel* is the result (*I* 87, 95).

Though Loy wrote *Insel* in the years spanning 1933–1936, the novel was not published until 1991 and has yet to garner sustained critical attention.[3] Andrew Gaedtke points out that *Insel* "has suffered the same disregard within contemporary modernist studies that it faced when Loy failed to find a sympathetic publisher" (143). However, several critics do offer insightful and valuable readings of this notoriously difficult text. Sarah Hayden reads *Insel* as a response to Fascist rhetoric about degenerate art and artists.[4] She refers to Insel himself as "a direct affront to Fascist body aesthetics," which laud clean, strong, able bodies, and she suggests that Insel's paintings are the type that would have been publicly ridiculed in *Degenerate Art (Entarte Kunst)* exhibitions common in Nazi Germany in the late 1930s (Hayden, *Curious Disciplines*, 191, 180). Hayden suggests, however, that Loy celebrates Insel *because* of his deviance, positing him as a radical "'degenerate' icon" (*Curious Disciplines*, 189). Tyrus Miller reads *Insel* as a response not only to the threat of Fascism but also to a confluence of events that left the modernist artist in a precarious position. Miller argues, "The internal exhaustion of the [modernist] movement" combined with the Depression, fear of a second world war, and the rise in reproduction technology created a "changed situation for artists" that Insel physically embodies (210).

I read Insel somewhat less sympathetically, as one who, despite his own perilous position, mistreats and maligns others, specifically women. Tyrus Miller, Andrew Gaedtke, and David Ayers variously note Insel's connection to optic technologies, automated machinery, and electric power. I draw on their discussions to show how, by connecting Insel to such technologies, Loy associates Insel with male modernists who use technology to subjugate women's bodies and senses. Loy links Insel to Surrealists in particular, many of whom used sight and visual technologies to violate and denigrate women in their art. Linda A. Kinnahan counts Insel among those Surrealists who participate in "an aesthetic legacy of using [and abusing] women's bodies" (Kinnahan 114) and who achieve this violent aesthetic through the camera. The Surrealists' problematic deployment of visual technology underscores the misogynist and eugenicist rhetoric that circulated during the modernist period. Such rhetoric called for the suppression of the sensuous body and enlisted technology in that suppression. I argue that Loy, however, reclaims the subversive potential of the so-called chaotic, sensuous female body and enlists technology not to fortify or dismantle it but to enliven and elevate it. As such, I read *Insel* as a dissensuous text, one that offers a feminist alternative to misogynist modernist practices that use technology to devalue women's bodies and senses.

To highlight Loy's feminist uses of technology and the sensuous body, I contrast her views with sexist narratives about the body and its senses. In the first two sections, I outline how fears about the body—coded as feminine and, therefore, considered unruly and unpredictable—gave rise to bodily reform movements. Technology played a key role in these movements and fueled fantasies of bodily control, sensory regulation, and female erasure. I examine how these fantasies manifest in Insel's paintings and argue that his sensory stifling and desire for disembodiment negatively impact his art—and, I think Loy would add, modernist art, more broadly. I offer Mrs. Jones's art as a contrasting, embodied alternative. While Insel conceives of the body and technology as mutually exclusive, Mrs. Jones does not divorce the sensuous body from technology but instead sees technology as a tool for expanding embodied experience and encouraging sensory play.

In the final two sections, I look more closely at misogynist and feminist uses of technology and how such uses involve, impede, or expand the senses. I illustrate how Insel violates women through haptic vision, touch, and taste and how that violence is often bolstered through or likened to invasive, masculinized technologies. These technologies sometimes perpetuate violence in the name of progress, which Loy illustrates through the character of a young girl with physical impairments who undergoes corrective surgery. Through this technological intervention, Loy reveals a fear of nonnormative bodies and senses that became increasingly common during the 1930s, as Hitler rose to power. Though Mrs. Jones sometimes shares that fear, she also works to combat sensory and bodily violence by fighting to retain her materiality and integrate the senses. Her "integrationist tendencies" (58)—a phrase that Suzanne Zelazo uses to describe Loy's poetry and visual art and that I borrow in examining Loy's prose—illustrate the power of the sensuous female body and the important work Loy does. I read Loy's integrationist tendencies as integral to her dissensuous aesthetic. By interrogating divisions between the sexes and the senses, Loy revalues the female body and makes a case for an integrated, feminist sensorium.

Misogyny, Technology, and Sensory Regulation

Mrs. Jones's and Insel have an odd, often-contentious relationship. In many ways, Insel is Mrs. Jones's muse. She studies and copiously details his every move: she finds his aura fascinating and his embodiment, or lack thereof, flabbergasting. From his "weird" walk to his seeming lack of gravity and "deflated" facial muscles, Insel is an endless curiosity (*I* 24). In addition to studying him, Mrs. Jones often mothers Insel, whose "role was helplessness personified" (21). She nurses him back to health, gives him advice (by recommending that he clean the suit he has worn for five years without washing, for instance), and provides him a place to live. Though they build a friendship and Mrs. Jones finds Insel's eccentricity amusing, even charming at times, she tires of his tendency to court disaster and "fabricate trouble" (19). Insel is not an altogether unsympathetic character, but, like many male modernists, he has a misogynist streak. He threatens to shoot his former lover "who left him for a lesbian" and, as later examples will show, he objectifies, condescends to, and abuses women (49). Insel finds many women menacing, and he gains power over them through female erasure. Such erasure was common in the art world, and in this way, Mrs. Jones's relationship with Insel resembles many of Loy's relationships with her male modernist contemporaries.

During the modernist period, discussions about art and who was capable of creating it often revolved around biology and gender. Concerns with male infertility are characteristic of some male modernists who coveted and, in turn, denigrated creative, female power and women's ability to reproduce. Loy engages themes of male reproductive envy in her poetry as well as in her prose. For example, in the poem "Parturition," Loy "vividly discloses how much of futurism is in effect an attempt to co-opt and expropriate a female and feminine territory . . . to supplant or incorporate the power of the *mater*" (Re 808–9). The Futurist F. T. Marinetti articulates this desire in his novel *Mafarka*, in which the hero "dreams of generating a mechanical son out of his own body and 'without the aid of the vulva' or the 'complicity and help of the female womb'" (Re 800). Likewise, Ezra Pound and T. S. Eliot commit erasure when discussing *The Waste Land* by describing themselves as pregnant mother and midwife, respectively (Armstrong, *Modernism, Technology, and the Body* 135).[5] In both instances, modernist fantasies of male motherhood exclude women from the reproductive process. They reject the female body as a necessary component of procreation and creation.

Insel is also threatened by and eager to deny women's bodies and their ability to create. Though he compliments and seems truly impressed by Mrs. Jones's paintings (which, it is worth noting, were rejected by an art dealer), he also seems suspicious of her talent. We see evidence of this in his comments about the so-called masculine mind versus the so-called feminine body. When Mrs. Jones tells Insel about her failed attempts to make "maquettes" for a ballet she is composing (*I* 85), Insel responds with no shortage of hubris, blaming her failure on her sex and lauding his own artistic abilities. In the words of Mrs. Jones, Insel "*thought at me*":

> "To make things grow," he conveyed on his silence, "you would have to begin with the invisible dynamo of growth; it has the dimension of naught and the Power of Nature. As a rule it will only grow if planted in a woman—But *my brain* is a more exquisite manure. In that time in which I exist alone, I recover the Oceanic grain of life to let it run through my fingers, multiple as sand." (*I* 86)

Like the misogynist modernists he represents, Insel conceives of the masculine brain as the site of growth and rejects the feminine body's role in creation. The first irony in this exchange is that Insel, an artist whose work is faltering and, in that sense, whose "dynamo of growth" is "invisible," mansplains the "rules" of creation to Mrs. Jones, a successful writer. Secondly, by contesting the "rules" of "Nature," Insel suggests that nature somehow got it wrong, that his mind offers more fertile ground for creation than women's bodies. Insel takes it upon himself to correct nature's mistake. He forgoes the body to create language and communicate; he speaks to Mrs. Jones telepathically, through his mind. He suggests that he "alone"—without woman, the female body, or even his own body—can "recover" the gift of creation denied him.

Insel's fantasy of disembodiment resembles those of other male modernists, and by attempting to suppress the female body, Insel also attempts to suppress (feminine) sensuousness. As Constance Classen notes, women are encoded as the more sensuous of the sexes—they are "all body, all feeling" (*The Deepest Sense* 203). In devaluing women and the sensuous body, Insel participates in a history of bodily and sensory regulation common to the modernist period and to male modernists in particular. Though popular thought holds that "the female body 'spills over' while the (idealized) male body has defined bounds," male modernists seemed less certain of said boundedness and expressed fear that their bodies, too, were fluid and given to spilling over (Henning 26). They attempted to mitigate this spillage by conserving seminal fluids that, according to popular thought, were a source of creative power. Ezra Pound, for example, viewed "The sexual act as a metaphor for artistic creation, and the brain's fluids as analogous to semen" (Armstrong, *MTB* 135).[6] To ensure these creative juices remained plentiful and potent, some turned to new medical technologies and treatments, such as the Steinach operation. A popular procedure in the early twentieth century, the Steinach operation claimed to redirect men's sexual fluid for creative purposes. Though, as Tim Armstrong notes, the operation was "simply a vasectomy [where] the vas deferens was severed and sutured," patients believed that the procedure "diverted [energy] from the production of semen to the production of hormone" (*MTB* 147).[7] Thus, "the system revitalized [itself] via a shift from external to internal secretion" (Armstrong, *MTB* 147). The fluids men once released could now be retained and repurposed for their own artistic benefit.

Marinetti and his followers took a similar approach to sensation, believing that one could redirect sensuous energy to reinvigorate a particular sense organ. For instance, in "Tactilism: Toward the Discovery of New Senses" (1924), Marinetti outlines a regiment for "Tactile Education" where he instructs his pupils to "every night, in total darkness, count and be aware of all the objects in [his or her] bedroom" (*Critical Writings* 375).[8] Abbie Garrington points out that this "familiar trope suggests that the tactile faculties will be sharpened by the absence of the visual sense" and that one can reappropriate visual energy into tactile energy (35). Although Marinetti breaks from sensory hierarchies by valuing touch over vision, his method is based on an either/or binary where one sensory act forecloses another—an aesthetics of denial that rejects multiplicity and the intersensory.

Marinetti was in the habit of distinguishing not only among the senses but also among people with particular sensuous proclivities. For example, he asserts that "painters and sculptors, who naturally enough tend to subordinate tactile values to visual ones, are unlikely to have the gift for creating tactile panels of any significance" (Marinetti, *CW* 375). Similarly, he differentiates between genders in his tactile program titled "Tactile Panels for the Different Sexes," where he describes "The two rival sensibilities" and "their competing sensations" (Marinetti, *CW* 374). Even in writings where Marinetti advocates for all five senses, he prescribes stringent, step-by-step instructions. For instance, in "A dish with sounds and scents," Marinetti writes, "Eating futuristically, one uses all five of the senses . . . We put to the reader a few other rules for the perfect dinner which will help us to fully enjoy the taste of all the courses to come" (*The Futurist Cookbook* 77). He continues with directions to "first use the art of perfumes" and "to next use in measured doses poetry and music" (Marinetti, *The Futurist Cookbook* 77). His instructions show an obsessive level of sensory control, even as he attempts to evoke diverse sensuous experiences. In short, while Marinetti's aims may be noble, even revolutionary, his means are problematic. His "sense-educative undertakings" dictate values that bolster sensory hierarchies (Garrington 35). In this way, Marinetti exemplifies what Loy conceives of as a male or masculine approach to the body and its senses, one founded on separation, exclusion, and restraint.

Such restraint was often inspired by machines and technology. Disciplinary movements, which gained popularity in the twentieth-century, coincide with the "start of the age of machinery" and offer a means of overcoming feminine softness and sensuousness—those "effeminizing poisons" that Marinetti feared would "turn men into gelatine" (Classen, *The Deepest Sense* 168; Burke, *BM* 157).[9] On account of women's perceived frailty—and in an effort to preserve that frailty—women were sheltered from physically aggressive, masculine forms of bodily discipline. Instead, to retain the soft sensuousness of the feminine body, women were subjected to domestic discipline and sometimes performed mock, "fancy drills" with brooms and mops instead of guns (Classen, *The Deepest Sense* 180–90). In contrast, military drill and marching disciplined male bodies in "precise, regular, and inflexible" movements and reflected "a major concern of early machine makers: the need for uniform components" (Classen, *The Deepest Sense* 168). Such uniformity differentiated machinal, male bodies from unpredictable female bodies and helped arm men against the sensory. According to Michelle Henning, "the armored [masculine] body" functioned as a "protective shell . . . that far from simply taking on board sensory information . . . actually guard[ed] against it" (28). Insofar as they served as models for fortifying the male body, technologies and machines were considered stereotypically masculine and were often employed to masculine ends. Through technological intervention, such as the Steinach operation, and through training programs that sought to render bodies more machinelike than human, men sought to discipline the body and to rid themselves of sensuous, feminine proclivities.

Modernists weaponized technology not only in actual war but also in the sex war, a point Loy communicates through *Insel's* sexually charged language. Acknowledging the popular belief that semen "could offer a power like electricity," Loy conflates sexual power and electric power in descriptions of Insel (Armstrong, *MTB* 148).[10] Mrs. Jones remarks, "One thing . . . as above all else menacing Insel was some climax in which his depredatory radioactivity must inevitably give out" (*I* 154). By describing Insel's rays as "depredatory," Loy calls to mind a predator-prey relationship, through which Insel pillages, plunders, and otherwise destroys his victims. Insel's fear that he will lose his power—that his radioactivity will "give out" or expend itself—mirrors that of modernist men who were afraid to waste their sexual and creative energy. By associating electric energy with sexual climax, Loy underscores the ways in which technology, like sex, is a source of power that Insel (and company) is determined to control.

However, technology, Loy suggests, is not so easily manipulated. At first glance, Insel enacts a male, machinal fantasy by becoming increasingly technological. Loy describes him as a hybrid being, a "gray man and an electrified organism at one and the same time" (*I* 77). Mrs. Jones remarks that Insel "might have served as his own fluoroscope . . . He had no need to portray. His picture grew, out of him, seeding through the inner-atomic spaces in his digital substance to urge tenacious roots into a plane surface" (*I* 82–83). The fluoroscope takes X-ray video, essentially, and here, the inorganic world of pictures and projections entangles with the organic substance of Insel. Loy's description naturalizes technology—fluoroscopic images seed and root—but this seeming naturalization is not entirely innocuous. The fluoroscope's ability to "seed through" and plant "tenacious roots" imply an infiltration, an unauthorized transformation, a slow taking over. Tyrus Miller notes this loss, commenting that "Insel's very body . . . [is] thoroughly penetrated by a technology of seeing and recording" (208).[11] With this penetration comes a threatened embodiment and a loss of agency. Insel has "no need to portray"; his portrayal is automatic and mindless, even out of his control. While David Ayers posits that Insel's "personal power—as electricity, magnetism, aura or rays—increases in proportion to his physical decay," Loy underscores the limits of that power (226). Insel does appear increasingly technological and disembodied, but by likening him to easily manipulated electric objects, "like a lamppost alight," and to various technologies, from the gramophone to the projector and the X-ray, Loy cautions against placing too much faith in technology, which can overwhelm the body (*I* 31).

In *Insel*, Loy does not glorify technology as a foolproof means of maintaining bodily integrity and power but instead highlights its proclivity to break down and the body's tendency to persist. As Gaedtke notes, Loy's "descriptions fixate on [Insel's] uncanny physiology, locating him somewhere between human and machine, but a machine that seems to be in an entropic state of decay and dissolution" (145).[12] Insel is, in Mrs. Jones's words, "a wound up automaton running down" (*I* 13). Machinal fortification fails when Loy portrays Insel not as the impenetrable, machine-hardened, masculine ideal but as a permeable vessel that springs leaks and fails to operate properly. Mrs. Jones, for instance, expresses an "intuitional curiosity as to the leak in Insel's magnetic coherence," noting a "perceptible seepage in [his] torpor" (49, 109). In crafting Insel as leaky, Loy both feminizes him and parodies male modernists' attempts at bodily mechanization—a mechanization, Loy suggests, that is bound to fail. For all his efforts at containment, Insel is unable to maintain and manipulate the "internal secretions" that male modernists so carefully guarded (Armstrong, *MTB* 147). In this way, Loy exposes the limits of the machine and the explosive persistence of the body.

In Insel's paintings, Mrs. Jones observes his attempts to regulate the male body and deny its sensuousness. His paintings exemplify Henning's notion of "bounded masculinity" in that they reject the body's permeability and exhibit extreme physical restraint and strain (26). Examining Insel's paintings, Mrs.

Jones notices "an obsessive absence of a mouth [that] implied an inconceivable constipation" (*I* 82). Insel denies his subject a mouth by which to ingest and to expel, creating an aesthetics of "constipation"—a toxic sensory and bodily environment that quells production and creativity. In Loy's characteristically biting tone, she suggests that, like the Futurists and Surrealists with whom she interacted, Insel and his art are, in impolite terms, full of shit. This fullness is most apparent in *die Irma*, the painting of a woman Insel raves about but Mrs. Jones finds offensive. When studying the painter and the painting, Mrs. Jones notices that "the gutter of [Insel's] upper lip was interrupted by a seam," while Irma's was not (111). Instead, "In this very same spot[, Irma] puffed to a swollen convergence." Loy's uncharacteristically succinct prose here conveys the surprise Mrs. Jones feels. "'But Insel,'" she protests, "'her upper lip is about to burst with some inavowable disease. You have formed her of pus. Her body has already melted.' 'Exactly,' he answered with mysterious satisfaction" (111). Here, Insel displaces embodiment—the "inavowable disease" of the abject female— onto Irma. While many of Insel's paintings lack a mouth, Irma's is "swollen" to the point of exploding, as if it contains all the fluids that Insel denies his other subjects. This overwhelming embodiment threatens to "burst" her and highlights Insel's attempts to "melt" the female form into diseased oblivion.

Insel's fixation on bodily fluids manifests as a denial of sensuous fluidity. In Insel's presence, Mrs. Jones notes the absence of fluids where they otherwise should be. She remarks, "Always in [Insel's] vicinity one had the impression of living in or rather of being surrounded by an arid aquarium," and she compares his mind to "the unreal tides of an ocean without waves" (43). Here, a perverse lack of water and movement render Insel dry and barren where he should be wet and fertile. Insel cannot think sensuously or create sensuous art, a point that becomes all the more obvious when juxtaposed with Loy's sensuous language and Mrs. Jones extra-sensory perception. Using a sort of sixth sense to view Insel's thoughts, Mrs. Jones comments that they,

> like drowned diamonds[,] blew out their rudimentary bellies—almost protruded foetal arms over all an aimless baton of inaudible orchestra—a colorless water-plant growing the stumpy battlements of a castle in a game of chess waved in and out of perceptibility its vaguely phallic reminder—. (43)

Loy invokes several senses in this description of Insel's sensuous lack: fetal arms and aimless batons invoke the sense of touch, diamonds and color-less plants invoke the sense of sight, and orchestras, even inaudible ones, evoke the sense of sound. However, on all sensory fronts, Insel falls short: from the fetal arms that almost protrude to the battlements that are mere stumps, this passage indicates incompletion, an inability to productively engage the sensorium. As if influenced by Insel's inability to finish, Mrs. Jones's observation itself stops short. The dash that ends the passage is only "vaguely phallic": it reflects Insel's feebleness and serves as a "reminder" of his creative deficiency.

If, as Loy believed, the senses invigorated one's art, then Insel's choice to forego the sensuous body does not bode well for his work. Using the rhetoric of male modernism against itself, Loy suggests that, if "Creative processes find parallels in sexual function," then fearing the body and its sensuous-ness renders men impotent on both fronts (Armstrong, *MTB* 134). Through repeated use of "consummation," Loy nods to the problem of finishing that plagues Insel and her male counterparts (*I* 104). She describes Insel as both unfinished and unable to finish. Mrs. Jones repeatedly refers to him as "em-bryonic" and "increate," and his incomplete physicality fascinates and mys-tifies her (3, 55, 69, 104). Additionally, Mrs. Jones notes that Insel "*never* paints": painting is "work he no longer seemed able to do" but that she en-courages him to continue (123–24). "You must *paint those pictures*," she urges (124). Loy herself paints Insel's inability in sexual terms, equating artistic ability with sexual ability. She declares, "[Insel's] conceptions were like seeds fallen upon an iron girder. . . . The visions emitted by the organism of this truly congenital surrealist were only a wasted pollen" (45). In a novel rife with references to spermatozoa, Insel's "seeds" and "pollen" serve as yet an-other symbol of wasted masculine and creative fluid. Insel, Loy emphasizes, can neither produce nor reproduce. He appears as both a failed technology and a failed procreator: the projector-like visions he emits, like the seeds he expels, only add to his stockpile of waste. By evoking the phallic, hard, "iron girder"—an impenetrable machinal/masculine ideal that proves use-less in the creative process—Loy further emasculates Insel and undercuts male modernist reverence of technology.

Loy acerbically asserts that Insel's valorization of technology and vilifica-tion of the sensuous body render him creatively impotent. Such impotence is most notable in the setting in which Mrs. Jones first encounters *die Irma*. Mrs. Jones observers that Insel "hung over *die Irma* like a tall insect and outside the window in the rotten rose of an asphyxiated sunset the skeleton phallus of the Eiffel Tower reared in the distance as slim as himself" (*I* 110–11). Just as Insel hangs over his painting, the word "asphyxiated" hangs over these lines, drawing attention to the stunted environment in which Insel works and the suffocated body that informs (or fails to inform) his aesthetic. Loy suggests that when nature, in the form of the rose/body, rots, culture, in the form of the Eiffel Tower/art, follows suit. Just as Insel sheds his humanity and becomes no more than mere insect, the Eiffel Tower loses its wonder and becomes no more than a skeletal shell of itself. Male creative power, as represented by the phallic tower, wanes, as does the figure of Insel, who appears "slim" and insubstantial. Loy attributes Insel's insubstantiality to sensory deprivation: a sensuous impotence that infects both his life and his art.

Sight and Sensory Impotence

Sensory impotence, Loy submits, results from channeling too much creative fluid into a single sense, in Insel's case, the visual.[13] Through the visual, Loy connects Insel to the Surrealists and their violent visual practices. Kinnahan notes an evolution in Loy's poetry, which moves from an "earlier feminist impatience with male representations of female sexuality" to "a serious critique of Surrealism's female imagery and the voyeuristic lines of power set into play by the violent manipulations of bodily forms" (111). This shift, Kinnahan insightfully observes, occurs during WW2, when "Surrealism's iconographic spectacle of violence against the female body" gains further resonance when viewed alongside images of concentration camps and large-scale human rights violations (111). I argue that *Insel* joins Loy's wartime poetry in its critique of the violence against the bodies and senses of women and those deemed inferior. In this section, I examine Loy's critique of the Surrealists' single-sense devotion and the problematic ways they conceive of sight. In the section titled "Technological Trauma and Visual Violation," I examine how sight and specular technologies are not as innocent as Surrealists often suggest and are instead weaponized against women and the so-called female sensorium.

As a visual specimen, Insel is, as Mrs. Jones notes, "organically surreal":

he would be "*worth* a little money to a surrealist" (*I* 108). His mere existence seems unfathomable, proof of the Surrealist notion that sight does not accurately capture reality. This is one reason Surrealists were so fond of visual technologies like the camera. The camera allowed Surrealists "to achieve a heightened realism," what they saw as a more "superior" depiction of reality (Kinnahan 83). Through the camera, Surrealists could "insist upon a vison freed from habitual conventions of perception" (Kinnahan 82). The camera offered a hyper, penetrating vision that allowed them to see and break free from social constructs. On their surface, Surrealist visual projects, in their desire to see anew, appear to resonate with the sensory projects of Loy and the women writers this book features. However, Surrealist visual reimaginings exclude the other senses, particularly the lower senses, and in that way differ from Loy and her dissensuous sisters. Though Surrealists set out to "disenchant sight," their efforts to dethrone the so-called noblest of senses (Jay 211) often reified its centrality, thereby perpetuating gendered sensory stereotypes.

Sight is certainly central to Insel's perception, often to an obsessive degree. Insel has an addictive personality (Richard Oelze himself was a suspected addict), and sight functions as his drug of choice. He possesses a "secretive in-looking twinkle" that preoccupies him endlessly (*I* 109). This urge to look within (not without) manifests as a narcissistic visuality on which Loy lengthily elaborates:

> Suddenly it dawned upon me that one thing about this man that made him so different to other people was that contrary to our outrunning holding-up-of-the-mirror self-consciousness, his was constantly turning its back on the world and tiptoe with expectancy, peeping inquisitively into its own mischievous eyes. Or, in some cerebral acrobatic recoil, that being who is, in us, both outlooker and window, in him, astonishingly, was craning back to look *in* at the *out*looking window of himself, as if there were something he might forget, some treasure as to whose lovely existence he wished to remain assured, some lovely illusion inside him, he *must* re-see to insure its continued projection. (109)

Insel does not see like others; in fact, he cares little about seeing others. By juxtaposing the inner and outer gaze, Loy draws attention to the barriers Insel creates between himself and the world, to which Insel's consciousness "was constantly turning its back" and refusing to engage. Insel's inward looking reflects his desire to protect and maintain interiority and his particular way of seeing. Considering the link between seminal economies and visual economies, his desire to "[peep] inquisitively into [his] own mischievous eyes" appears not only self-involved but autoerotic. This is no easy task. Insel must force his vision to withdraw from the world by "recoil[ing]" and "craning back" into himself. His "visual acrobatics" are further reflected in Loy's acrobatic language. Bending back on itself, Loy's prose communicates a masculine anxiety about sight and men's place as seers. By looking "*in* at the *out*looking window of himself," Insel "re-sees" himself in the position of the looker and maintains the "illusion" of masculine visual power.

Despite conceiving of sight as masculine and therefore denying women this sensory privilege, Surrealists frame their relationship with sight as innocent, even noble. Martin Jay notes that Surrealists "sought to recover the virginal sight, the *jamais vu*, that would be the uncanny complement of *déjà vu*" (237). Jay goes on to say that

> If the Surrealists radically defied visual conventions, they did so, at least initially, in the hope of restoring the Edenic purity of the "innocent eye" ... By violently disturbing the corrupted, habitual vision of everyday life, the visionary wonder of childhood, so they believed, might be recaptured. (243–44)

Jay's description of the Surrealist agenda suggests a purification of both the visual and the feminine: a sensuous transformation likened to sexual ablution. Insel enacts this Edenic, childlike, Surrealist vision, but Loy conceives of such seeing as child*ish* and overly simplistic. After listening to Insel fantasize about "the joy of *watching* [her daughter] evolve," Mrs. Jones "realized there was nothing, nothing, in all the world elementary enough to serve as an object for such simplified observation as [Insel's]. Everything must henceforth for him drowse in an impotence of arrested development" (*I* 123). Here, Loy critiques the "joy of watching" as immature, shallow, and unproductive. Such seeing "arrests development" by looking backward to the past for sensory inspiration. Such backward-looking does not inspire new ways of seeing but impedes them, a point Loy emphasizes through language that connotes ineffectuality, namely "drowse" and "impotence." By equating such "simplified observation" with male impotence, Loy genders vision: by exposing the inadequacies of such seeing, she short-circuits the male visual fantasy.

Mrs. Jones's words express Loy's distaste for common modern visual practices. "For years," Mrs. Jones laments, "I had been submitted to the tedium of the imaginative living among races conceiving no final outlet for their dynamism but destruction, forced to inertia by the rush of intellect in the wrong direction" (*I* 165). Loy expresses a similar sentiment in the essay "Psycho Democracy." She envisions an ideal society where

> man has the conceptual power to create a substitute for war, having the same stimulus to action as the hazard of death, the same spur to renassence [*sic*] as devastation . . . [where] his mentality will evolve new forms of expressive action to inspire him to such ebullitions of enthusiasm as does the call to arms. (19)

Loy illustrates the consequences of man's misdirected thinking and the destruction that results through Insel. Both obsessively inward looking and obsessed with idealized notions of seeing, Insel is blinded by his fixation on the visual. Sitting outside the Lutetia hotel with Mrs. Jones, Insel becomes something of an idle flâneur:

> "I can see right into these people," [Insel] asserted, indicating the crowd gathered around the Hotel. "I know exactly what they are; I know what they do." And that was all. As if satisfied by his sense of insight, he needed not to perceive anything specifically, his mind exposed these people as brightly illuminated "whats." A reaction he accepted for entire comprehension. (*I* 44)

"And that was all," one of the shortest sentences in the novel, echoes Insel's own shortsightedness. Contrary to Insel's "satisfied," smug assertion otherwise, Loy's dismissive tone suggests that he gains no new insight or comprehension through seeing. In this respect, Loy again connects vision with impotence. Insel lazily "accepts" a sort of seeing that Mrs. Jones finds not only ridiculous but also restrictive. His brand of seeing is both limited and limiting: it violates by "exposing" people and dehumanizes by deeming them mere "whats." Instead of "seeing into," Insel sees through, as if the people he observes are invisible or unworthy—as if "he needed not to perceive anything specifically." However, Mrs. Jones sees through Insel's visual posturing, characterizing it as an empty practice—a missed sensory opportunity—and a damaging use of vision.

Insel's writing, which he attempts when he fails at painting, also suffers because of his devotion to the visual. The few lines he manages to write reflect his single-sense agenda: "My sister and I walked along the road. Coming to the town gate we gave it a good thump . . . All of the townsfolk came out of the gate, swarming about us to look" (125). Mrs. Jones responds to Insel's writing with little surprise, noting, "As ever, with Insel, 'to look' was a deadlock, he had written no more" (125). Vision, here, dead-ends perception. Like the gate in Insel's story, sight blocks the way and impairs further sensuous exploration. Mrs. Jones, a productive writer, finds such limited uses of sight naive and inhibiting. Loy seems to agree, positing sight alone as an insufficient sensory modality. *Insel* embodies Loy's "aesthetic of the 'inconceivable'—of what cannot be fully visualized about the subject" (Walter, "Getting Impersonal" 670). The novel foregrounds other ways of conceiving and perceiving that surpass vision and single-sense perception. Loy suggests that there is more to be written and other, more sensuously convergent ways of writing.

Science and the Sensuous Body

Loy's approach to technology, the body, and the senses invokes and revises those approaches of the Futurists, Surrealists, and many of her male contemporaries. In contrast to Insel's writing, which reflects his limited view of perception and sensation, Mrs. Jones's writing is markedly complex and multisensual. However, it is also scientific. Indeed, *Insel* itself acts as an extended "scientific" observation of Insel by Mrs. Jones. Combining scientific language with sensuous language, Loy challenges assumptions about the function of the sensuous body in scientific observation. As scientific technologies became more sophisticated, their presence in the laboratory increased and the role of the human body dwindled. In the aptly titled "The Death of the Sensuous Chemist: The 'New' Chemistry and the Transformation of Sensuous Technology," Lissa L. Roberts explains that from the late eighteenth century onward, scientists began to think of the human sensorium as untrustworthy, even obstructive. Roberts notes moments when "the presence of chemists' bodies were deemed a downright nuisance" (117). For example, Antoine

Lavoisier, often referred to as the father of modern chemistry, "advised his readers to keep their hands off the vessels that held test-substances, lest their body heat alter experimental circumstances" (Roberts 117). Women's bodies, because of their perceived volatility and their associations with the lower senses, were a particular nuisance. As Roberts notes, "In the 'new' chemistry, taste and smell virtually disappeared as formal media of chemical analysis" (123). The body, scientists proclaimed, interfered with objectivity and the intellect, and women's bodies, ever-inclined to touch, taste, and smell their surroundings, were deemed especially disruptive.

Not only were their perceptive aparati deemed more flawed than men's, but women's very presence in the laboratory signified a breach of a theretofore male-dominated, public space. In this way, the struggles of female scientists mirror those of modernist women writers. In an effort to discourage women from taking up space in the laboratory, the media often vilified women in the sciences. Marie Curie, for instance, was one of the most renowned and ridiculed women of her time. She received two Nobel prizes for her research in radiation, yet French newspapers focused on her sex life rather than on her scientific discoveries. The media labelled her an adulteress, a foreigner who "systematically destroyed" the home of an honest Frenchwoman (Reid 305).[14] Such sexualization of female scientists was common. As Colbey Emmerson Reid describes it, "the public manifestation of [women's] mental life became a sign of sexual impropriety" (306). Loy herself was no stranger to such claims. By making the female body public in her poetry, and by inhabiting a public female body, Loy incurred critical backlash. Critics, for instance, famously lambasted her poem "Songs to Joannes" for its lewd references to the "mucous-membrane" and female orgasm (Burke, *BM* 19).[15] Often, Loy's audience was flabbergasted by her explicitness. They cast her language not as anatomically correct and scientific but as promiscuous and pornographic. Alfred Kreymborg, Loy's longtime friend and editor, remarked, "Had a man written these poems, the town might have viewed them with comparative comfort. But a woman wrote them, a woman who dressed like a lady and painted charming lamp-shades" (489). As patriarchal society fought to maintain a feminine ideal, along with the mutually exclusive categories of masculine intellect and feminine embodiment, women suffered the consequences. Reid notes, "To protect their virtue, [female] intellectuals would have to retreat to the study, a figurative closet designed to narrow the scope of the mind, abandoning the body and its encounters with others" (306). Loy, however, refuses the closet. Instead of abandoning the body, she "inaugurates a poetics of self-abandonment [that contrasts] the rigid protection of bodily integrity characteristic of Futurism" and other male-dominated artistic movements (Armstrong, *MTB* 118–19). The body, Loy suggests, contains its own sensuous intellect, one that is worth exploring through sight, sound, smell, taste, and touch.

In *Insel*, Loy both utilizes and examines the entire embodied sensorium—nothing is off the table in her sensory laboratory. Mrs. Jones assumes the persona of a sensuous scientist or anthropologist and, inverting "the Surrealist tendency to view women as [their] passive muses," takes Insel as her object of sensuous study (Arnold 174). She remarks, "The casual accident of chance threw me a dope-fiend—guinea-pig for experiment—in research on the *spirit*" (*I* 165).[16] This spirit, however, manifests materially, via what Loy refers to as "the fourth dimension." In the fourth dimension, "matter exists outside of normative spatial and temporal parameters" and, in turn, lends itself to nonnormative sensuous study (Zelazo 59).[17] While laboratory research of the time adopted a hands-off approach, leaning more firmly on technology for collection and calculation, Mrs. Jones's methods are notably tactile. Curious about the "aura that enveloped [Insel] with an extra external sensibility," Mrs. Jones carries out a series of experiments using touch as the instrument and object of study:

> To investigate, I tapped him lightly on the arm in drawing his attention—and actually in a tenuous way I did feel my hand pass through "something" . . . the effect on Insel was unforeseeable—jerking his face over his shoulder, he twitched away from my fingers with the acid sneer of a wounded feline . . . Later I repeated the gesture, but as if my hand in its first contact had got coated with the psychic exudence it would seem there was no longer any hurt in it. He was calm under my touch. (*I* 46)

Repeating her tests and noting their effects, Mrs. Jones appears a proper scientist, thoroughly investigating Insel's response to sensation. Touch, arguably the most feminine of senses and often the most maligned, is central to her methodology. Physical contact alters her relationship to Insel, allowing for familiarity and empathy. The influence of Henri Bergson's ideas about the body as "conductor" and his call to "think matter" are visible in this exchange (qtd. in Zelazo 55, 61). Loy's hand serves as conduit between herself and Insel by intercepting and conveying communications. Her hand also acts as a conduit between body and mind by channeling the intangible into the tangible. Her hand is "coated" in matter from Insel's mind—his "psychic exudence"—which is no longer merely cerebral but concrete and felt. Such unexpected amalgamations "signal new forms of sensitivity" and illustrate new modes of sense perception (Gaedtke 156). Gaedtke suggests that Loy's interest in "new sensitives" corresponds to those of Frederic Myers, Henri Bergson's "occasional colleague" (155). Myers found "evidence of psychological abilities yet to come" in schizophrenics, hysterics, and others deemed mentally ill. "What was generally regarded as mental illness," Gaedtke writes, "was, for Meyers, evidence of new mental faculties . . . which were to be encouraged and fostered through proper scientific means, rather than stigmatized as failure of self-control or as 'feminine weakness'" (155–56). Loy, too, finds productive potential in new sensory modes and presents them as alternatives to limiting sensory and scientific practices.

Loy further promotes subversive sensory practices through sensuous, scientific prose. Remarking on the "technical language" of Loy's poetry, Suzanne Zelazo observes, "For Loy, it is from in-between sensual registrars that meaning emerges" (58). The same is true of *Insel*, where Loy blends the so-called softness of feminine sensation and sensuous language with the so-called aggressiveness of masculine scientific thought and technical language. Such prose breaches exclusionary gendered and sensory boundaries and revels in possibility. In this in-between space, signification is less valuable than the process of signifying, which involves exploring the sensory means at one's disposal and considering the sensuous combinations that might result. Loy illustrates sensory exploration in Mrs. Jones's observations of Insel. Mrs. Jones claims that the

> very word, *Entwicklung*, was so much Insel's word; its sound seemed to me onomatopoeic of his intellectual graph. For my alien ear, it had a turn of the ridiculous as though a vast process had got twisted in a knot of tiny twigs, haply to unravel and root, and branch against the heavens. (*I* 123)

Loy's reference to Mrs. Jones's "alien ear" speaks less to her grasp of foreign language and more to her foreign way of listening. Loy combines the visual graph of a scientist or engineer with the specialized, "alien ear" of a poet, who not only listens to sounds anew but also finds new ways to represent those sounds. The aural and visual merge as Loy translates the sound of "*Entwicklung*" into an image, a "graph" that charts sonicity visually. Sound and vision also manifest as touch—the tactile quality of knotting, unraveling, rooting, and branching out through which sensory experience, ultimately, multiplies. This rhizomatic image illustrates what Zelazo calls Loy's "multisensual aesthetics" wherein "language . . . an arboreal, fixed, and thereby truncated medium, becomes instead imminent possibility" (57). Loy accesses language, here the word "*Entwicklung*," through her body. Through an unfolding process of sensuous understanding, she reclaims the body and its senses as valuable sources of intellect and discovery.

Instead of burying the body and the senses under the weight of technology, Loy employs technology to highlight the sensuous body's capaciousness. According to Zelazo, Loy responds to "the technological innovations of modernity and the increasing mechanization of [modern] experience" by not only "hold[ing] on to the body in the face of the machine, but also us[ing] the machine as a body, expanding the limits of normative sensual experience" (49). Throughout *Insel*, Loy asks us to take stock of so-called normal sensory experiences that we might otherwise take for granted. Mrs. Jones observes one such everyday occurrence as Insel leaves her apartment. She records, "He shut the door, an act I have heard an authoress describe as so banal it is unfit for publication. But shutting the door, like all automatism we take for granted, is stupendous in its implications" (*I* 32). The "act" to which Mrs. Jones draws our attention has a mechanic, routine feel, but Loy suggests that the "authoress" who overlooks it also risks becoming mechanized and desensitized. With her perception on autopilot, she has the air of an automaton. Mrs. Jones is wary of this automatism and evokes the machine to interrogate her sensory surroundings, to register the "stupendous . . . implications" of the everyday. "When Insel shut the door," Loy writes, "infinitesimal currents ran out of him into the atmosphere, as if he were growing soft invisible fur [so] that . . . Even before he came into one's presence, one received a draughty intimation of his frosty approach" (*I* 32–33). Mrs. Jones perceives Insel's "infinitesimal currents" by herself becoming a sensory technology—not a visual technology, like those modern science privileges, but a tactile technology that feels the "invisible" electricity of Insel's "fur." Like a weather barometer or a seismograph, Mrs. Jones senses the atmospheric changes Insel effects, the draughts and frost that surround him. In this moment, Mrs. Jones acts as both the scientist and the scientific instrument. Her body does not hinder but enables this act. In fashioning Mrs. Jones's body as a technology but allowing it to retain its sensuousness, Loy subverts the traditional sensorium and invites new identifications between human and machine.

Technological Trauma and Visual Violation

While Loy associates Mrs. Jones with productive uses of technology—as a means of affirming the body's value, expanding sensory practices, and rethinking human and nonhuman relationships—she associates Insel with violent uses of technology. Loy underscores the connection between technological and sensory violence by likening Insel's vision to invasive machines. Like H.D., Loy conceives of vision as intersensory, and she emphasizes its ability to penetrate and violate. In *Insel*, as in H.D.'s *HERmione*, sight is haptic, and the male gaze manifests as a tactile, physically felt threat. To understand Insel's relationship to these violent visual technologies, we should first consider the role vision plays in Surrealist art featuring women.

Many Surrealists viewed their relationship with the female art object through the lens of courtly love. In this paradigm, a Knight strives to win the affections of a Lady, but "the fulfillment of erotic love . . . is constantly delayed by obstacles" (Bate 153). As such, the Lady herself becomes less an "actual woman" and more an unattainable ideal: she functions merely to fuel the Knight's quest (Bate 154). Thus, the so-called elevation of woman to the status of "Lady" renders her a vacuous entity, what Lacan refers to as "the Thing" [*das Ding*] (qtd. in Bate 156). Women function as "the Thing" not only by reminding the Surrealists of their desire but also by congratulating them for not acting upon that desire: they can look, but they cannot touch.[18]

And yet, Surrealists enact touch through a violent male gaze that maims, delimbs, disfigures, and otherwise empties female bodies of their agency and worth. As Linda A. Kinnahan observes, "violated feminized bodies" are prevalent in Surrealist photography and painting (Kinnahan 88). One example of the violent, male Surrealist gaze can be found in Salvador Dali's *Woman with Drawers* (1936), a painting that was showcased in Loy's son-in-law's gallery. *Woman with Drawers* depicts a woman whose head is a hollow cavern, akin to a carved-out gourd. Where the woman's eyes would be, a drawer stands open and empty: she cannot see, nor does she have a thought in her head. The woman has no nose or mouth—nothing that grants her agency or identity. A fine hair, much like the setae I discuss later in this section, covers the woman's skin, rendering her beastlike. Her most prominent features are her breasts, which hang below the frame of the painting. Dali later used this painting on the cover of an announcement for his exhibit in Julien Levy's gallery. In the announcement, the woman's breasts open, like flaps, to reveal tiny renditions of Dali's paintings (Kinnahan 102–3). Where woman's creative fluids could be, male Surrealist art spills forth instead.

Visual technologies often aided Surrealists in sexualizing and subjugating the female body, a trend that Loy critiques in both her poetry and her prose. Loy's unpublished, autobiographical novel *Islands in the Air* features a male photographer named Holyoak, whose vision she links to both the camera and the X-ray. According to Kinnahan, Holyoak embodies "the continuing power of the male who controls the technology of vision" (50), through which he exerts the "power to wound, shape, penetrate, and reveal the body concealed and the body vulnerable in its exposure" (48). Loy links Insel to similarly threatening technologies, thereby underscoring the hapticity of the male gaze. Mrs. Jones remarks that Insel's "petrified eyes drill" into walls and into people (*I* 48). In this short phrase, Loy emphasizes the fossilization of damaging acts of visual perception and of Insel's participation in a long-standing tradition of men whose eyes bore through things and people. Insel's gaze, like the gaze of Surrealists more broadly, appears scopophilic; in other words, he derives sexual pleasure and power through the gaze. In scopophilia, the eye functions as a "sadistic weapon" that ingests or subsumes the object upon which it fixes (qtd. in Bate 189). Such is true of many Surrealists, who weaponized the eye against women, thereby turning artistic subjects into sexualized objects.

Mrs. Jones herself is a frequent victim of Insel's piercing, scopophilic stare. She describes an incident when

Insel gathered himself together for some voluntary magnetic onslaught . . . Shafts from his eyes became so penetrating I could feel myself dissolve to a transparent target, they pierced me, and traveling to the further side, stared through my back on their return to his irises. (*I* 72)

Here, Loy envisions sight as a form of technologically derived power—a "magnetic" force that man wields against woman. Insel's ability to "stare through" and "penetrate" Mrs. Jones's body recalls that of the X-ray. Like the invasive eye of the X-ray, Insel's boomerang-like vision slices through Mrs. Jones: she becomes the "target" of premeditated haptic violence. Her resulting dissolution and feelings of transparency communicate trauma, the subject who disappears as the result of a violent sensuous attack.

Insel's appropriation of the "mechanical eye of the X-ray" and his veneration of technology not only deprive him of his capacity for empathy but also cause him to take pleasure in others' pain (Danius 74).[19] Mrs. Jones judges him a sadist, who feels "utter joy at sight of [her] disablement" (*I* 120). Mrs. Jones is not the only target of Insel's mechanomorphic and unfeeling gaze. He targets women, in general, as seen in the following recollection by Mrs. Jones:

> We sat around the Dôme and Insel x-rayed. All the girls, as they giggled along the Boulevard, he disrobed—more precisely, he could not see that they were dressed. As if on an expedition for collecting ivory, he *handed* me their variously molded thighs—weighed them with an indescribable sensitivity of touch. (137)

Mrs. Jones's comment that Insel "could not see" the women's clothing suggests an intentional blindness, an inability or unwillingness to see the girls' humanity—yet another instance when Insel classifies humans as mere "whats" (44). Loy implicates touch in this erasure, emphasizing Insel's hands as instruments that enable destructive vision. Likened to a butcher and a poacher, Insel uses his tactile vision to sever women into pieces, weigh them to identify the most valuable parts, and discard the rest—just as a poacher would discard an elephant for all but its ivory tusks. Insel's precision—his disturbingly careful, visual measurement and his "sensitivity of touch"—make the violence he commits all the crueler and more unusual. The emphasis on the word "*handed*" indicates Mrs. Jones's surprise at the haptic qualities of Insel's vision, the way his eyes work like hands.

If the hand serves as "the *best* example of what characterizes the *human being*, at the top of an ontological hierarchy—for attaining, taking [*prendre*], comprehending, analyzing, knowing," as Derrida suggests, Insel's hand does not prove promising (qtd. in Garrington 30). Through his hands, Insel resists touch, the most proximate of the senses, which Derrida says most closely "entangle[s] [man] in the world" (qtd. in Henning 26). Through a study of Insel's hands, Loy communicates fear of losing touch with one another and of losing the sense of touch itself. Garrington suggests that this fear was common in the modernist period, during which touch "sees its power wane, set aside by scientific and technological discovery" (30). Her critique reads as a response to Futurists and Vorticists, whose love of technology threatened to render touch obsolete. Loy invests Insel's hands with both evolutionary potential and an unrealized and already-waning power. Contemplating Insel's hands, Mrs. Jones observes:

> Out of [an] atavistic base his fingers grew into the new sensibility of a younger generation, in his case excessive; his fingers clung together like a kind of pulpoid antennae, seemingly inert in the superfine sensibility, being aquiver with such miniscule vibrations they scarcely needed to move—fingers almost alarmingly fresh and pink for extremities of that bloodless carcass, the idle digits of some pampered daughter; and their fresh tips huddled together in collective instinct to more and more microscopically focus his infinitesimal touch. (*I* 118)

Here again, Insel's hands and fingers, like the man himself, linger in an "alarming" state of embryotic preformation. His hands have the air of an amphibian—they are a pulpy mass more akin to a webbed foot or the yet-unseparated, webbed fingers of a human fetus than to a fully formed human hand. His fingers, the "almost alarmingly fresh" fingers of a not-yet-newborn, "cling" together protectively. The hands demand further protection because they are inexperienced and virginal—the yet unused, "idle digits of some pampered daughter." Loy's feminization of Insel's hands reads as an affront to his hypermasculinity. Because of their feminization and lack of use, Insel's hands possess an "atavistic" quality that lends them a "superfine," childlike "sensibility." While this childlike sensibility gestures toward perceptual potential, ultimately this potential goes unrealized. Through Insel's hands, which are both inhibited and emergent, Loy alludes to the untapped sensory potential contained in this particular sense organ.

While Insel's hands appear "aquiver" with sensory potential and budding ability, he wards off touch in an effort to ward off the feminine. This struggle is apparent in the way his touch is sometimes nurturing and sometimes harmful. Sometimes, Mrs. Jones feels "regalvanized" by Insel (*I* 57). She recalls a moment when Insel "laid a fluttering hand on [her] shoulder" and "the torture in [her] body ceased" (*I* 57). Other times, Insel's touch unsettles Mrs. Jones, the feel of his arm like a "dried branch across [her] shoulder" (*I* 153–54). However, to touch or to be touched by Insel is rare. Mrs. Jones remarks that Insel "warned off contact less he crumble": "excruciation . . . [,] in him [,] took the place of a sense of touch" (*I* 45, 70). While Insel's aversion to touch is not without pity, it also signals what Henning refers to as a masculine "closing-down of the senses" (in contrast to a feminine "openness and responsiveness . . . and lack of control") (26). It is a state of being "sense-dead and self-contained" (Henning 26). Insel's lifeless, "dried branch" of an arm and his "constricted fingers" appear both "sense-dead and self-contained," as do further characterizations of his hands (*I* 39; Henning 26). Mrs. Jones describes Insel's hands as "fearsome . . . narrow, and pallid like his face, with a hard, square ossification towards the base of the back, and then so tapering as if compressed in driving an instrument against some great resistance" (*I* 118). Insel's hands take the offensive: they are frightening and weapon-like in their "driving" force. Their "ossification," "tapering," and "compression"—what Mrs. Jones later refers to as their "cruel difficulty of coming apart"—suggest masculine sensuous posturing, a means of protecting against feminine "passiveness" and "susceptibility" (*I* 118; qtd. in Henning 26). Ultimately, Insel's inflexible hand mirrors his reductive worldview—his unwillingness to know the people and things around him—and accounts for his callous sensory interactions.

In turning against touch, Insel often turns his touch against women. Mrs. Jones describes Insel's scuffle with some prostitutes to whom he owes money as an "apologetic sacrifice" where Insel "hurl[ed] off the negresses" and "beat one of them up" (*I* 69). Here, sex, power, and violence go hand in hand. Insel refuses to acknowledge the rights of the women by denying them money. When addressing the reader, Mrs. Jones condemns Insel's bigotry, comparing him to the brutal slave owner in Harriet Beecher Stowe's *Uncle Tom's Cabin* (*I* 70). However, when addressing Insel, she is far less condemnatory of the violence he commits. Mrs. Jones glosses over the physicality of the abuse Insel inflicts, casting it in banal language, as if "beating one of them up" is an everyday, unnoteworthy occurrence. She proffers a similar, blasé attitude toward sexual violence, suggesting that Insel has "an approach of continent rape" (*I* 72). The implication is that abstaining from sexual violence is applause-worthy—that violating women is a right Insel generously denies himself. The playful tone Mrs. Jones uses to discuss physical and sexual violence against women—from "teasing" Insel about his woman-trouble to jokingly nicknaming him "*macrusallo*" (a play on *maquereau*, meaning pimp, and *salaud*, meaning bastard)—paradoxically makes Insel more threatening (*I* 71). By dismissing his aggressions as misdirected flirtations, Insel's touch becomes all the more dangerous.

Though Mrs. Jones and Loy often share similar experiences and points of view, when it comes to Insel's acts of violence, the two diverge. Mrs. Jones downplays Insel's actions, and Loy attributes this response to the violence Mrs. Jones experiences at Insel's hands—and his eyes that act like hands. When Mrs. Jones dons a new red coat, for instance, Insel responds by "Churning [her] with his eyes into the colorless vapors of his creation" (*I* 39). Insel's eyes violently toss Mrs. Jones about and, under the pressure of his gaze, her body evaporates. Using his eyes as weapons, Insel robs Mrs. Jones of her colorful vitality and asserts power over her: she becomes "his creation." This sensuous violation continues through violence committed more directly via Insel's hands. Bit by bit, against Mrs. Jones's will, Insel picks apart her red coat:

> The cloth of my coat, a *fantasie*, was sewn with lacquered red setae—wisps, scarcely attached, which caught the light, and all through the evening unusual manifestations of consciousness occurring outside the Lutetia were punctuated by Insel's staccato spoliation of that hairy cloth. He could not desist. Like an adult elf insanely delousing a mortal, whenever I laughingly reprimanded him for ruining my coat, with an acrid cluck of refutation he would show me what he had instantly plucked from the cloth—it was always a *white* hair—He did not trouble to contradict me—the evidence was clinching—But in the end the side of my coat sitting next to him was bare of all its fancy setae. (39–40)

Language of violation permeates this passage. Insel's "spoliation" of Mrs. Jones's yonic, "hairy cloth" signals an act of desecration akin to rape. The "evidence" of the crime, Mrs. Jones suggests, is "clinching": by removing the wisps of setae—the stiff, bristle-like hairs of her coat—Insel forcefully removes the protective layer that covers Mrs. Jones, effectively laying her "bare." Setae are not just hairs but sensory organs that enable sensation or locomotion in nonhumans (like spiders and earthworms), and when Insel depletes Mrs. Jones of her setae, he further divests her of sensory agency. Likened to a chicken after slaughter, Mrs. Jones is "plucked" at and picked apart. Insel's fingers strike at her with percussive persistency, and their disruptive, staccato quality denote a disconnected, dehumanizing touch. Insel himself appears inhuman here, clucking like a chicken and "delousing" like an elf. Though delousing might otherwise imply care, here it implies an obsessive cleansing and forced refashioning. Insel removes white hairs—symbolic of Mrs. Jones's age—and he shows Mrs. Jones his spoils as if gloating. Forcefully reminding Mrs. Jones of her spoiled youth, Insel happily plucks her down to a prepubescent hairlessness, which, again, functions as a critique of her womanly maturity.

In this way, Insel inflicts harm not only tactilely but also visually. He rids Mrs. Jones of the ability to fashion herself—to assert her own visual agency—and instead fashions her to his liking, thereby claiming that power for himself. This removal, then, is both literal and metaphoric: Insel destroys not only the "fantasie" of Mrs. Jones's coat but also the fantasy of woman's control. Cloaking the event in metaphor, Mrs. Jones tries to distance herself from the trauma of Insel's touch. She uneasily, "laughingly reprimands" Insel, thereby gaining emotional distance from the shocking act. Loy further communicates shock and distance through the dash. Dashes cut through the final lines, serving as a reminder of tactile violence. Dashes also cordon off the crime scene, emphasizing Mrs. Jones's final acknowledgement that "in the end" Insel has violated her, the pile of setae at his side proof of his plunder.

Masticating Men and Consumable Women

By describing Insel as "delousing," Loy connects Insel to parasitic acts of eating and violence committed through taste. Taste and Insel's appetite structure much of the story, and Loy introduces both Insel the character and *Insel* the novel through the sensory site of the mouth. In the opening lines, Mrs. Jones remarks,

The first I heard of Insel was the story of a madman, a more or less surrealist painter, who, although he had nothing to eat, was hoping to sell a picture to buy a set of false teeth. He wanted, he said, to go to the bordel but feared to disgust a prostitute with a mouthful of roots. (*I* 3)

Loy conflates Insel's ability to consume food with his ability to consume, or purchase, products and services. Insel displays power through his ability to buy teeth just as he can buy sex and women. However, he also feels anxiety about his mouth as a public, sexualized representation of his masculinity (or lack thereof). He frets over it, worrying what women will think of his mouthful of impotent "roots." To compensate for his insecurity, Insel aggressively pursues women, exhibiting an alarming taste and insatiable desire for the opposite sex. Women become the foodstuff upon which the clochard parasitically feeds.

Insel's mouth is an inescapable source of sensuous violence: an always-threatening, ever-consuming sensory faculty. Loy likens his mouth to a consumerist machine that never sleeps. It works, ceaselessly and inexplicably, with inhuman regularity. Upon waking Insel one morning, Mrs. Jones confronts his mouth as one would a monster:

With the unforeseen ugliness opening up suddenly emerging hippopotami *the gums* in their hideous defenselessness *observed* me—an obscene enjoyment of ill-will pleated his clamped lids. His teeth had not decayed. They were *worn* down. (*I* 94)

The rapid-fire pace of Loy's nearly punctuation-less syntax communicates the terror Mrs. Jones feels. Insel features as what the Surrealist painter Paul Nougé referred to as a "bewildering object" (qtd. in Jay 238). Such objects, Andre Breton contended, "*bewilder sensation*" through "the systematic derangement of all the senses" (qtd. in Jay 238). Loy achieves this bewilderment by rearranging Insel's sensory faculties—his "clamped lids" gain the mouth's ability to grimace in "ill-will," just as his mouth perversely gains the eyes' ability to see.[20] Insel's clamped lids suggest a blind consumerism that is itself nightmarish. However, the bulk of the violence in this scene comes from the gum's observatory powers: Loy shifts the male gaze to the mouth. This serves again as a poignant illustration of scopophilia, which psychoanalyst Otto Fenichel describes (in multisensuous metaphor) with the equation "to look at = to devour" (qtd. in Bate 189). Rather than threatening outright consumption, Insel's toothless mouth threatens brazen grotesquerie, one that looks back at the horrified viewer. Mrs. Jones is appalled that Insel's teeth have not "decayed" from lack of hygiene, as one might expect, but are *"worn down"* as if from ravenous grinding or gnashing. Likewise, the sonic persistency with which Loy crafts this passage wears down the ear: word pairs like "unforeseen" and "obscene," "observed" and "emerging," and "ill-will" confuse sounds and meanings, disorienting the reader just as Insel disorients Mrs. Jones. The confluence of sensations in this passage suggests that "getting in touch with Insel" runs not only "the whole itinerary of Good and Evil" but also the gamut of sensation (94). Eyes and mouth work in tandem to illustrate Insel's cross-modal, consumptive desire. However, by depicting Insel's desire in terms that are as visually stimulating as taste invoking, Loy dismantles ideas about the separation of the senses. She renders the masculine, "distant" sense of sight just as bodily as the feminine, "proximate" sense of taste, thereby resisting male sensory violence.

In *Insel*, Loy inverts the parasitic structure she outlines in her "Feminist Manifesto." In the latter, Loy writes of women's dependence on men and the limited choices available to them. As "conditions are at present constituted," Loy proclaims, "you have the choice between **Parasitism**, & **Prostitution**—or **Negation**" (*The Lost Lunar* 154). Loy suggests that to survive in the world, women must either live off men, through marriage or sex work, or deny men and, in so doing, deny themselves social agency. In *Insel*, however, women do not rely on men for their survival; instead, Insel lives off and feeds on women. Loy depicts this feeding quite literally. Like his "vampiric" art, Insel depends on others for food and energy (*I* 82). As mentioned, Insel is near-starving, and many of his encounters with Mrs. Jones involve food. Not only does Mrs. Jones frequently buy Insel dinner and feed him—lifting the fork to his mouth when he is too weak to do so himself—but she herself becomes food-like in Insel's presence. She variously refers to herself as "an undiminishable steak" and "his beefsteak," a slab of meat upon which Insel's preys, but also to which he "prays" (*I* 69, 45). Notably, Insel worships Mrs. Jones's body only when it functions to nourish him. By conflating his acts of preying/praying, Loy underscores the perversity of Insel's so-called reverence.

Insel orchestrates a moment of reverse transubstantiation, wherein Mrs. Jones becomes mere meat. "Suddenly," Mrs. Jones recalls, "I felt myself sag; become so spineless, so raw—. I, a red island with its shores of suet" (45). The verbs and adjectives in this passage connote Mrs. Jones's meatiness. She "sag[s]" like a "spineless" carcass on a butcher's hook; she appears "red" and "raw" like a bloody piece of meat. Loy draws attention to Mrs. Jones's edible organs by enveloping her in "suet," the fatty tissue that lines the organs of livestock. Mrs. Jones's isolation, which Loy emphasizes through the words "I" and "island," cast this not as a moment of spiritual communion but as a sacrificial act that is alienating and objectifying. Mrs. Jones, however, appears somewhat oblivious to her objectification. She comments that "her condition as undiminishable steak" made her feel "almost sublime," and she seems to revel in both her materiality and her untouchability (45). This reads as a moment of situational irony. Unlike Loy's reader, Mrs. Jones cannot see the full extent of the damage that Insel, or the systems he upholds, can do.

Mrs. Jones herself sometimes perpetuates this system through her reaction to and fear of disability. This is most apparent in her descriptions of Fifi, a young French girl whom she briefly befriends. Mrs. Jones describes Fifi, in less than delicate terms, as "a little girl whose intelligence was like a jewel in a case too tightly closed. A backward child, one of those partial imbeciles, who, not being 'all there,' showing only half their human nature, are either angelic or diabolic" (*I* 129). Through her either/or language, Mrs. Jones perpetuates reductive narratives about disability and gender. She utilizes what disability studies scholars David T. Mitchell and Sharon L. Snyder refer to as the "contrasting deployment of disability—as a device of artistic innovation that entrenched disability's associations with corruption" (5). Because Mrs. Jones is devoted to expanding sensory and bodily ability, she fears the conditions that corrupt and inhibit Fifi's mind, which is "too tightly closed" and constricted. This fear becomes a reality when she psychically inhabits Fifi's mind. "As if a flash of sympathetic insight 'put me in her place,'" Mrs. Jones recalls, "I suddenly found myself imprisoned in Fifi's mind . . . My brain, like a bird in ceaseless hurt, beat its wings for the conscious liberation against a cage" (*I* 130–31). Through this moment of shared pain and imprisonment, Loy evokes sympathy for Fifi. This sympathy is both problematic and productive. Loy does not allow Mrs. Jones, or her readers, to retain a comfortable distance from disability; instead, she emphasizes its nearness. Mrs. Jones's negative response to that nearness, however, reifies disability as undesirable—it is a "cage" from which one must escape. At the same time, confronting the immediacy of disability enables Mrs. Jones to feel compassion for Fifi and anger at the unjust treatment she receives.

Through Fifi's disability, Loy criticizes the systematic suppression of non-normative minds and bodies. Like Fifi's mind, Fifi's body is also caged, a point Loy illustrates through the image of Fifi being as "rigid as bygone queens in her orthopedic corset" (*I* 128–29). Doctors promise to make Fifi like "average children" by grafting a bit of her leg into her spine, "thus rectifying her crookedness and relieving her pain" (130). Though this operation is somewhat altruistic, it is also corrective: it will realign Fifi with acceptable physical standards by straightening her "crooked" body. Fifi's crookedness underscores her marginality; her body is a warped version of the physical ideal. The desire to normalize Fifi applies not only to her body but also to her mind. Mrs. Jones recalls that she had "only once . . . seen [Fifi] unhappy . . . A drip of anguished words revealing how she received as an awful animosity her mother's solicitous efforts to get her to 'make sense'" (130). Because others do not understand Fifi—because she does not "make sense" by typical standards—they deem her unfit. Instead of accepting her difference, they attempt to alter and erase it.

Loy depicts this erasure as a consumptive act: like Mrs. Jones, who she so often makes meaty, Loy offers up Fifi as food for thought. Because her spinal condition leaves her body stiff and inflexible, Fifi envies the duck because, she says, "*Il dort dans son dos* [He sleeps on his back]" (*I* 130). The connection between Fifi and fowl further entwines when, after undergoing surgery to correct her "crookedness," "Fifi died most uncomfortably, lying very much like a trussed duck, only on her tummy—her leg being bent up behind her for the grafting and bound to her back—screaming in a nursing home until she had no more breaths" (*I* 130). By likening Fifi to a "trussed duck," Loy not only highlights her less-than-humane treatment but also effectively renders Fifi a dinner dish. Hers is another sacrificial body, one that died on the altar of surgical intervention and technological improvement. Caught under the scalpel of medical imposition, Fifi becomes a spectacle, a perverse body served on a platter for visual consumption. Loy makes the reader complicit in this consumption, crafting a subject-object relationship between a human and her food that shocks and horrifies. In so doing, Loy positions Fifi as a vulnerable and powerless victim of systemic bodily violence.

(Re)Integrating the Sensuous Body

While Mrs. Jones is also subject to the same system that robs Fifi of her body, imperfect though it may have been, she acknowledges that "—unlike Fifi, I could get out" (*I* 131). While Fifi had little to no say in her future, Mrs. Jones defies male imposition by fighting against the "dissolution" of the sensuous body (107). Just as doctors dismantle Fifi's body, Mrs. Jones undergoes an "incredible dematerialization" via contact with Insel (128). Insel's lack of materiality is well-documented by Mrs. Jones. She notes his "air of friability" and comments that "his body—what was left of it—seemed less ponderable than it should have been" (46). Insel, Mrs. Jones declares, "was made of extremely diaphanous stuff" (45). While this disembodiment exemplifies a social ideal, Loy positions it as undesirable. Challenging rhetoric that characterizes bodies as infectious and dangerous, Loy suggests that the absence of Insel's body is itself a disease and a social threat. As if contagious, "Insel, whose illness was dissolution," passes his dissolving disease to Mrs. Jones (107). She explains that one night, "I unexpectedly disintegrated. My body, which had hitherto made upon itself the impression of a compact mass, springing a multiplicity of rifts, changed to a fractional covering I can only compare to the spines of a porcupine; or rather vibrant streamers on which my density in plastic undulation was being carried away—perhaps into infinity" (127). Though Insel is not with her when this occurs, Mrs. Jones attributes her experience to him and compares her embodiment—or lack thereof—to his. Just as Insel springs leaks, Mrs. Jones springs "rifts" from which her materiality seems to seep. She no longer feels like a corporeal, solid substance but experiences only a "fractional covering" that leaves her body exposed and unprotected. The hairlike setae of which Insel robs Mrs. Jones return here in the form of porcupine quills, recalling and emphasizing Mrs. Jones's diminishment. The "vibrant steamers" and wavelike "undulation[s]" transmit electric currents that shock Mrs. Jones. In this electrically charged moment, she appears to encounter what Loy refers to, in the unpublished essay "Notes on Metaphysics," as the "Electrolife" (qtd. in Parmar 71). Sandeep Parmar describes Loy's "electrolife" as "an essential, universal current that connects the mortal body to the creator by means of conduction" (71). Though this connection is meant to recharge the individual, here, it overpowers Mrs. Jones, reducing her "density," causing her body to "disintegrat[e]," and leaving her fragmented and fractured. Being closer to the life force, paradoxically, brings her closer to death. Loy's language reflects the liminal state Mrs. Jones's body occupies. Like the interrupting phrase "—perhaps into infinity," Mrs. Jones's body hangs in the balance.

In an act of feminist defiance, Loy does not dissolve Mrs. Jones's body, as she does Insel's, but retains her materiality. This is not an easy feat, however, and the assault on Mrs. Jones's body and senses attests to the strength of the social and material forces against which she battles. "Climbing slowly up the hill to the station to buy a newspaper," Mrs. Jones explains,

> I was cleft in half. Like the witch's cat when cut apart running in opposite directions, suddenly my left leg began to dance off on its own. Thoroughly frightened at this bisectional automatism, I somehow hopped to the fence on my right and clung to it in an absurd discouragement. (*I* 128)

Here, the female body that inspires so much divisiveness becomes divided and "bisectional." Loy demonstrates how the binary logic of opposites—left/right, male/female, technology/body, desirable/undesirable—generates fracture. Such polarities leave Mrs. Jones feeling torn in "opposite directions." Like "the witch's cat cut apart," she undergoes a sort of vivisection; like Fifi, she falls victim to a cruel experiment. One difference between Fifi and Mrs. Jones is that the latter's experience occurs not in an institution but in an everyday setting through which Loy emphasizes the anti-feminine, anti-corporeal, and anti-sensuous ideologies women must contend with in their daily lives. By locating such contention in the female body, Loy also illustrates the way social pressures manifest as tangible physical forces. Such forces threaten to reshape Mrs. Jones's body and dispossess her of corporeal power. Mrs. Jones, however, reclaims her bodily agency through the hand. Touch, a so-called lower sense, serves a higher purpose, anchoring Mrs. Jones in the material world. Through it,

Loy combats male sensory violence and resists those forces that attempt to dissolve, disfigure, and dismember the sensuous female body.

In the face of forces that attempt to disintegrate and divide, Mrs. Jones seeks to integrate and unify the senses and sensing bodies. She realizes her vision in a rare moment when she and Insel sensuously and psychically connect. This moment illustrates what Re calls a "true futurist (r)evolution," which "resides . . . in the transformation of sexual codes to liberate both man and woman by ending the false opposition of feminine body vs. masculine mind" (813). These oppositions are put to rest when Insel sleeps. After helping the restless man fall asleep, Jones receives "an invitation to wholly exist in a region imposing a supine inhabitance" (*I* 88). It is important to note that Insel consents to this communion. While Insel's incursions into other people's materiality are often uninvited and intrusive, Mrs. Jones enters Insel's mind only at his beckoning, via psychic "invitation." What unfolds thereafter is an experience of "interpenetration" (Loy, "Feminist Manifesto").[21] Mrs. Jones "participat[es] in the ebullient calm behind Insel's eyelids, where cerebral rays . . . were intercepted by resonant images audible to the eye, visible to the ear; where even ultimate distance was brought within reach, tangible as a caress" (*I* 89). This description illustrates how Loy collapses the distance between Mrs. Jones and Insel, the barriers between inner and outer, and the space among the senses. She grants hearing to the eye and vision to the ear, loosening stringent definitions and broadening sensory capabilities. This productive state, however, is available only when Insel sleeps—when he lets his guard down and does not attempt to contain or control the sensuous body. His subconscious, freed from social restraints, becomes a fertile breeding ground for sensation. Behind Insel's closed eyes, where the hegemony of vision is temporarily stilled, Mrs. Jones notes an "ebullient calm"—the possibility for a bubbling up or boiling over of sensuousness that Insel rejects when awake. The synesthetic "outburst," then, remains the realm of the subconscious and the feminine, a capacious sensuousness that the masculinized social consciousness continues to refuse.

The final exchange between Insel and Mrs. Jones illustrates this difference, which Loy characterizes as a choice between death and life, destruction and creation. Insel, "passionately in love with Death," often repeats, "*Sterben—man muss*" [To die—one must] (*I* 55). Mrs. Jones, however, counters Insel's morbid mantra with her own affirmation: "*Man muss reif sein*—One must be ripe" (153). Her assertion causes Insel to "crack as if he had been *shot* alert. 'Could she possibly mean it,' I could '*hear*' him asking himself . . . 'Here is a woman with whom there is absolutely *nothing* to be done'" (153). Mrs. Jones's assertion that "one must be ripe" suggests that one must be fertile, willing, and able to bear fruit: one must be female. With this claim, she establishes herself and her words as weapons that "crack" Insel's walls of resistance. If she is "a woman with whom there is absolutely nothing to be done," as Insel thinks, it is because she refuses to be done away with. Just as she frustrates Insel, she commits to continue frustrating social and sensory norms.

In the beginning of the novel, after remarking that her paintings had been rejected by an art dealer, Mrs. Jones expresses a desire to "Forget all form I am familiar with, evoking a chaos from which I could draw forth incipient form, that at last the feminine brain might achieve an act of creation" (*I* 20). She claims that Insel "had done this very thing . . . But with a male difference" (20). *Insel* is evidence of Mrs. Jones's struggle and achievement, "but with a [fe]male difference." In revaluing the female brain and body, Loy reappropriates the masculine rhetoric that associates femininity with chaos. Chaos, she suggests, has the power to disintegrate not the sensuous body but the systems that inhibit the sensuous body and, by extension, women. She enacts what Burke, referring to Loy's infamous "Love Poems," calls "the disintegration of an ideal, or, more positively, the process of 'deconstruction' that Gertrude Stein described to Loy as the aim and technique of modernist art" ("The New Poetry" 51). Unlike Insel's disembodied art, *Insel*, in its messy sensuousness, illustrates the productive chaos of the body and its senses. Loy's dismantling makes way for new, feminist forms and intelligibilities. While Insel's embryonic emanations never come to fruition, Mrs. Jones successfully "draw[s] forth incipient form." Through it, she maps the difficult terrain modernist women traversed when attempting to "at last" realize and receive recognition for "an act of creation."

Loy shares her act of creation, and her battle, with womankind. In writing *Insel*, she releases "myriads upon myriads of distraught women" who share her feelings of being "*choked by a robot*" (*I* 134). By exposing how technology was masculinized and weaponized against women—smothering their voices and depriving them of bodily and sensory agency—Loy undoes the masculine stranglehold on the sensorium and the female body. She combats woman's erasure by repurposing technology to feminist ends. Under her direction, technology does not barricade bodies and bolster divisions but promotes integration and exploration. While misogynist modernist rhetoric demeans the sensuous female body and stifles sensory experimentation, Loy's writing births new linguistic and sensory forms. Disorienting, nonlinear, and non-logocentric, *Insel* does not invite mastery but continues to generate meanings and multiplicities.

3

" . . . A zoom severed it"

Sensory Interruptions in Virginia Woolf's
Between the Acts

In the previous chapter, I discussed Mina Loy's subversive use of technology and sensation to counter masculine violence, which became increasingly more threatening in the context of WW2. Virginia Woolf, also writing during the war, commits similarly subversive acts not only to confront masculine violence but also to resist Fascism's bodily and sensuous control. Where Loy works to expand sensory thinking, Woolf works to ensure sensory practices remain spontaneous, not standardized. To do this, Woolf, like H.D., who I discuss in chapter 1, invokes nonhuman sensations that challenge patriarchal and anthropocentric sensory paradigms. For both Woolf and H.D., the nonhuman inspires sensuous possibility. By elevating nonhuman animals alongside other so-called inferior sensory beings, Woolf celebrates alternative sensory practices and the too-often-devalued bodies associated with them. Unlike H.D. and Loy, Woolf pays special attention to aural technologies, which played an important role in Fascist attempts to homogenize sensory experience. By reappropriating these technologies and aligning them with the sounds of nature, Woolf disrupts Fascism's dangerous biopolitics. In its stead, she proffers a sensuous hybridity in both the content and the form of her writing.

"Are machines the devil, or do they introduce a discord . . . Ding dong, ding . . . by means of which we reach the final . . . Ding dong . . ." (*Between the Acts* 136).[1] So ponders one of the "old cronies" in Woolf's 1941 novel, *Between the Acts*. Interruptions like the dinging of the bell appear frequently in Woolf's final novel, which was itself interrupted and not quite finished at the time of her death.[2] In this bit of dialogue, Woolf voices a modernist concern about disruptive machines, a concern that became more pressing as suspicions regarding modern technologies, like the warplane and the radio, intensified during WW2. The ever-growing body of technology—ranging from the telephone to the gramophone to the motorcar—interfered with life as usual. Such interferences were often sensory, as in the aural "ding dong" of the clock bells that sounds in the passage above. While it may be tempting to dismiss such interruptions as mere nuisance, emblematic of an all-too-common modernist dissonance, Woolf advises differently. In *Between the Acts*, Woolf draws attention to the productive potential of technological and sensuous disruption and posits such disruption as a source of sensory liberation. By exploring the sensory dimensions of the various interruptions Woolf stages, this chapter highlights the ways in which Woolf features subversive technologies, deviant sensory characters, and new, often-nonsensical sensations of modernity to advocate for alternative sensory practices.

Sensory practices include the various ways humans respond to and make sense of, or process, sensations: the way, for instance, one categorizes scents as pleasant or unpleasant or sounds as desirable or undesirable (mere noise). Over time, sensory practices become sensory habits, which we enact automatically. These habits are reinforced by society and culture, with social norms dictating which senses and sensory practices are accepted and valued and which are not. In this way, sensory practices are performative: they are socially supported and socially constructed, and they vary from society to society. *Between the Acts*, itself a story about a stage performance, draws attention to sensory performativity and the process of making sense of sensation. Woolf highlights the performativity of sense-making through the performance that takes center stage in her novel. As the novel begins, auteurs, actors, and audience members gather for the annual charitable play, sponsored by the Oliver family. Hereafter, the stage production and the production of sense-making ensue. However, by featuring various sensuous and technological interruptions in and around the play, Woolf prompts characters and readers alike to dwell in the space "between the acts" of sensing and sense-making.

The act of sensing, and sensation itself, are pre-performative. In its raw, unprocessed form, before humans categorize and hierarchize it, sensation is "the direct registering of potential" (Massumi 97). Brian Massumi defines it as "a sheerness of experience, as yet un-extended into analytically ordered, predictably reproducible, possible action" (97). In other words, sensation can inspire endless reactions, and only through social processes and pressures are such reactions shaped and limited. With its myriad possibilities and potentials, sensation is similar to affect. The term "affect" is particularly useful for theorizing the liminal space that exists between categories, where much of *Between the Acts* takes place. Like sensation, definitions of affect are elusive and varied. Firstly, affect can denote emotion. An affective turn seems fitting for a novel that questions, "Did the plot matter?" And answers, "Don't bother about the plot; the plot's nothing . . . The plot was only there to beget emotion" (*BA* 63). A more nuanced definition of affect, however, proves even more useful in reading *Between the Acts*. According to Melissa Gregg and Gregory J. Seigworth, affect "arises in the midst of *in-between-ness*: in the capacities to act and be acted upon" (1). They further explain, "Affect marks a body's belonging to a world of encounters [. . .] but also, in non-belonging, through all those far sadder (de) compositions of mutual in-compossibilities" (Gregg and Seigworth 2). Woolf herself spoke of such encounters and "in-compossibilities" in the oft-quoted "A Letter to a Young Poet." Advising her nephew Quentin, Woolf writes, "Let your rhythmical sense wind itself in and out among men and women, omnibuses, sparrows—whatever comes along the street—until it has strung them together in one harmonious whole. That perhaps is your task—to find the relation between things that seem incompatible yet have a mysterious affinity . . . to rethink human life . . ." ("A Letter to a Young Poet" 192). By situating *Between the Acts* in an affective, in-between space, Woolf tunes into those unexpected relationships and productively rethinks sensation.

Woolf wrote *Between the Acts* during WW2, and the theater of war influenced Woolf's sensory theater. During the war, when so much already made so little sense—with "Everything uncertain," as Woolf writes in her diary—abiding with seemingly nonsensical sensations like the sounds of sirens and the reverberations of bombs was unnerving and painful (D5: 225).

In this disorienting atmosphere, Woolf's characters exhibit a tendency to categorize, rationalize, or otherwise make sense of sensation. Woolf, however, stages various interruptions that disrupt the sense-making cycle. The resulting liminal state prevents her characters from blindly repeating sensory habits. Thus, Woolf harnesses the destabilizing potential of sensation to "puncture our received wisdoms and common modes of sensing" and to "interrupt our conventional ways of perceiving the world and giving it value" (Panagia 2). Such interruptions ask us not to take sensory practices for granted; they are, in the words of Davide Panagia, "political moments because they invite occasions and actions for reconfiguring our associational lives"—for rethinking our automatic responses to sensation (2–3).

To interrupt these automatic responses, Woolf invokes disruptive technologies. I start this chapter by discussing how Woolf, her fellow modernists, and her characters view technology. While many of Woolf's contemporaries and characters perceive technology as threatening, Woolf values technology for its potential to unite diverse senses and bodies. In the next sections, I examine two of Woolf's most sensuous characters, Mrs. Manresa and Miss La Trobe. Mrs. Manresa's outsider status allows her to break rules and revel in sensations of all kinds. I argue that Woolf posits Manresa as a dissensuous role model because of her willingness to defy sensory conventions. I pay particular attention to how Manresa relates to taste and sound. Through taste, she challenges social norms that divide the senses and sensing bodies; through sound, she illustrates how technologies of war create productive moments of sensory alterity and questions which sounds count as meaningful. While Mrs. Manresa is a dependably disruptive character, Miss La Trobe is more conflicted. La Trobe sometimes revels in and encourages sensuous spontaneity and other times seeks to control the sensory responses of others. Her desire to exert this control is most obvious in her direction of the play, with its carefully crafted sensory acts. Through La Trobe and her play, Woolf draws attention to and discourages habitual sensory performances. Instead, she exposes both her and La Trobe's audience to new sensations and new ways of engaging their senses. Though both Miss La Trobe and Mrs. Manresa fail to make sense by conventional standards, Woolf reappropriates their failure for feminist and inclusive ends. They join Mina Loy's Mrs. Jones, who I discuss in the previous chapter, as female characters who subvert logocentric ways of sense-making. They are helped by various disruptive technologies, as well as by unexpected intrusions from nonhuman animals. As mentioned, Woolf follows H.D. in lauding nonhuman sensory practices, and the nonhuman animals Woolf features further challenge anthropocentric and masculine sensory norms. Together, the nonsensical, nonhabitual sensory practices of women and nonhuman animals alike contribute to the discovery and acceptance of new modes of sensing. Through them, Woolf realizes her multisensuous vision.

Technology and Sensory Possibility

While some of Woolf's contemporaries considered technology threatening or counterproductive to their craft, Woolf found creative potential in technology. As Tim Armstrong explains, thinkers and artists like Sigmund Freud, Walter Benjamin, Paul Valéry, and Wyndham Lewis felt the need to defend themselves against what they perceived as energy-sapping, sensuously overwhelming technologies. They feared overstimulation and neurasthenia, as well as energetic and seminal depletion, and these fears likely only intensified during the war (Armstrong, *Modernism: A Cultural History* 93).[3] For Woolf, however, technology had the power to prompt new sensations, make possible unlikely sensory relationships, and productively interfere with habitual sensory practices. A common source of interruption in the twentieth century, and an increasingly violent one during the war years, technology provided fodder for rethinking sensuous praxis. In "A Letter to a Young Poet" Woolf relays, "There are a thousand voices prophesying despair. Science, they say, has made poetry impossible; there is no poetry in motor cars and wireless" (191). But, Melba Cuddy-Keane notes, "Woolf herself does not endorse these hostile views, and there are other, stronger indications that she connected technological development with a liberating expansion of space" (76).[4] Such space was of particular importance to women, and Makiko Minow-Pinkney reminds us that the "liberating effects of new technologies introduced into the household were perhaps far greater for women than for men" (180). Such technologies exposed women to sensory experiences and sensations they were once denied. Technologies like the bicycle and omnibus granted women mobility and, in turn, wider access to the world outside the domestic sphere. Likewise, the need to produce technologies of war brought women to the once-dominated male workforce.

Those technologies that did not physically transport could sensuously transport, creating unlikely opportunities for connection. The gramophone, for instance, "allowed the high modernists, Eliot and Woolf, to go 'slumming' in the intimacy of Woolf's drawing room" (Scott 103). By disseminating new sensations across once uncrossable borders—economic, geographic, and otherwise—the gramophone changed how, where, and with whom auditors listened. Bonnie Kime Scott notes Woolf's concern with not only "the potentially democratizing force of the new availability of music," specifically, but also "the social impact of the new technologies" generally (73). Woolf voiced this positive view in an argument with Harold Nicolson, which she details in a diary entry from 1927: "'But why not grow, change?' I said. Also, I said, recalling the aeroplanes that had flown over us, while the portable wireless played dance music on the terrace, 'can't you see that nationality is over? All divisions are now rubbed out, or about to be'" (D3: 145).[5] Though Woolf makes this statement some time before WW2 begins, a similarly hopeful tone echoes throughout *Between the Acts.* In her final novel, Woolf channels the disruptive energy of technology and war's "recklessness—part good—part bad" to blur social divisions and celebrate sensory diversity (D5: 304).

In contrast to Woolf, many of the characters in *Between the Acts* do not appreciate technology's ability to "rub out divisions"; instead, they see technology as a threat to the traditional social order. *Between the Acts* is set in and around Pointz Hall, a country estate inhabited by the Oliver family: the patriarch, Bartholomew Oliver (Bart); his widowed sister, Mrs. Lucy "Bossy" Swithin; Bart's son, Giles; Giles's wife, Isabella (Isa); and their two children. When the novel opens, the Olivers are preparing to host the annual play, performed by local villagers. As people trickle onto the estate, the narrator notes their class differences:

Among them [. . .] were representatives of our most respected families—the Dyces of Denton; the Wickhams of Owlswick; and so on. Some had been there for centuries, never selling an acre. On the other hand there were new-comers, the Manresas, bringing the old up to date, adding bathrooms. And a scatter of odds and ends, like Cobbet of Cobbs Corner, retired, it was understood, on a pension from a tea plantation. Not an asset. He did his own housework and dug in his garden. (51–52)

In opposition to the "most respected families," these "odds and ends" are either amusing, as in the case of the Manresas with their new-fangled ideas, or useless, like Cobbet of Cobbs Corner. Either way, they are outsiders, marked by a sense of unbelonging. The narrator attributes their undesirable, or, at best unnecessary, presence to technology. She remarks, "The building of a car factory and of an aerodrome in the neighbourhood had attracted a number of unattached floating residents" (*BA* 52). These "unattached floating residents" illustrate the view that technology incited "disorderly movement, a slipping of self from its proper moorings" (Trask 22). Technology not only granted bodies physical mobility but also inspired what many saw as a perverse desire for class mobility and social status. It changed the social landscape, bringing into contact the old and new monied, the wealthy and the working class.

Technology not only fosters the uncontrollable, often unpredictable movements of marginalized people but also encourages perverse movements among the mainstream. For instance, "attached" residents no longer viewed Sundays as sacred days. Instead, "there were absentees when Mr. Streatfield called his roll call in the church. The motor bike, the motor bus, and the movies—when Mr. Streatfield called his roll call, he laid the blame on them" (*BA* 52). The motorbike and the motor bus, as technologies of transportation, enabled churchgoers to shirk their civic duties in favor of joyrides, just as they permitted the lower classes to travel and intersperse with the leisure classes. Film technology, perhaps the most blameful of all, offered all individuals, regardless of class, an escape from realities and responsibilities. In the eyes of many of Woolf's characters, and the contemporary populace they emblematize, technology distracts and displaces, allowing privileged bodies to make themselves marginal and granting marginalized bodies unprecedented access to privileged spaces.

Increasingly, modernity's ever-shifting bodies heterogenized once-homogenized spaces. While the city is most often considered the modernist zone of heterogeneity par excellence, Woolf also positions the country as a zone of anxious mixtures. Outsiders alter the visual landscape of the village surrounding Pointz Hall, causing long-established villagers to bemoan "That hideous new house at Pyes Corner! What an eyesore! And those bungalows—have you seen 'em?" (52). Here, changes in the architecture create new sensations that impact not only the view of the countryside but also the sensory experience of rurality itself. City bodies, specifically, threaten to bring perverse city sensations, thereby interfering with the so-called natural sensory space of the country estate. When writing of the city, Woolf notes its often-overwhelming sensuousness, as she does in "Oxford Street Tide":

> Oxford Street . . . is a breeding ground, a forcing house of sensation . . . The mind becomes a glutinous slab that takes impressions and Oxford Street rolls off upon it in a perpetual ribbon of changing sights, sounds and movement. Parcels slap and hit; motor omnibuses graze the kerb; the blare of a whole brass band in full tongue dwindles to a thin reed of sound. Buses, vans, cars, barrows stream past like the fragments of a picture puzzle. (21)

Woolf deems Oxford Street a "place of perpetual race and disorder." In contrast to this urban cacophony, the rural setting of Pointz Hall, with its beloved Barn, "chuckling" birds, and "empty, empty, empty; silent, silent, silent" rooms, at first seems to offer a sensory reprieve from urban sensory excess (*BA* 1, 26).

Such sensorially opposing characterizations of city and country were common of the modernist period. Tim Edensor explains that "the country-side was conceived as a privileged setting in which the sensory intrusions of such non-traditional rural dwellers were not welcome" (52). These non-traditional, polluting bodies took various forms—the religious or racial other, the queer, the androgynous—and were denied access to "the more stable, allegedly authentic setting of the village and the countryside" (Edensor 50). According to Edensor, "The rural thus served as a venue from which to express judgments about the inferiority of the spaces, practices, and bodies of others according to sensory criteria, where noise, smell, appearances, and textures were key markers of cultural difference" (52).

Pointz Hall and its surroundings are the venues from which Woolf's elite characters observe cultural differences and critique their so-called sensory inferiors. However, the sensuous space of Pointz Hall is not always idyllic. Consider, for instance, the following description, with its aggressive verbs and undertones of gluttony and violence: "[Lucy] has been wakened by the birds. How they sang! Attacking the dawn like so many choir boys attacking an iced cake" (*BA* 6). Animals, not humans, enact these sensuous impositions, which may be considered natural, not cultural, and therefore some-what less intrusive. However, by likening the birds to boys and the organi-cally occurring dawn to a man-made cake, Woolf begins to challenge and complicate the binaries of nature/culture, country/city, human/technology, and superior/inferior. I discuss the function of animals further in the section titled "Crossing Sensory Borders: Humans, Animals, Technology, Nature." For now, I focus on the various ways Woolf's human characters trespass on guarded sensory ground.

"Admirable woman, all sensation": Mrs. Manresa as Sensory Role Model

One of the most prevalent sensory outsiders is Mrs. Manresa, who en-acts the most nettlesome sensory interference at Pointz Hall. Manresa is a gaudily bejeweled Londoner of whom little is known. Gossip suggests she was born in Tasmania, and her questionable origins and Jewish hus-band underscore her alterity. Manresa's otherness is especially obvious in relation to more reputable characters like Lucy Swithin. Lucy's name, meaning "light," suggests that she is not burdened by corporeality, and Woolf juxtaposes Lucy's embodiment with Manresa's. Of Lucy, her brother Bart wonders, "Was it that she had no body? Up in the clouds, like an air ball, her mind touched ground now and then with a shock of surprise. There was nothing in her to weight a man like Giles to the earth" (80). In contrast, Manresa is solidly grounded and firmly embodied. Of her, Bart thinks, "Giles would keep his orbit so long as [Manresa] weighted him to the earth" (82). Where Woolf aligns Lucy with ether, she casts Manresa as earthy and primitive: she is "the wild child" who "squats on the floor" (*BA* 39, 75). Manresa's untamable, unladylike body offends feminine and sensory decorum.

Manresa commits the most egregious offense through the so-called lower senses, namely the sense of taste. Women have long been negatively associated with taste. Dating back to Eve and her forbidden fruit-eating, the consuming woman posed a threat not only to herself but also to society. In the late twelfth century, for instance, Andre le Chepelain contended, "Woman is such a slave to her belly that there is nothing she would be ashamed to assent to if she were assured of a fine meal, and no matter what she has, she never has any hope that she can satisfy her appetite when she is hungry" (qtd. in Classen, *CA* 79). Depictions of the eating woman are equally unflattering in modernity, where woman's so-called insatiability is a maker of sexual and economic desire. Andrea Adolphi remarks that the figure of the "oversexed, consuming woman . . . is intimately connected with middle-class fears of being displaced from the socio-economic order through the class mobility that occurred between the world wars" (445). While Manresa's presence among high society shows that she has meta-phorically eaten her way up the social food chain, her physical acts of eat-ing are equally transgressive.

Manresa publicly indulges in food and drink which, for a woman, is in especially bad taste. Classen explains that "in order to atone for the femi-nine failing of sinful taste, virtuous women were expected to lead lives of gustatory restraint" (*CA* 79). Manresa, however, is and does the opposite. Promptly after her arrival at Pointz Hall she proclaims, "We have our grub" and proceeds to eat not out of necessity and with little enjoyment, like a proper lady, but unapologetically and with gusto (*BA* 27). She is "the first to drink, the first to bite," and though taste is a characteristically female sense, eating so eagerly in public, and not while confined to the private space of the home, masculinizes her and perverts the sanctity of taste as a domestic sense (71).[6] By using food and taste for personal gratification, not to nurture others, Manresa commits a crime against sensuous femininity.[7] Femininity, however, seems the least of Manresa's concerns. The narrator comments that she had "given up dealing with her figure and thus gained freedom" (30). Manresa's personal freedom comes at a price to the larger, male-dominated, socio-sensory order. Adolphi notes that "her position as a consuming female subject makes her an agent of destabilized potential—one of that feared club of 'man-eaters'" (445). Because she eats like a man, Manresa is encoded as a man-eater, a monstrous, consuming woman. Through acts of eating that disregard gendered sensory norms, Manresa gnaws at the sensory order and threatens men's place within it.

Manresa further destabilizes the sensory order by violating sensory di-vides and emphasizing the intersensory. Intersensory experience, or the min-gling of sensations—the experience of simultaneously touching and tasting, or seeing and smelling, for instance—interferes with hierarchies that order sensation, giving each sense (and each sensing body) a value. For Manresa, however, sensation is wonderfully mingled and messy. Observing Manresa, Woolf's narrator notes, "She looked before she drank. Looking was part of drinking. Why waste sensation, she seemed to ask, why waste a single drop that can be pressed out of this ripe, this melting, this adorable world? Then she drank. And the air around her became threaded with sensation" (*BA* 39). By denying sensuous exclusion—by embracing a sort of no-sense-left-behind mentality—Manresa not only reconfigures sensory interactions but alters sensory space, transforming the very atmosphere of Pointz Hall into a buzz of sensation. The resulting environment is one of sensory plurality and equality, where the high and low sensory orders collapse as sight, taste, and touch melt together.

The same impulse that drives Manresa to suck the marrow out of sensation earns her associations with sensory excess and immodesty. Woolf crafts Manresa as an overtly visible spectacle: "Her hat, her rings, her finger nails [*sic*] red as roses, smooth as shells, were there for all to see" (27). She is also an overtly visual spectator—she unabashedly "ogles" Bart and Isa, which is rude behavior for a man but inexcusable behavior for a woman (29). Woolf further illustrates her sensuous impropriety when, during a conversation about Chinese theater, Manresa "interrupted, *scenting* culture" (97, emphasis mine). Manresa's disruptive socio-sniffing interrupts the conversation and, in meta-gesture, the novel's dialogue. Manresa connects high culture and the low sensorium, perverting the former and elevating the latter. By responding to sound (Lucy's voice and the chatter about Chinese theater) with scent, she challenges traditional sensory associations. "Goddess-like, buoyant, abundant, her cornucopia running over," Manresa is a wealth of sensation who refuses to be contained or controlled (82). Like an invasive species, she disrupts the pastoral with the chaos and disorder of her urban sensory milieu.

Manresa disrupts not only sensory hierarchies but also larger gendered, identarian categories. She is both natural and wild and unnaturally mobile and mechanized—a hybrid sensory force with which others must reckon. Isa's reaction to Manresa juxtaposes the two women: "Isa was immobile, watching her husband. She could feel the Manresa in his wake" (76). While Isa is fixed and unreactive, Manresa is transient and empowered by motion. She is not quite human but, instead, "the Manresa." This title befits the dynamism of her character. Because she problematizes gender norms through her masculine behavior, Manresa cannot easily or merely be labeled "woman." Though, in this instance, Isa feels Manresa in her husband's wake, more often than not, Manresa is the commanding vessel. She tows Giles along, tugboat like, and he feels "less of an audience more of an actor, going round the Barn in her wake" (74). Giles is perhaps most susceptible to her will, and their affair is less noteworthy than the way in which Manresa perceives her role in the relationship. Manresa, "woman of action as she was," pursues Giles (76). He is her "little boy" and "Taking him in tow, she felt: I am the Queen, he my hero, my sulky hero" (120, 74). In so doing, Manresa inverts the gendered power structure. Woolf emphasizes this disruptive movement through kinetic language: the towing action and the tugboat's wake signal displacement and underscore Manresa's transgressive nature. Woolf fashions her as a character who gravitates toward movement and away from stasis and whose transgressive motions cut across normative dictates.

Manresa's Productive "Chatter"

Manresa further troubles gendered sensory norms by destabilizing associations between language and sound. Sound studies have gained popularity among Woolf scholars, who are more frequently turning away from the visuality of Woolf's work, of which scholarship abounds, and tuning into the rhythms, vibrations, musicality, and noisiness of Woolfian soundscapes.[8] While the sensory turn in Woolf scholarship is important, approaching aurality intersensorially, rather than in sensory isolation, allows me to articulate a more fully embodied aesthetic in Woolf's work. Woolf herself acknowledged that sound is wrapped up in other sensations, and she describes many of these "colour and sound memories" in the autobiographical essay "A Sketch of the Past" (67). Woolf recollects one such "highly sensual" memory of St. Ives, when "the buzz, the croon, the smell" combine in a multisensuous chorus ("A Sketch of the Past," 67). Her attention to sensory interconnectivity foregrounds what Adriana Varga lauds as the "synesthetic quality Woolf remained interested in exploring . . . throughout her life" (75). Such synesthesia is apparent in *Between the Acts*, a noisy novel that "hail[s] the reader as an eavesdropping spectator" and asks us to observe not only our listening practices and sensory proclivities but also how we categorize sound and sensation (Harris 69).

Woolf took particular note of the changing soundscape of modernity, which governments increasingly attempted to regulate. The twentieth century saw the first efforts at noise control in public spaces with ordinances "prohibiting the excessive ringing of church bells . . . limiting the practice of bagpipes to certain hours of the week [, and] forbidding the use of whistles to call cabs" (Flint 186). Edensor notes that the management of sensation "came at a cost to sensory diversity and excitement, producing sterile, over-regulated spaces and unstimulating blandscapes" (Edensor 53). Woolf herself points to a similar "blandscape" fostered by the BBC, which attempted to regulate sound by, for instance, forbidding certain accents on air. "Listening and speaking," Pamela L. Caughie observes, "became skills propagated through broadcasting schools, radio discussion groups, and how-to manuals advertised in *The Listener* [the journal of BBC]" (340). Woolf found such restrictions troublesome and hoped, instead, to have what she referred to as "an individual, not communal BBC dictated feeling" (D5: 306).[9] In contrast to what Cuddy-Keane calls the "dispassionate, authoritative mode" of the BBC, for whom "spontaneity was considered too dangerous," Woolf expressed a desire for sensory alterity as a productive alternative to conventional sensory responses (77).

Sensory alterity, Edensor explains, occurs when we enter new environments that emphasize sensory difference and allow us to break from our daily sensory routines (32). Such environments are replete with new sensations that prevent usual sensory responses. Tourism is perhaps the most obvious form of sensory alterity, but it can manifest less noticeably in everyday activities such as entering a crowded place, facing unexpected weather, or confronting smells on the street. War also incites sensory alterity—a traumatic, involuntary alterity—during which individuals are subject to "many disagreeable sensations" (Woolf, D5: 243). For Woolf, many of these "disagreeable sensations" were sonic—the blasts of explosions, whir of warplanes, and drone of air raid sirens. She documents them in her diary while writing *Between the Acts* and grapples with them in the novel. Amid sonic alterity and upheaval, *Between the Acts* asks, how do we distinguish between sounds that are dangerous and those that are desirable? What kinds of sounds do we deem valuable, and which do we dismiss as mere noise?

Woolf brings these questions to the fore through the character of Manresa, who often makes sounds that are more akin to animal, musical, or technological noises than discernable human language. In so doing, she underscores an important distinction Woolf makes between sound as a sensory impression and sound as a unit of language. Woolf critics and sensory scholars note that Western societies often denigrate sound and privilege language. Cuddy-Keane describes the difference between sound and language as the "linguistic representation of sound and the linguistic conceptualization of it (sonicity as opposed to semantics)" (70). The urge to order sound into language is common of patriarchal societies, where the so-called masculine mind is valued over the so-called feminine body. Such societies "treat the utterance as if its sole purpose is to present a cognitive claim" (Panagia 17). Woolf, however, resists this ordering. As Ralf Hertel contends, by "reaching for impressions before they are structured . . . according to masculine logic . . . Woolf invites [readers] to open up to a feminine perception of the world" (183).

Woolf gives new value to the aural dimensions of sound through Manresa's often nonsensical utterances, which distance her from the cognitive, semantic dimensions of sound. Manresa's associations with affective sounds abound. She has a "fluty" voice that she uses to sing and hum throughout the novel (*BA* 42). She produces dramatic sound effects, as when she mimics the "noise like a cork being drawn from a ginger-beer bottle. Pop!" (97). The narrator notes the way "the coins in [Manresa's] bead bag jingled," and Bart comments, "You could trust [Manresa] to crow when the hour struck, like an alarm clock" (120–21). Manresa's noises gain value when we consider how Woolf's "welcoming of noise of various kinds is repeatedly bound up with the desire to acknowledge human connections" (Flint 188). Since sound and human interactions are both "inescapable," Kate Flint suggests, "One's response to noise may, therefore, in Woolf's fiction, be read as an index to a character's degree of comfort with that condition" (188). Manresa—who makes and welcomes not only various sounds but also various sensations—figures as one of the more inclusive, adaptable, and admirable characters in *Between the Acts*. Her openness to sound signals her openness to new ways of sensing, knowing, and communicating. Through Manresa's so-called unintelligible noises, Woolf promotes new, feminist sensory modes that reassert the value of sensation itself by resisting the masculine impulse to translate sensation into language.

Woolf suggests that there are less logocentric, more embodied ways of making meaning. One such moment occurs when, before the play begins, Manresa acknowledges her inability to write, while (incorrectly) attributing the play to Isa:

> "I'm sure *she's* written it, haven't you Mrs. Giles? For myself," Mrs. Manresa continues, "speaking plainly, I can't put two words together. I don't know how it is—such a chatterbox as I am with my tongue, once I hold a pen—." She made a face, screwed her fingers together as if she held a pen in them. But the pen she held thus on the little table absolutely refused to move. (42)

Manresa's attempt to produce meaning through writing fails. Even when speaking, she considers herself a "chatterbox," someone prone to incoherent babbling. However, though Woolf emphasizes Manresa's inability to produce language, she is still able to make meaning. She conveys meaning by performing failure: by beginning to write and then stalling. The stasis of her pen contrasts the motility of her tongue and creates tension between the written word and the language of the body. Manresa uses her body as pen: it makes meaning as she silently pantomimes. Adolphi suggests that by denying Manresa the power of words, Woolf subsequently denies her cultural capital, an honor that she reserves for Isa, the poet. However, in a novel where, as Hermione Lee notes, "language is in decay," Manresa's seeming lack works to her benefit (210).

Manresa's failure to produce traditional, masculine forms of language and to heed sensory norms serve as examples of how, in the words of Anne Cunningham, "feminine failure can provide us with an affective reorientation," an unorthodox way of perceiving ourselves and our world (184). Woolf provides an example of affective reorientation in the oft-noted mirror scene. As the actors gather on stage for the finale, "The Present Time. Ourselves," they carry with them all manner of reflective materials. Splintered mirrors, "tin cans," "bedroom candlesticks," "old jars," and "the cheval glass from the Rectory" serve as mirrors for the audience (*BA* 125). The surprising appearance of the mirrors captures the audience "as [they] are" in an affective, liminal state "before [they've] had time to assume . . . And only, too, in parts" (125). In this moment, the mirrors interrupt habitual sense-making and traditional modes of seeing, an imposition the narrator calls "cruel [. . .] distorting and upsetting and utterly unfair" (125). Instead, the audience members find themselves in a semiotic state of becoming, before language shapes sensation and before bodies take shape through sense-making acts. They are forced to see and sense differently, and this leaves them feeling uncomfortable and intruded upon. Except for Manresa. The narrator acknowledges, "All shifted, preened, minced . . . Even Bart, even Lucy, turned away. All evaded or shaded themselves—save Mrs. Manresa who, facing herself in the glass, used it as a glass; had out her mirror; powdered her nose and moved one curl, disturbed by the breeze, to its place" (126). While this might be easily dismissed as superficial or vulgar behavior, Manresa accepts the sensory invitation others reject, thereby illustrating not only her taste for new sensations but also her ability to reorient herself within an otherwise unnerving affective space.

Manresa's alterity proves advantageous: her "wild child" nature frees her from stifling sensory dictates and grants her access to sensory spaces and identifications otherwise denied more so-called civilized bodies (*BA* 39). Because of, not in spite of, Manresa's disruptive and at times irreverent alterity, she emerges as a productive sensory role model. Where others are caught, Manresa, as the later part of her name suggests, yields.[10] If she seeks to "raze" "man," as Adolphi notes, and as the latter part of her name suggests, it is less to destroy men than to disrupt the social and sensory hierarchies on which mankind depends (445).[11] When viewed through a sensory lens, the narrator's assessment of Manresa gains new resonance:

> Vulgar she was in her gestures, in her whole person, over-sexed, over-dressed . . . But what a desirable, at least *valuable*, quality it was—for everybody felt, directly she spoke "She's said it, she's done it, not I," and could take advantage of the breach of decorum, of the fresh air that blew in, to follow like leaping dolphins in the wake of an ice-breaking vessel. (28–29, emphasis mine)

In her fondness for taste, enthusiasm for the intersensory, and willingness to interrupt the process of sense-making, Manresa breaks the ice of tradition, paving the way for new modes of sensing. She crosses sensory thresholds, encouraging others to follow in her wake.

Undoing the Spell of Sense-Making: Miss La Trobe and Sensuous Intrusions

Another character who draws attention to habitual sensory practices is the novel's playwright, Miss La Trobe. Like Manresa, "Very little was actually known about" La Trobe (*BA* 40). Characters question her sexuality since "Rumor said . . . She had bought a four-roomed cottage and shared it with an actress" (40). They also question her nationality, wondering, "Where did she spring from? With that name she wasn't presumably pure English" (40). Predicated on difference, La Trobe is "an outcast. Nature had somehow set her apart from her kind" (143). This is, in part, because she deviates from her feminine "nature": "Outwardly she was swarthy, sturdy, and thick set; strode about the fields in a smock frock; sometimes with a cigarette in her mouth; often with a whip in her hand and used rather strong language . . . perhaps, then, she wasn't altogether a lady?" (40). The inverse of Joyce's "womanly man," La Trobe is a manly woman who resembles the stalwart Lady Millicent Bruton in *Mrs. Dalloway*. Just as Lady Bruton dreams of an "imaginary baton such as her grandfathers might have held" with which she "commands battalions," Miss La Trobe "command[s]" her actors with an "attitude proper to an Admiral" (Woolf, *Mrs. Dalloway* 112; *BA* 43). Unnervingly androgynous, La Trobe invites questions not only about gender performance but also about sensory performance.

Like Manresa, La Trobe promotes a feminist sensorium by valuing sensation for sensation's sake and devaluing language. Though a writer, La Trobe seems distrustful of words and often resists the masculine impulse to make sense of sensation. Instead, she praises "Words without meaning—wonderful words" that are more sensuous than cognitive (144). These "wonderful words" come to her in a haze of sensation at the end of the novel while, sitting in a bar amid "the acrid smell of stale beer," La Trobe envisions her next play. In a moment of reverse sense-making, that which was once imbued with meaning diffuses into pure sensation:

She raised her glass to her lips. And drank. And listened. Words of one syllable sank down into the mud. Words rose above the intolerably laden dumb oxen plodding through the mud . . . The cheap clock ticked; smoke obscured the pictures. Smoke became tart on the roof of her mouth. Smoke obscured the earth-coloured jackets. She no longer saw them, yet they upheld her, sitting arms akimbo with her glass before her. There was the high ground at midnight; there the rock; and two scarcely perceptible figures. Suddenly the tree was pelted with starlings. She set down her glass. She heard the first words. (144)

This passage begins and ends with intersensory activity. As La Trobe drinks and listens, taste and sound converge to produce words that are more sensuous than lingual: they are one-syllable sounds imbued with tactility, embodied words that sink and rise and pull La Trobe along with them. Woolf pairs these intersensory sensations with various obstructions—mud, darkness, and smoke—that emphasize La Trobe's inability to sense as usual. Her inability to see is especially noteworthy. Since sight is often associated with cognition and masculinity, by denying La Trobe access to this faculty, Woolf again interrupts masculine modes of sense-making. This interruption makes room for new, feminine sensory practices: La Trobe, like the "dumb oxen," forgoes traditional acts of hearing in order to hear anew. She lets her vision go blurry in order to see what was otherwise not visible; she sinks into the mud of messy, unprocessed sensation and, herein, finds artistic inspiration.

La Trobe's desire to realize her artistic vision and to influence the sensory experiences of others through her writing renders her suspicious. She gains associations with another infamously deviant and dissensuous female figure, the witch. As Constance Classen notes, witches "defied sensory and social norms by using the feminine senses of touch, taste and smell as media for self-gratification, rather than self-sacrifice, and as avenues for empowerment, rather than instruments of service" ("The Witch's Senses" 71). Similarly, La Trobe wields sensation like a wand to alter her audience's sensory experience. Woolf alerts readers to La Trobe's witchiness in various ways. For example, Lucy points to La Trobe's misuse of touch to manipulate her audience. She calls La Trobe "not merely a twitcher of individual strings" but "one who seethes wandering bodies and floating voices in a cauldron, and makes rise up from its amorphous mass a re-created world" (*BA* 105). Through the re-created world La Trobe conjures, she hopes to empower her audience, whose sensorium she finds frustratingly limited. Of her audience, La Trobe laments: "Swathed in conventions, they couldn't see, as she could, that a dish cloth wound round a head in the open looked much richer than real silk" (45). Though this speaks to a lack of mental imagination, it also emphasizes how sensory conventions and traditional sense-making acts physically limit bodies and foreclose perceptual possibility. La Trobe attempts to strip her audience of these conventions, so they can see and sense anew.

While La Trobe may be good-intentioned, her sensory project reflects a desire to exert control over what Woolf will reveal to be an uncontrollable sensescape. La Trobe encourages new sensory acts by interrupting the performance of the play with unexpected sensations. This is most apparent in her plans for "The Present. Ourselves." In this act, "'After Vic.,' [La Trobe] had written, 'try ten mins. of present time. Swallows, cows, etc.' She wanted to expose them [her audience], as it were, to douche them, with present-time reality" (122). La Trobe envisions a pure state, marked by quaint pastoral sounds, wherein she can rid her audience of sensory pretense and "douche" or cleanse them of sensory habits. By stopping the performance of the play, La Trobe also hopes to suspend habitual sensory performance. Abuzz with affect, La Trobe's "Present" occupies the temporal space between sensing and sense-making. In this space, the playwright plans to douse her audience in sensation and force them to confront their perceptual praxis.

While elsewhere in the play La Trobe successfully manipulates technological sounds, in "The Present," the sounds of machines interrupt her sensory agenda, serving as a reminder of the invasive and often-puzzling sounds of modernity. As the audience unwittingly confronts these sounds, La Trobe's planned sensory disenchantment morphs into affective entrapment. The narrator describes the audience as

> Prisoners . . . all caught and caged . . . watching a spectacle. Nothing happened. The tick of the machine was maddening . . . All their nerves were on edge. They sat exposed. The machine ticked. There was no music. The horns of cars on the high road were heard. And the swish of trees. They were neither one thing nor the other; neither Victorians nor themselves. They were suspended, without being, in limbo. Tick, tick, tick went the machine. (120–21)

The identifiable language of "swallows and cows" in La Trobe's ideal act are replaced by the "tick" of the gramophone and the noise of car horns—the unpredictable, unintelligible sounds of modernity. Woolf emphasizes the droning quality of these sounds through clipped sentences and monotonous syntax—"[t]he tick," "the machine," "the horns." This intrusive sense-escape forces the audience "to confront the medium—that is, the technical apparatus—divested of its message" (Pridmore-Brown 414). Here again, Woolf immerses her characters and reading audience in the Real of sensation. In this amorphous Real, the "swish of trees" and the "tick" of the gramophone create a disturbing admixture, where sounds cannot be easily parsed. So-called natural and mechanical blur and, like the audience, become "neither one thing nor the other." The resulting environment is one of suspension where "nothing happens," and the audience hangs in-between sensing and sense-making. The sounds they encounter are equally in-between and not-easily-categorized, a point Woolf underscores via the category-obsessed Victorians of the preceding act, which linger in the audience's memory. Though Woolf bids her audience dwell in this space of sensory declassification, La Trobe and the playgoers respond negatively to her direction. Their feelings of imprisonment convey what Cuddy-Keane describes as "a new apprehension of sound as sound rather than as a conceptualized or narrative meaning; or more precisely, a heightened focus on sound as aural experience rather than intermediary for a nonaural signified" (90). This apprehension reflects an audience grappling with the sounds of modernity, for which "everything carries effects . . . including background sounds and the humming of the machinery itself, but not everything *means* something" (Caughie 341).

The urge to make meaning remains, however, and Woolf's characters' discomfort with difficult-to-parse sounds underscores the social impulse to categorize sensation and enact sensory habits—to make sense of things. This urge occurs, Panagia explains, when we encounter a new or unfamiliar sensation that does not "make sense to us" and "we try to make sense of it by fitting it into some kind of context or over-arching life schema" (2). La Trobe embodies this struggle and the desire for the familiar, lamenting, "If only she'd a backcloth to hang between the trees—to shut out cows, swallows, present time! But she had nothing. She had forbidden music" (*BA* 122). Here, unexpected sensations distress an already sensuously overtaxed La Trobe. "Reality [is] too strong," La Trobe mutters, and she attempts to weaken the Real by blocking sensation and lessening sensory possibility (122). Anything, she implies, would do the trick, even a backcloth, a mere black screen, would direct the audience's senses, allowing them to organize themselves around the act of seeing (an organization that she later disrupts and diffuses through the splintered mirrors). In short, instead of deterring habitual modes of sensing by letting herself and her audience dwell in sonic possibility and uncertainty, La Trobe scrambles to make sense of sensation.

La Trobe acknowledges that music—which she initially forbid because it is too familiar a sound—would be an especially effective means of sensuous organization. Unlike the aforementioned, unintended sounds to which the audience responds negatively—of which Pridmore-Brown notes, "It is as if their bodies do not know how to move"—music is familiar and soothing (414). It functions as, what Trina Thompson calls, "a metaphor for and catalyst of harmonious security" (210). Music brings order to what the audience perceives as affective chaos. Woolf's narrator describes the audience's relief when the gramophone begins: "Like quicksilver sliding, the filings magnetized, the distracted united [. . .] all comprehending; all enlisted. The whole population of the mind's immeasurable profundity came flocking [. . .] from chaos and cacophony measure" (*BA* 128). Unlike the disorienting affective sounds that mark "The Present," music—composed, constructed, "measured"—contains deliberate, easily identifiable sounds around which La Trobe's audience can sensuously arrange themselves. The audience's reception of sound is notably passive, however, as are the verbs that connote their movements. The pull of the music is "magnetized," a sensuous conscription in which the audience "enlists" and to which they mechanically or passively "flock." Music, then, seems to have the opposite effect of earlier un-intended noises, which "can be viewed as short-circuiting the instantaneous connection among rhythm, emotion, and collective action" (Pridmore-Brown 412). Collective action, with its herd mentality, fosters the mindless, reflexive habituation of those "common sense" practices that Woolf discourages. Unlike the affective, disorderly "tick, tick, tick" of the gramophone's machinery, music does not short-circuit sensation but offers the audience a sensory reassurance that "[t]he first note meant a second; the second a third" (*BA* 128). Music orders time, providing the safety of progression and anticipation. When La Trobe and her audience cannot anticipate what comes next, they respond with anxiety. Music lulls their anxious, over-saturated sensory minds and underscores their desire for familiar sensations of which they can easily make sense. Through La Trobe and her audience, Woolf exposes their resistance to sensing differently and their hesitance to confront sensations that require them to take an active role in sense-making: she highlights their fear and unwillingness to sense anew, in the now. Recognizing the need for sensory familiarity but wishing to interrupt passive sensory ingestion, Woolf continues her sensory dance, leading her characters and audience between safe sensory territory and less trodden sensory grounds.

After observing "The Present," La Trobe quickly notes, "Something was going wrong with the experiment . . . Every second they were slipping the noose. Her little game had gone wrong . . . This is death, death, death, she noted in the margin of her mind; when illusion fails. Unable to lift her hand, she stood facing the audience" (*BA* 122). The noose symbolizes La Trobe's paradoxical attempt to free her audience but underscores the violence of her approach: she attempts to strangle habitual sense-making practices. She laments that she cannot contain her audience in a sensory bubble and that they escape the forced act of sensing that she stages. Her fears illustrate the difficult task of the artist, whose sensory experimentation does not go unchallenged. At the end of the act, La Trobe is "unable to lift her hand" to orchestrate sensation, and the scene ends on a note of impotence.

La Trobe's inability to raise her hand becomes a way for Woolf to show her hand, so to speak, and to expose sense-making as a constructed, socially driven act. She does this by juxtaposing culture, namely La Trobe's efforts to direct the sensorium, and nature. Shortly after La Trobe succumbs to failure, rain intervenes: "the shower fell, sudden, profuse . . . Hands were raised. Here and there a parasol opened. The rain was sudden and universal" (*BA* 122–23). Rain, like music, is familiar sensuous territory. It shakes La Trobe's audience from their sensory stasis, prompting them to perform their typical sensory habits—sheltering themselves from the rain. The rain provides sensory relief from the incomprehensible sensations that precede it and, in so doing, frees La Trobe, too, who, "wiping away the drops on her cheeks . . . sighed, 'That's done it,'" (122–23). Though La Trobe wanted to douche her audience in reality, in pure sensation, "The eruption of reality, the rain show, the 'douche,'" Laura Marcus notes, "provides, paradoxically the necessary illusionism" to continue the play (185). The rain does not cleanse La Trobe's audience members of their sense-making habits but re-immerses them in sensory performance. The rain is a welcome distraction, an atmospheric intervention. It releases the audience from the cultural state of affective liminality the playwright foists upon them. Woolf's audience, however, sees the rain as a purposefully contrived element Woolf conjures in her own act of sensuous direction. When the narrator comments, "Nature once more had taken her part," readers are made privy to the rain's function as an element of theater and of the novel (123). Woolf provides her reader with a behind-the-scenes glimpse of sensory production, where the so-called natural seems not-so-natural. The rain becomes another actor in Woolf's sensory drama. So, while La Trobe fails to "douche" her audience of their sense-making habits, Woolf successfully deconstructs sensory acts and douses her audience in the Real. Rain exposes the sensory scaffolding upon which sensory habits are built and illuminates the hand that pulls the often-invisible sensory strings.

Recovering Sensory Technologies, Reconfiguring Sensing Bodies

Woolf's choice to expose sensory control in miniature speaks to concerns about biopolitics more broadly. Biopolitical control, or the state-sanctioned and -supported control of human bodies, was an especially prominent threat during the late 1930s and early 1940s when Woolf wrote *Between the Acts*. Though Hitler and the Third Reich often romanticized the premodern past and criticized modernity's decadence, they relied on modern technologies, built on and operated by the forced labor of non-Aryans, to manifest their vision of an ideal Germany. Fueled by eugenicist thinking, the Third Reich invented technologies not only to build a new Germany but also to rid it of anyone who might dirty the genetic pool with physical, mental, or emotional impurities. As Roger Griffin notes, "The same perverted ethos conflating technological advance with a lethal biopolitical agenda" gave rise to devasting technologies like the atom bomb (326). For Fascists, technology went hand in hand with the elevation of the Aryan race and the eradication of so-called degenerates.

Under Fascist control, technology perpetuated violence in more subtle, but no less harmful, ways. Hitler exerted biopolitical control over the sense of sound, for instance, by colonizing technologies like the radio, through which he sanitized sensation and controlled what people heard. Michele Pridmore-Brown and Michael Tratner both persuasively discuss how *Between the Acts* encourages various forms of "distracted listening" as a way to resist Hitler's hegemonization of hearing. In this section, I build on their analysis by further exploring how Woolf champions diverse sensations, sensuous bodies, and sensory practices at a time when the purification of the races and the standardization of sensory experience were inextricably linked. As I hope to show, Woolf's choice to champion seemingly nonsensical sounds and beings stands in direct contrast to Fascist rhetoric that deemed such sounds, and the beings that produce them, unintelligible, worthless, or dangerous. Acoustic technology aids Woolf in this work by opening her ears to nonhuman, nontraditional sounds.

During WW2, the manipulation of sound through acoustic technologies became a source of anxiety for Woolf and her contemporaries. "Fascism's emphasis on acoustic communion, its rootedness in the dramatic orchestration of emotion" (Pridmore-Brown 411), led listeners to mistrust aural mediums, a suspicion *Between the Acts* both conveys and quiets. Sound technology, Woolf suggests, though often used to dehumanize or convey dehumanizing messages, is not without humanity. As several Woolf scholars observe, the gramophone in *Between the Acts* "operates on a human scale," and sometimes, quite eerily, emotes (Harris 70).[12] The gramophone, for instance, feels joy, its "tune . . . reel[ing] from side to side as if drunk with merriment" (*BA* 59). Likewise, it expresses grief by "moan[ing]," "lament[ing]" and "wail[ing]" (66, 68). In these instances, the gramophone appears more feeling and human than the audience members, who mechanically follow its direction—"*Dispersed are we*"—to leave at the end of the play (68).

Woolf's technological recovery also extends to the megaphone, a somewhat notorious sound technology. La Trobe introduces the megaphone in the final act when she subjects the audience, already shifting uncomfortably under the scrutiny of the mirrors, to a "megaphonic, anonymous, loudspeaking affirmation" (*BA* 127). This voice—presumably La Trobe's—mysteriously "asserted itself" (127). The audience responds to it much as they respond to other affective sounds, and the narrator "thanks heaven" when "the bray of the infernal megaphone" ends (128). Their reaction mirrors modernist thinkers like Walter Benjamin who viewed the megaphone as an instrument of Fascism. Woolf would have been familiar with this view and with Hitler's use of the megaphone, and other sound media, to promote his cause and homogenize his audience. Under Fascist control, the megaphone made "the multiple and varied into the controlled, the unified, the rigidly shaped" (Tratner 128). La Trobe, however, diverges from this common use and encourages dissent in her audience. The megaphone, and megaphonic aurality, emerge as sources of sensory potential. Speaking through the megaphone, she urges, "*Let's talk in words of one syllable, without larding, stuffing, or cant. Let's break the rhythm and forget the rhyme. And calmly consider ourselves*" (*BA* 127). Here again, La Trobe defers to sonicity over semantics. The sounded syllables of the words she bids her audience speak matter more than the words themselves. She encourages her audience to trim the fat and remove the "stuffing" from their words, to strip down language to a primitive, monosyllabic form. The goal is to "break" from old patterns and speak in new "rhythms"—to sound differently. By advising her audience members to consider themselves—to take stock of their sensory habits and make note of the ways they respond to certain sensations—La Trobe breaks the trance of the dictator's voice. In so doing, she discourages automatic responses and sensory habituation.

La Trobe's subversive use of sound maps new sensory territory, disrupting not only common technological associations but also common sensory associations. With its emphasis on breaking and forgetting, La Trobe uses the megaphone to encourage dissensuality and sensory reflection, the latter of which she literalizes through the splintered mirrors that accompany the megaphonic voice. Together, the scraps of mirrors and the reconstituted megaphone signify a productively broken sensorium, through which the audience hears and sees differently, thus illustrating Harris's observation that "[t]he pageant at the heart of *Between the Acts* can be read as an audiovisual apparatus aimed to provide a defamiliarizing recognition in the audience through a reframing of reality" (72). This defamiliarization is apparent in the audience's uncertain response to their reflection, at which they wonder "... Ourselves?" (*BA* 125). By joining forces between megaphone and mirror, Woolf disrupts organoleptic organization.

Organoleptic organization refers to "the correspondences that bind a sense organ to an act of perception" (Panagia 155). Such organization occurs when, over time, repetition of sensory acts solidifies the eyes as organs of sight, the ears as organs of sound, and so on. In contrast, organoleptic *disorganization* challenges these overly simplistic correspondences and foregrounds the intersensory. For instance, organoleptic disorganization submits that the skin is not merely an organ of touch but "could become a nodule of sensation: my finger touches your arm and you can at once see, hear, and smell my touch" (Panagia 7). Panagia draws attention to the repercussions of such disorganization and asks, "What would happen if our senses of skin were interrupted and we experienced skin as an organ of disfiguration? What if we went even further and stopped thinking organically so that the shape of our bodies was no longer determined by the disposition of our organs?" (7). Woolf answers these questions and enacts disfiguration through the mirrors, which visually disarrange and fragment bodies, leaving "Here a nose . . . There a skirt . . . Then trousers only . . . Now perhaps a face" (*BA* 125). Misshapen, the audience members must grapple with their Cubist reconfiguration, as they see "themselves, not whole by any means" (126). Instead, they are "scraps, orts, and fragments" (128). Sound contributes to their fragmentation and acts as the sonic equivalent of the mirrors, reflecting organoleptic disorganization aurally.

When the megaphonic voice mysteriously issues "from the bushes," it is simultaneously invisible and omnipresent, disembodied and felt—it is the "voix acousmatique" that "insofar as it is not anchored to a specific source, localized in a specific place . . . functions as a threat that lurks everywhere" (*BA* 127; Zizek 127). The sound of the megaphone cannot easily be localized in the body, and the audience cannot comprehend how to listen to the anonymous megaphonic voice. Tratner's observation about the mirrors is true of the megaphone as well: both "suggest that one of the goals of the pageant is to fragment everyday reality so it can be assembled in some new way" (117). By disorganizing bodies and introducing unfamiliar sensations through disruptive technologies, Woolf encourages new sensuous arrangements and alternative ways of processing sensation.

Crossing Sensory Borders: Humans, Animals, Technology, and Nature

Woolf discourages habitual sense-making rituals and warns against those forces that condone them. While Fascism is an extreme example of the threat of sensory sterilization and standardization, Woolf draws attention to seemingly benign, everyday acts and social institutions that can be equally inhibiting. Religion, Woolf suggests, is one such institution. When, at the end of the play, Reverend Streatfield attempts to discern "what message . . . [the] pageant was meant to convey," the narrator protests:

> What an intolerable constriction, contraction and reduction to simpli-fied absurdity he was to be sure! Of all incongruous sights a clergyman in the livery of his servitude to the summing up was the most gro-tesque and entire. He opened his mouth. O Lord, protect and preserve us from words the defilers, from words the impure! What need have we of words to remind us? Must I be Thomas, you Jane? (*BA* 129).

The megaphone unexpectedly releases the audience from the spell of sensory habituation, which the narrator and audience come to appreciate, but the Reverend—the capital F Father—again attempts to make sense through language, relying on its overly simplistic "Thomas and Jane" binaries to do so. His actions threaten to "defile" the experience of pure sensation. Woolf positions Rev. Streatfield as a man of sensory habits and rituals. As a servant of the cloth, he submits to a higher power and his servitude runs averse to Woolf's challenge to authority. Woolf undercuts his orderly desires stylisti-cally, jumping from the Bible to children's books, from Doubting Thomas to plain Jane.

In contrast to Woolf's radical sensory agenda, the reverend—who the narrator calls "a piece of traditional church furniture"—and the church he represents appear old-fashioned, a point Woolf underscores when noting, "The profits [from the play] . . . all go to a fund for installing electric light in the Church" (*BA* 129, 10). The metaphorical need for light undercuts the au-thority of Rev. Streatfield and the institution he represents, but the physical need for light positions the Church as a place of sensory deprivation. It is a place that has remained in the dark (literally and figuratively) and, until this point, valued ritual over progress. The Church and its followers preserve sensory traditions, as does the novel's most devout character, Lucy. Lucy's association with light gains new meaning as Woolf connects Lucy's faith with her sense of sight. Lucy maintains her particular way of seeing when "every morning, kneeling, she protected her vision" (*BA* 139). While Woolf does not appear unsympathetic to sensory ritual and the desire to protect the old ways—to continue to see, smell, and otherwise sense as usual— she simultaneously suggests that these ways are outmoded and ineffectual.

Lucy's sensory habits, while a comfort, allow her to turn a blind eye on an ever-changing sensory world—a world in which, Woolf suggests, the same old ways of sensing simply will not do.

Certainly, one cannot read Woolf in the "same old" way, and *Between the Acts* disrupts the formal elements of the novel, even more than Woolf's previous works. By blending prose, drama, and poetry, Woolf interrupts traditional sense-making processes. Combining the rhythms of prose, the visual and kinetic elements of drama, and the aurality of poetry, Woolf creates new sensory experiences for her reader. She does this, in part, through aural idiosyncrasy—by inserting unexpected sounds in the novel. Taking a note from the gramophone, quite literally, Woolf infuses her prose with contemporary cadences:

> The tune changed; snapped; broke; jagged. Fox-trot, was it? Jazz? [. . .] What a cackle, a cacophony! Nothing ended. So abrupt. And corrupt. Such an outrage; such an insult; And not plain. Very up to date, all the same. What is her game? To disrupt? Jog and trot? Jerk and smirk? Put the finger to the nose? Squint and pry? Peak and spy? (124)

While the play's audience members find this "jagged" tune suspect and wonder what hand La Trobe had in this mischief, the novel's readers, jolted by the rhythmic changes in their reading, become cognizant of Woolf's hand in this disruption. We might think of this as Woolf responding to her narrator's claim that "[s]urely it was time someone invented a new plot, or that the author came out from the bushes" (146). Woolf stages a sonically felt authorial intrusion through playful rhymes, repeated interrogatives, and short fragments of sentences. Along with the abrupt semicolons, these elements trouble an easy reading and sense-making experience. Woolf's "game," then, as the above passage suggests, *is* "to disrupt," and the surprising rhythms of her jazz-inspired lines thwart readers' expectations for reading prose. Interrupting prose with meter, Woolf "smash[es] to atoms what was whole," leaving behind sonic fragments of the traditional reading/listening experience (*BA* 124). Such fragmentation, Thompson says, "is an artistic blessing," since, in musical composition, "the act of fragmentation frees a motive from its initial context to become a different type of building block" (213). In other words, deconstruction paves the way for reconstruction.

Freed from the imperative of sense-making, Woolf builds a new cast of sounds through which she desensitizes, in order to resensitize, the trained ear of her reader. Woolf's reading audience, in attuning to the revolutionary sensations of *Between the Acts*, becomes complicit in Woolf's dissensuality, themselves enacting alternative sensory practices. Woolf encourages such practices by eliding language and emphasizing sensation. This elision occurs through the repeated use of ellipses, and the phrase "etc., etc." "etc., etc." poses a challenge to traditional acts of reading and sense-making. The following passage—a poem within a play within a novel—already disrupts generic expectations, but Woolf's use of "etc., etc." further interrupts the otherwise recognizable rhythm and rhyme pattern of the poetic line. She writes,

> "*Armed against fate,*
>   *The valiant Rhoderick,*
> *Bold and blatant,*
>   *Firm, elatant, etc., etc.*"
>
> (*BA* 66)

Woolf's use of "etc., etc." is dismissive. She could have as easily said "blah, blah, blah." The phrase "etc., etc." shifts the emphasis from the meaning to the sound of words and draws attention to the process of listening. This process, Elicia Clements posits, has the potential to "change political circumstances" (59). By "leaving something out" ("Elision") and gesturing toward but not specifying the "extras" or "sundries" to which she refers ("Et cetera"), Woolf makes space on the page for the unheard, the misheard, and the unsaid.[13] Woolf's inclusivity applies not only to sounds but also to the people who make them: the so-called unintelligible, the invisible, and the ignored. Making space for once-excluded sensing bodies creates more inclusive sensory circumstances within which divisions among people and senses increasingly dissolve.

By promoting inclusivity and the intersensory, Woolf undoes sensory segmentation and interferes with sensory hierarchies. Through elision, this time in prose, she rewrites sensory interactions. During a brief intermission between scenes 1 and 2 of the play, the audience ponders the view around them with the gramophone as accompaniment. The gramophone's tune tells a story of an idyllic pastoral where "Eve lets down her somber tresses brown and spreads her lucent veil o'er hamlet, spire and mead, etc. etc. And the tune repeated itself once more. The view repeated in its own way what the tune was saying [. . .] The cows, making a step forward, then standing still, were saying the same thing to perfection" (*BA* 92). By refusing to fill space with language, other than the gestural "etc.," Woolf opens the way for sensation. "etc." again dismisses the story the gramophone tells and accentuates, instead, the dispersion of sound not only among different sensuous actors—the gramophone, the view, and the cows—but also among different sensory faculties. Sight and sound enmesh as the view finds its voice and "repeat[s] in its own way"; touch and sound intertwine with the movement of the cows, who "step forward," "stand still," and "say the same thing to perfection."

When "the cows joined in," the narrator declares, "the reticence of nature was undone, the barriers which should divide Man the Master from the Brute were dissolved" (*BA* 125). There are many moments throughout the novel when "the Brute" participates and, by privileging the perceptions of animals, Woolf champions unconventional means of communicating and sensing. Woolf's elevation of animals reflects her personal interest, which she developed as a child, as well as a wider cultural interest in animal studies.[14] According to Caroline Hovanec, early-twentieth-century biologists, psychologists, philosophers, and artists alike "were deeply invested in the question of how to represent animal subjectivity" (Hovanec 3). Hovanec notes that Woolf's specific approach to ethology borrows from comparative psychology, which "aimed to understand human and animal minds from the inside" and "viewed animals, including humans, as diffuse bundles of sense impressions" (160). For Woolf, Hovanec asserts, "the question of what animal subjectivity is like . . . is principally a question of what sensations animals feel" (Hovanec 160). Rasheed Tazudeen contends that Woolf "attunes to the sensuous dimensions of animal being" in order to "imagine a futurity beyond the time of the human, when the absence of human consciousness . . . would allow new nonhuman forms of sensory experience to thrive" (491, 492).[15] However, Woolf does not seem to predicate nonhuman contributions on human absence. Instead, by blending human and animal sensations, she gestures toward the "humanimal," what W. J. T. Mitchell describes as a "hybrid creature predicated on the refusal of the human/animal binary" (qtd. in Wolfe xiii). Binaries collapse further when Woolf invites technological sensations to the table, and Cuddy-Keane's observations about Woolf's short story "Kew Garden" ring true for *Between the Acts* as well. It is a novel in which Woolf "shifts between mechanical and natural noises and discovers a new integrated polytextural music" where "the human, natural, and mechanical, are notated together in a comprehensive environmental soundscape" (Cuddy-Keane 84). More than just a soundscape, Woolf creates a polytextural sensescape that resists reifying sensory hierarchies or relying on traditional social value systems: sight does not undermine touch, just as the technological does not outweigh the natural. The resulting "triple melody" reconfigures the human sensorium and provides a fitting example of Woolf's egalitarian, multisensuous aesthetic (*BA* 92).

Woolf acknowledges, however, that achieving such an aesthetic is not always as idyllic a process as the above passages suggest. Shifting sensory paradigms is often a violent endeavor. Woolf illustrates this when, after the play ends and everyone disperses, La Trobe begrudgingly gathers her things, convinced that "she hadn't made them see" and that the play was "a failure, another damned failure!" (*BA* 68). Her thoughts, however, are interrupted:

> suddenly, the starlings attacked the tree behind which she had hidden. In one flock they pelted it like so many winged stones. The whole tree hummed with the whizz they made, as if each bird plucked a wire. A whizz, a buzz rose from the bird-buzzing, bird-vibrant, bird-blackened tree. The tree became a rhapsody, a quivering cacophony, a whizz and vibrant rapture, branches, leaves, birds syllabling discordantly life, life, life, life without measure, without stop devouring the tree. (142)

Animal and technological sensations pierce the literary line and interrupt La Trobe's anthropocentric sensuous agenda. Rohman points to the potential for animal sounds to disrupt linguistic hegemony, describing them as an "eruption of psychic forces that were repressed or contained within traditional literary conventions" (27). Her description brings to mind the cultural containment and repression of the senses, which "erupt" in *Between the Acts* through this mixture of animal and technological sounds. When Woolf allows nature and technology to imprint on and alter her prose, she enables not only a "remapping of literary language" (Rohman 27) but also a remapping of sensuous perception. Woolf electrifies the senses sonically through the "whizz" and "buzz" of fricatives, tactilely through the vibratory "hum" of the tree, and visually through the charged imagery of wires alive with energy. Her conflation of electric and natural imagery again cuts across nature/culture dichotomies and interrupts easy distinctions. Distinctions among the senses also fade as Woolf levels the sensory hierarchy and grounds the once-elevated sense of sound. By locating sound—a so-called higher, masculine sense—in the birds and trees, Woolf brings sensation and sensory agency down to earth, quite literally. Nature exercises its agency by "syllabling" or consciously articulating its dissent. Such dissent is not without violence, a point Woolf emphasizes through the aggressive verbs "attack," "pelt," and "devour" and through the series of hyphens that strike the page and the ear with percussive rhythm. The birds themselves are weaponized— "winged stones"—that dive like fighter planes and sound an important alert: the natural (as opposed to socially curated) sensorium is "vibrant," inclusive, and ever-changing. The "ecstasy" of that sensorium lies in the untamed discord of sensuous diversity. La Trobe's perceived "failure" is an opportunity to welcome new actors and admixtures to the sensory stage and to embrace the disruptive power of discordant sensuality.

In drawing on the frenetic energy and sensations of war, Woolf attempts to reappropriate war's violent and nonsensical interruptions. These interruptions, because they provide a break from the usual sensory program, function as sites of sensory potential: they grant readers and characters alike the space to reconsider "what counts as common sense" (Panagia 7). In an effort to expand "what counts," Woolf stages a sensory intervention in one of the final interruptions of the play. As Rev. Streatfield declares, "'Each of us who has enjoyed this pageant has still an opp . . . ,'" Woolf interrupts him. "The word," she writes,

> was cut in two. A zoom severed it. Twelve aeroplanes in perfect formation like a flight of wild duck came overhead. *That* was the music. The audience gaped; the audience gazed. Then zoom became drone. The planes had passed. " . . . portunity," Mr. Streatfield continued, "to make a contribution." (*BA* 131)

The most notable contribution in this scene comes from the airplanes, whose interruption creates an "opp . . . portunity" to revisit sensory habits and to reconfigure sensory practices. The unintended noise of the airplanes' zoom disrupts these practices by cutting through the stale sounds of the Reverend's speech. Such interruptions were common in the modernist period, when, as Jane Lewty describes it, "Acoustic interference was beginning to impede words on the page" (157). While it may be tempting to read such interference as negative, here, by impeding "words on the page," technological interruption gestures toward new forms of communication and reinvigorated acts of listening. Such listening anticipates the interruptions, disturbances, and surprises of a modern, and modernist, sensescape. Within this newly expanded sensorium, once-threatening noises transform into unexpected melodies, as evidenced by the narrator's surprise that "*that*"—the airplanes' zoom—"was the music." While we might read this statement as fearful that the sounds of warplanes may one day become as commonplace as music, we might also read Woolf's words as hopeful. Technology, Woolf suggests, can "sever" the instantaneous, knee-jerk reaction to repeat sensory habits, thereby liberating the modern subject to hear, see, touch, taste, and smell anew.

In *Between the Acts*, Woolf illuminates the unpredictable sensory landscape of a country at war and the sensuous disruption that accompanies it. Modernist subjects were often unsure of how to respond to the parade of new sensations that altered the modern sensescape, and Woolf's final novel both reflects and responds to this uncertainty. As she attends to those "bindings and unbindings, becomings and un-becomings, jarring disorientations and rhythmic attunements" of interruptive sensory moments, Woolf offers an answer to the question that opens this chapter: "Are machines the devil, or do they introduce a discord . . . ?" (Gregg and Seigworth 2; *BA* 136). Machines, Woolf seems to say, while often used for devilish purposes, are not the devil. Though mechanical and technological discord have the potential to assault and anesthetize the senses, they also have the potential to invigorate our eyes, ears, and noses and open them to new ways of sensing, and understanding, ourselves and others.

Just as the play within the novel urges its audience members to take stock of their sensory habits, Woolf encourages her reading audience to survey its sensory past, present, and future. By featuring animals, Woolf draws inspiration from a primal, prelingual time before sensation was so highly constrained and constructed. In so doing, she challenges sensory norms that fuel our impulse to categorize and exclude, to value certain sensations and sensory practices and to denigrate others. By aligning herself with sensory deviants like Manresa and La Trobe, Woolf promotes alternative sensory practices and taps into their disruptive potential: she cleaves a space between sensing and sense-making. In that space, she interjects new sensuous narratives that rattle the sensory structure. Expressing a wariness of both change and convention, *Between the Acts* arises from an intersection of emotions—a place between fear and possibility, loss and liberation—where Woolf exercises the freedom for which La Trobe, "a slave to her audience," hungers (*BA* 65). By resisting the urge to make sense for her audience, Woolf flouts conventions and refuses to "act [her] part" (Woolf, "A Letter to a Young Poet" 184).

4

Sensory Dystopia

Stifling Sounds, Sights, and Technologies in Elizabeth Bowen's *Eva Trout*

In the previous chapters, I discuss various ways women writers challenge patriarchal and anthropocentric sensory norms. I examine how H.D. resists a masculinist, unisensory worldview, how Mina Loy advocates for women's unbounded sensuous experimentation, and how Virginia Woolf rebels against Fascist sensory control. The threat that technology might be used to discourage or denigrate diverse sensory experiences and experimentation undergirds each of these writers' projects. In this chapter, I examine a writer for whom such threats become a reality. Elizabeth Bowen offers a glimpse into a thoroughly technologized world where the so-called masculine senses reign and where sensuous possibility withers.

In Elizabeth Bowen's unfinished memoir, *Pictures and Conversations*, she fondly reflects on her first bicycle, a "glittering brand-new Raleigh" (42). "Now *this* is yours," Bowen's aunt said when she gifted her niece the bicycle (42). From then on, the thirteen-year-old was enamored of her new possession. "First riding the Raleigh," Bowen recalls,

I dismounted, often, simply to stand and look at it. This, my first machine, had an intrinsic beauty. And it opened for me an era of all but
flying, which roads emptily crossing the airy, gold-gorsy Common en-
hanced. Nothing since has equaled that birdlike freedom. (42–43)

As Bowen encountered and acquired more machines, however, her relationship with them became less idyllic and more complicated. By 1967, when
Bowen wrote *Eva Trout, or Changing Scenes*, a new era of technological
change had prompted her to again ask, how does technology not only liberate but dominate? To what extent do we possess our machines, and to what
extent do *they* possess *us*?

In *Engineers for Change: Competing Visions of Technology in 1960s America*,
Matthew Wisnioski asserts that "questions of agency and identity" are "at the
center of technology and social debates" (Wisnioski 128). The debates of the
mid-1960s begin after several years of what Wisnioski describes as "a near-
utopian belief in technology's beneficence" (3). The period from 1945 to 1964
saw technological advancements that allowed for increased space exploration,
life-saving medical interventions, and ever-expanding global communication.
During this period, people on both sides of the Atlantic came to associate technology with progress and possibility: the chance to see farther, hear better, and
live longer. However, as technology became more prevalent, public feelings
about technology became less certain. According to Wisnioski, "technology
took on ambiguous and ultimately sinister connotations in American thought
and culture" (3). Norbert Weiner's 1960 article "Some Moral and Technical
Consequences of Automation" illustrates this shift in prevailing attitudes toward technology. Weiner, an MIT mathematician and the "father of cybernetics," cautioned against the belief that "a machine which man has made must remain continually subject to man" (1355). He goes on to say that though "many
people have pooh-poohed the dangers of machine techniques" and "flatly con-
tradicted . . . predictions . . . that the machine might take over the control of
mankind," this assumption "should be rejected in its entirety" (1355). He warns
that "machines can and do transcend some of the limitations of their design-
ers, and . . . in doing so they may be both effective and dangerous" (1355).

One danger technology posed was its increased propensity for destruction. While this was not a new concern—indeed, it was a concern many
voiced during WW1—it was amplified by the cultural context of the 1960s.

Technology fueled the military industrial complex and, during the Cold War and Vietnam Conflict, global citizens lived under the threat of atomic bombs, nuclear missiles, and chemical warfare. Such technologies harmed not only humans but also animals and the environment, a point Rachel Carson emphasized in her foundational environmental treatise *Silent Spring* (1962). Pressure to rethink human uses of technology did not only come from outside technological communities, however. Engineers joined antiwar and environmental activists to demand more humane, socially responsible technologies (Wisnioski 1). Their demands became increasingly important as technology became further divorced from human control. Unlike technologies of the Industrial Revolution that were largely dependent on human operators, or early-twentieth-century technologies that were semiautomatic, technologies of the 1960s were fully automized (Hong 51). Sungook Hong notes, for instance, that from 1951 to the mid-1960s, the number of digital machines in the manufacturing industry increased from seven to 7,500 (Hong 51). The rapid increase of destructive and automatous technologies caused humans to rebel against them. Sociological studies like Herbert Marcuse's *One Dimensional Man* (1964) and Jacques Ellul's *Technological Society* (translated into English in 1965) warned against man's over-reliance on technology and of technology's dehumanizing effects. "Not since the machine-breaking uprisings of the early nineteenth century," Wisnioski asserts, "ha[d] so many citizens perceived technology as a force to be resisted" (4).

Concerns about technology and human agency were further complicated by technological interventions in the human body. Advancements in the fields of genetic coding and biomedical engineering led to the creation of electronic prostheses and artificial organs, making technology's imprint on the human body and senses all the more immediate (Hong 55–56). Not only was technology intertwined with the human body and mind, but so, too, was it developing its own body and mental faculties. In the late 1950s, advancements in the fields of cybernetics and artificial intelligence (AI) led to the creation of various "thinking machines" (Hong 56). These machines possessed the ability to imitate, communicate, translate, and teach. Especially meaningful to this manuscript is the development of technologies with "emergent sensory capabilities," like Gordon Pask's "electrochemical devices," which could not only hear but also evolve their hearing (Cariani

1). Such technologies contributed to an already uncertain atmosphere—a time when technologically laden "contemporary life was becoming more alienating, more destructive, more totalitarian, and less human" (Wisnioski 4–5). Within this contentious technological and sensuous milieu, Elizabeth Bowen wrote *Eva Trout, or Changing Scenes.*

Bowen's interest in technology is visible throughout her oeuvre, in both her fiction and her non-fiction. A self-proclaimed fan of the cinema and a longtime contributor to the BBC, Bowen wrote frequently about film and radio.[1] Likewise, she found, as the other writers in this book did, that technology could invigorate art by piquing the senses. Speed's "intensifications," Bowen proclaimed, "were good for art . . . [Speed] alerts vision, making vision retentive with regard to what only may have been seen for a split second" (*Pictures* 44). While Bowen found creative potential in technology, she also acknowledged that much of society felt differently. Bowen recognized that, by the beginning of the twentieth century, society was already growing tired of technology.[2] "The age of speed," she wrote, "was not . . . cordially welcomed in" (Bowen, *Pictures* 43). Bowen attributes this inhospitable attitude to a society already inundated by technologies—steam, electric, and otherwise—"a world which already had cause to regard itself as completely modern" (42). This already modern world viewed technology as irksome, at best, and threatening, at worst. Bowen devotes a long passage in her memoir to explaining prevailing attitudes toward technology at the turn of the century:

> About motor-cars and their offspring motor-bikes there continued, for longer than may be realised now, to be something mythical and phenomenal—even hostile? "Flying machines," at the start were less ill-seen; few and freakish, they constituted a threat only to aeronauts who took off in them. Motor-cars, which spawned at a greater rate, looked at once Martian and caddish. Their colour spectrum and flashing fittings of brass were themselves offensive. The combustion engine, with its splutterings and roarings, was at once disagreeable and enigmatic. (*Pictures* 43)

Not only were these "hostile," "freakish," and "offensive" technologies unwelcome, Bowen suggests, but they were also dangerous. "Enough was enough," she imagines the public proclaiming. "Anything further, one felt, might annoy God" (44).

God's annoyance is apparent in Bowen's later fiction, which has a dystopian air. Spencer Curtis Brown, Bowen's friend and literary executor, observes:

> In her last two novels, she no longer conveyed that there were earth-tremors beneath the feet of her characters; we knew that the earthquake had already come . . . it was now a world in which the Serpent was already on the advance towards moments of triumph everywhere, over the society of man, the body, and the mind. (xxxviii)

I suggest that the triumphant Serpent in Bowen's final novel, *Eva Trout, or Changing Scenes*, takes the form of acoustic and visual technologies. Though characters attempt to harness the power of such technologies—from the radio to the recorder, the telephone to the television—time and again, technology prevails. Bowen sometimes fashions this power struggle as comical, other times as concerning. However, underlying all interactions with technology is a weariness and wariness of its power and influence over the senses and sensing bodies. *Eva Trout* details how (seemingly benign) acoustic and visual technologies reify the privileged senses of sound and sight to the detriment of all other senses. The result is a sensory dystopia, marked by disconnection, displacement, and an artificiality that disables social and sensuous progress.

Eva Trout is another notoriously difficult novel, in part because it resists easy categorization. It is, as Claire Connolly notes, "a misunderstood novel which confronts contemporary readers with a memory of an in-between space in literary and cultural history" (137). Emily Bloom argues that, while the novel "gestures towards postmodernism" (105–6), *Eva Trout* is "late modernist" in its "desire to forge links, connections, and associations" (126). I follow Bloom in reading *Eva Trout* as a late modernist text that encapsulates an epoch of explosive technological change, resulting in unforged links and unrealized connections. In writing *Eva Trout*, Bowen inhabits a rare position of reflection, providing a backward glance at a period that both lionized machines, speed, and innovation and became increasingly disillusioned by them. As such, Bowen's novel serves as a fitting end to this study of modernism. The concerns H.D., Mina Loy, and Virginia Woolf share come to a head in the 1960s, and *Eva Trout* shows us what happens when the sensory restraints they fought to loosen are pulled taught.

Other scholars have aptly read *Eva Trout* as a novel that foregrounds disturbance, in both content and form. In *Elizabeth Bowen and the Dissolution of the Novel*, Andrew Bennett and Nicholas Royle famously call *Eva Trout* "awkward, disjunctive, [and] convulsive" (142). Similarly, Neil Corcoran conceives of *Eva Trout* as a "disfiguration," a deformed version of Bowen's earlier works (131). Corcoran comments that *Eva Trout* makes "a final return, with a difference, to the material of Elizabeth Bowen's earlier fictions of childhood: a return in which the relationships . . . are all now destabilized in a way productive of panic rather than release" (Corcoran 135). I attribute this instability and panic to the influx of technologies in the 1960s and a prevalence of acoustic and visual technologies in the novel. By examining the technologies in *Eva Trout*, I add to the critical conversation about the various objects that populate Bowen's oeuvre.[3] However, unlike Bowen's earlier novels, where houses and furniture are often charmingly personified, *Eva Trout* features technological objects that inflict bodily and sensuous harm. Situated in the context of the 1960s, Bowen's depiction of technology reflects a period when the public began to view "technological systems [as] embodied arrangements of power and authority" and to fear that "those systems could take on a life of their own" (Wisnioski 9).

To better understand how technology empowers or impairs Bowen's characters and their sensory practices, I engage with scholars who examine issues of agency and subjectivity in *Eva Trout*. I view the novel through a psychoanalytic lens to articulate how 1960s technologies informed late modernist conceptions of self. I seek to illustrate how, during this pivotal decade, "machine and technology became part of what it meant to be human" (Hong 50). Questions about human agency in a hyper-technological world also gave rise to questions about human ability; thus, I privilege scholars who discuss sound and deafness in Bowen's work. While I, too, bring attention to Bowen's soundscapes, I do so to highlight the broader sensorium, which scholarship on *Eva Trout* and Bowen largely neglects. By linking these camps of critical discourse, I articulate how late-twentieth-century society conceived of technology and the senses, and how those conceptions impacted their ability to form personal connections. Specifically, I illustrate how fixating on the distant senses of sight and sound, as well as visual and acoustic technologies, alienates Bowen's characters from the larger sensorium. This, in turn, divides them from one another, ultimately contributing to society's collapse.

I begin by discussing the ever-shifting society Bowen and her characters inhabit—a society where technology continually evolves and, therefore, continually changes how and what people see, hear, smell, taste, and touch. This changeability creates a desire to control one's sensuous environment, and Eva attempts and fails to gain agency through sound and sound-producing technologies, like the telephone and the radio. In focusing on the radio, my argument echoes Bloom, who asserts that, unlike Bowen's other postwar novels, *Eva Trout* "bids adieu to radio as a medium that enables connection" (125). Through such failures, and through the deaf figure, Jeremy, Bowen draws attention to the disabling effects of acoustic technologies and the frighteningly mutable boundaries between human and machine. Her commentary calls into question traditional understandings of ability and disability that I explore in the next section, which examines how vision and visual technologies further deprive Eva of empathy and agency. Eva's preoccupation with sight and sound, and visual and acoustic technologies, negatively impacts her relationships with other characters, a point that Bowen amplifies through the absence of touch. I highlight how Bowen uses the absence of touch to signal sensory foreclosure and to imagine a dystopic society—one that searches for answers in all the wrong places and through all the wrong senses.

Bowen's novel traces the comings and goings of Eva Trout, a recently orphaned ingenue. On her twenty-fifth birthday, the "big heiress" comes into an equally large inheritance and, with this money, Eva embarks on a series of adult firsts: she lives alone for the first time, buys her first home, and adopts a son (*Eva Trout* 9).[4] Eva's attempts to live a "normal" life are, in large part, a response to her tragic and unstable upbringing. Eva's mother, Cissie, abandons her as an infant and dies shortly thereafter. Eva's father, Willy Trout, also neglects her while traveling the world with his lover (presumably the reason Eva's mother left the marriage), Constantine Ormeau. Eva gains some semblance of stability while at Lumleigh, an all-girls school, where she befriends (and becomes somewhat smitten with) Iseult Smith, her English teacher. After finishing school, Eva moves in with the newly married Iseult and her husband, Eric Arble. However, her time there, like her time in all the other places she inhabits, is fleeting. Eva leaves the Arbles, spends a short time in Broadstairs at Cathay (which is supposed to be her new, permanent residence), then leaves for America. She travels across America before briefly returning to London and then moving to Paris. This list of locales is intentionally disorienting. Through Eva's shiftlessness, Bowen highlights the transitional quality of her novel and of the time and technologies of which she writes.

Technology and Transition: *Changing Scenes* and Sensescapes

In *Eva Trout*, technology changes not only what people see but how they see. The automobile, in particular, makes for ever-shifting seeing, where one's vision is not allowed to linger. Bowen portrays this phenomenon during a meeting between Iseult and Constantine, Eva's guardians. While the two discuss what to do about their unruly ward, they travel from Constantine's office to lunch by car. "Change of scene was," Bowen writes, "thanks to the chauffeur-driven Daimler, a matter of minutes, glided through smoothly. Huge creamy porticoes, lit-up little luxury shops were registered by Iseult. News-flashes from vendors' corners, orchidaceous flashes from florist windows" (*ET* 33). The smoothness of the Daimler contrasts with the suddenness of the "news-flashes," and Bowen depicts seeing as a speedy and distancing act. Iseult cannot stop to smell the roses but instead experiences them as fleeting "orchidaceous flashes." The passive construction Bowen uses puts Iseult in the backseat, so to speak. She can only passively "register," not actively process, the sights she sees. The automobile is a technology that carries Iseult away from intimate, embodied sensory experience and immerses her in a visually oriented, sped-up sensory environment. The automobile-induced "flashes" to which Iseult finds herself subject characterize a society in motion and out of control. Bowen found such changes of scene significant enough to title her final novel after them: *Eva Trout, or Changing Scenes*. Like the society of which she writes, the title of Bowen's novel remains unsettled.

Bowen associates perpetual motion with perceptual and sensuous change. Just as the automobile changed the way we see, radio changed the way we hear. Like Virginia Woolf in *Between the Acts*, Bowen recommends a new way of listening, one that does not privilege logocentrism. In an essay on the BBC's "Third Programme," Bowen writes,

> My own feeling is that in listening to spoken (or broadcast) speech, we have listened for sense too much and for sound too little . . . Language can put out a majesty in its sheer sound, even apart from sense: in poetry and, at its greatest, prose, this becomes apparent. (205)

Understanding the technological and sensuous impacts of which Bowen speaks requires listening differently to her novel and engaging in sensory play.

Through slant-like listening, for example, one can recognize the likeness between Iseult and Eric Arble and the arbors with which Bowen associates them.

Through references to the Arbles and their arbors, Bowen illustrates the way technology changes not only sensescapes but also landscapes. Briefly, at the novel's beginning, Bowen grants her readers a rare look at a prelapsarian sensorium—an idyllic, multisensuous Eden before the technological Fall. Bowen suggests that such spaces are unsustainable in the face of the machine. She underscores the Arbles/arbors' prelapsarian connection by titling the first section of *Eva Trout* "Genesis." Genesis brings to mind Eve and the flowering arbors of Eden, which Bowen represents through Eva and Larkins Orchards, the name of the land the Arbles once owned. Larkins Orchards was once an Edenic place, the realization of Eric's lifelong dream to be a fruit farmer. Iseult was equally enchanted by the orchard. The narrator remarks that Iseult

> never foresaw [her] marriage, its days and nights, other than as embowered by dazzling acres, blossom a snowy blaze and with honeyed stamens, by sun then moonlight, till came later—fruited boughs bowed, voluptuous, to the ground, gumminess oozing from bloomy plums. (*ET* 16)

This description brings several senses to the fore. "Boughs bow" heavy with fruit and flowers glow in a "snowy blaze," invoking hapticity, both the visual and the tactile. The "ooze" and "gumminess" Bowen describes bring to mind different textures and types of touch, while Bowen's "honeyed" prose leaves readers, like Iseult, salivating for want of taste. Iseult imagines the land to be ripe—an "embowered" haven of sensuous possibility.

Eva Trout never realizes its sensuousness potential, however. Multisensuous descriptions like those of Larkins Orchards appear infrequently in the novel, which Bowen attributes to the advent of technology. Bowen illustrates this sensuous lack when the machine, in the form of a hay baler, intervenes on natural space, leaving the narrator nostalgic for the sensory-rich past. "Hay-making was at its height," Bowen writes,

> a mechanized whirring sounded over the country six days a week— when distant enough, it was in a contemporary way poetic. Restricted by the positions of orchards, the operation had about it something not only seasonal but tactical, military: summer manoeuvers. (*ET* 275)

The "mechanized whirring" of the hay baler is one of many acoustic interferences Bowen introduces in the novel. "Six days a week," the incessant noisiness of the hay baler impedes on the sensescape of the orchards, snuffing out the other senses. Using words like "operation," "tactical," and "manoeuvers," Bowen conceives of the machine as threatening and purposeful: it wages a militant attack on one's daily sensory experience.

The only reprieve from this mechanical attack on the senses occurs at evenings and, presumably, on Sundays, the biblical day of rest. During these times, the ears rest and the orchards return to their original, multisensuous state. Bowen writes, "The cessation at evening brought with it humid silence scented by exacerbated grass-roots and mangled wild-flowers. How sweet, how haunting new-fallen hay smells. Its mauve-bronze living shimmer is but a memory" (*ET* 275). In this passage, the senses are as wild and lush as the landscape. Touch and sound mingle through a felt, "humid silence"; sight and smell intertwine in the "mauve-bronze shimmer" of "new-fallen hay smells." Still, the effects of the mechanical violence remain in the "exacerbated" grass and "mangled" flowers. Bowen contrasts the oppressive, sonic whirr of technology in the field with the multisensuous lushness of the orchard. She posits the former as an extractive mechanics that is important in the ways it contributes to damaging and overworking the land. Eric, too, spurred on by an overeager Iseult, overworks and mismanages Larkins Orchards and is eventually forced to sell the fruit fields. He leaves the natural space of the orchards for a mechanized space, becoming the foreman of a garage. Importantly, Eric does this at a time when automobiles were increasingly recognized as pollutive and when public protests forced automobile manufacturers to acknowledge their role in environmental degradation (Wisnioski 34). The shift from the natural to the mechanical that Bowen describes represents a larger cultural and sensuous shift with which Bowen's contemporaries and characters grapple.

No one experiences this shift more keenly than Eva, the most unsettled of the novel's characters. Throughout the novel, technologies of transportation magnify Eva's feelings of disconnection and displacement. Eva's relationship with these forms of technology seems vexed from birth when, just two months after she is born, her mother dies in a plane crash. As a child, and as an adult, Eva is constantly moving, and technologies of transportation haunt the novel. Eva's father often uproots her, leaving her with unfamiliar people in unfamiliar places. For instance, after forcing Eva from the failed, experimental school that served as a temporary, albeit suspect home, Willy Trout took his daughter

> to Mexico, where they were joined by Constantine; then, business call-ing him to the Far East, dropped her off with a Baptist missionary fam-ily in Hong Kong, reclaimed her, left her in San Francisco with some relations of his chiropodists, caused her to be flown to him in New York, flew her from thence to Hamburg, where he picked her up later and asked her if she'd like to become a kennel-maid, decided it might be better for her to go to Paris and was about to arrange things on those lines when [Eva] said she would like to go to an English boarding school. (*ET* 55)

This is only one instance of the many frenetic rhythms of Eva's youth, which carry into adulthood. Implied in these epic travel lists are the grand ma-chines that magically transport Eva, enabling her constant movement and perpetually severing her connections to places and people. Keri Walsh makes a similar observation in her analysis of Bowen's *To the North* and *The House in Paris*, the latter of which she calls a "melancholia of intervolved tran-sit, exile, homelessness, and displacement" (26). Walsh suggests that Bowen "re-purposes Futurist technique" in these 1930s novels by de-romanticizing technological destruction (21). The same could be said of *Eva Trout*. Eva's constant movement sets the tone for a frenetic novel, which is made only more frenetic by the many technologies she encounters.

Claiming Sensory Space: Technology, Displacement, and Disconnection

Technology, like Eva's constant movement, further severs her connections to people and places, exacerbating her feelings of displacement and discon-nection. Because Eva does not have a place to call her own, she becomes territorial of those spaces she does temporarily claim for herself, and that possessiveness manifests through sensory control. In a society where sound, in particular, permeates everyday life, Eva seeks freedom from acoustic op-pression and copes with sound by attempting to suppress it. Namely, Eva seeks to control the sounds of the first (and only) house she buys, Cathay. Her noise control efforts call to mind Roland Barthes's contention that the appropriation of space is also a matter of sound: domestic space, that of the house, the apartment—the approximate equivalent of animal territory—is a space of familiar, recognized noises whose ensemble forms a kind of household symphony. (qtd. in Flint 191)

Eva, having never had a home of her own, understandably wants to direct that symphony and to manage the music of her house. This becomes apparent in Eva's emotional reaction to even the most common of household sounds. Bowen notes that, at the mere mention of installing a telephone, Eva "flew into a panic" and yelled, "I WON'T have one!" (78). Though Eva's opposition to the telephone stems, in part, from wanting to avoid contact with the Arbles and Constantine, the telephone's noisiness and unpredictability make it particularly undesirable. Other household sounds also invite Eva's indignation. As Mr. Denge shows Eva around the house, he "g[ives] a tug to the [toilet] chain" that throws Eva into a rage: "the resultant roar, cataclysmic, stampeded Eva, who pushed nay fought her way violently past him, shouting: 'That is enough! Go—go away at once! You take liberties . . . You make too many noises in my house'" (*ET* 81–82). Eva suffers the sound of the flushing toilet physically, as if being run over by wild animals. To her, the sound of the flushing toilet is itself wild—it is a rogue noise, evidence of the not-yet domestic soundscape that needs taming. The toilet, a site of waste disposal, prompts Eva to dispose of sensory waste within her home, through efforts at noise control.

Despite Eva's efforts at noise control, sound persists, and Bowen portrays it as undesirable and disruptive. For example, when Constantine arrives unexpectedly at Cathay, tracking down Eva as is his custom, he violently disturbs the quiet of the house merely by ringing the doorbell. Bowen describes the all-out auditory assault at length:

Cathay, long untroubled, was appalled by the bell—the stygian service quarters, most affected, went on as though stung by a hornet. Elsewhere the baronial woodwork crepitated; vibration made any electric candles left in their sockets between the antlers appear to flicker, as might the genuine kind. The owner was no less outraged than was her property; halting, she looked down the stairs aggressively. This attack from the bell . . . it intended never to cease. (*ET* 102)

Cathay's response to the bell mirrors Eva's: both are "appalled" by this unexpected, uninvited sensory visitor. Shockwaves, along with sound waves, ripple throughout the house, which "crepitates" and shudders as if "stung." Sound threatens to overload the sensory circuit of her home, causing the electric candles to "flicker." It figures as an attacking enemy intruder that Eva must "thwart" and against which she must defend. Protective of her home, her first real possession, Eva wants to control its soundscape, but quickly finds that sound is a persistent and untamable houseguest.

Eva's desire to dictate the sounds of her home stems from an inability, so to speak, to dictate her own aural output, and she covets technologies that possess this ability.[5] Due to her constant moving, Bowen explains, Eva acquires an odd manner of speaking and "express[es] herself like a displaced person" (*ET* 10). By the time she arrives at Lumleigh at the age of sixteen, "her outlandish, cement-like conversational style had set," and she "was unable to speak—talk, be understood, converse" (10, 62). Until Eva meets her teacher, Iseult (then Miss Smith), she is largely isolated and unaware of her "communication deficit" (10). Iseult, however, does not mince words with Eva: she derides her pupil's speech as "pompous, unnatural sounding . . . wooden . . . deadly . . . hopeless . . . shutting-off . . . misbegotten!" (64). Though Iseult "proposed to tackle Eva's manner of speaking," she feared she arrived "too late on the scene" to make a difference (10).[6] Abandoned by Iseult, just as she improved her speech—or in Eva's words, just as she "was beginning to be"—Eva turns to technology as teacher, and the objects she acquires further illustrate her desire to gain power through technology (*ET* 203).

Fittingly, Eva's former teacher is the first to encounter this technology, which Eva has begun stockpiling. During her first and only visit to Cathay, Iseult discovers:

> Outstanding examples of everything auro-visual on the market this year, 1959, were ranged round the surprised walls: large-screen television set, sonorous-looking radio, radio-gramophone in a teak coffin, other gramophone with attendant stereo cabinets, 16-millimetre projector with screen ready, a recording instrument of BBC proportions, not to be written off as a tape recorder. Other importations: a superb

typewriter shared a metal legged table with a cash register worthy to be its mate; and an intercom, whose purposes seemed uncertain, had been installed. (124–25)

A computer, scheduled to arrive the following week, completes Eva's collection. When Iseult asks Eva why she needs a computer, Eva curtly responds, "It thinks . . . That is what you used to tell me to do" (125). Eva believes that by possessing technology she can possess its qualities as well—or perhaps, that she need not possess such qualities but can depend on technology to enact them for her. Maren Linett suggests that Eva's "defensiveness about the computer also indicates to readers how to understand the 'purposes' of the intercom. Eva hopes, in her inchoate way, that the intercom will compensate for her inability to communicate" (271–72). Not just the intercom but the other technologies in her stockpile serve as prostheses: they can see, hear, and speak for Eva. In this way, Bowen enacts a fear that Mina Loy alludes to in her novel, *Insel*. Loy associates her antagonist with technologies that distance him from other characters, namely, women. Through these technologies, he often dehumanizes and disempowers women. Bowen turns this harm inward. She illustrates how Eva's overreliance on technology creates self-detachment and dependency, depriving Eva of her own sensuous power.

Technology changes not only the way Eva sees and hears herself but also the way Bowen's readers see and hear her novel. If "In the 1930s and 1940s, acoustic effects in novels—gramophones, street noise, radios, telephones— follow technological changes," then Bowen's novel of the late 1960s appears even more impacted by these technological changes (Hepburn, "Acoustic Modernism" 153). This impact is most obvious during a scene in Cathay, when Eva selects a recording device from her "long line of instruments" and demonstrates it for Iseult (*ET* 126). "Shall I record us?" Eva asks, to which Iseult emphatically replies, "Not on any account!" But she proceeds with the recording anyway. Eva responds, "It has recorded, 'Not on any account.' And now it records me saying, 'It has recorded, 'Not on any account'" (126). Through the echo-chamber of this repetition, the recording device changes not only the way Eva hears but also the way *Eva*, the novel, sounds. Through meta-gesture, Bowen links the recording function of the page in the reader's hand to the recording of the recorder. Hepburn observes a similar effect in Bowen's *The*

Little Girls, where "The novel functions as a recording device in which sounds are laid down and replayed" ("Acoustic Modernism" 159). In *Eva Trout*, this replaying stabilizes Eva while destabilizing the novel. N. Katherine Hayles suggests that in Bowen's work, as in Beckett's, "Manipulating sound through tape recorders . . . becomes a way of producing a new kind of subjectivity . . . [Tape recorders] create a new subject ambiguously located in both the body and the recorder" (94). By capturing Eva's voice, the recording device stills the transient ingénue in ways no human has. And yet, the recording device moves the prose line, altering its look and feel, creating a techno-prose hybrid.

Just as technology infiltrates and transforms the space and sound of the novel, so, too, does it encroach on Eva's home space. Eva's dependence on technology takes a dangerous turn, and Bowen portrays technology as all-powerful and all-consuming. In and around Cathay, technology stages a takeover. Along with the plethora of technologies Iseult observes, she also notes, "Drums of copper casting obstructed the hall . . . portions of the stair-way were cut away, leaving oubliettes, over which cables flowed upward towards the gallery" (*ET* 124). Eva's new technological possessions require rewiring that eats away at her home, leaving cavernous holes and creating dangerous obstacles. Cables flow or stream upward like an invasive species of vine. Further invasions occur in the living room where "Electronics had driven the old guard, the Circe armchairs, into a huddle in the middle of the floor" (125). Most notable, however, is the way in which technology trans-forms not only the domestic space but also the outside space. The narrator notes, "Glaring in upon all this, the June sun took on the heightened voltage of studio lighting. All windows were shut" (125). Here, Bowen underscores technology as aberrant and overpowering: in Eva's electronic world, even the sun becomes electric, no more than a giant bulb lighting a photo shoot. The short, emphatic clause "All windows were shut" further underscores the damage technology causes. The resulting environment is one of insularity that seals in Eva and blocks out the sensuous world.

Failures of Transmission: Acoustic Technologies, Disability, and Distortion

Acoustic technologies, in particular, contribute to Eva's alienation, a point Bowen illustrates though Eva's contentious relationship with her beloved transistor radio. Eva's transistor makes an appearance early in the novel as one of her cherished possessions, but also as one that continually defies her. The transistor follows Eva to her first home. While Eva waits at the train station for Mr. Denge, her realtor, to escort her to Cathay, Bowen notes, "Her transistor [Eva] grasped" (77). Syntactically, Bowen places the transistor in a position of power: though not the subject of the sentence, the "transistor" appears in the subject position, not Eva. This reversal complicates the relationship between the actor and the acted upon, subject and object. This reversal is further apparent in Eva's reliance on the radio for comfort. Notably, in a twist on renée hoogland's reading of maternal voice in *Eva Trout*, Eva looks to the radio as one would a mother, an action that further highlights the transistor's agency, as well as Eva's perverse, yet pitiable, dependence on technology.[7] While Eva is sick and has no one to check on her, the transistor seems to hold vigil by her side. "With a gleam like a forehead's," Bowen writes, the transistor "stood by her bed" (*ET* 43). Here, again, Bowen grants the transistor human properties, but, like many of the humans Eva encounters, the transistor is dismissive. When Eva turns to her transistor for sympathy, it turns against her:

> —at a moment, [Eva] was constrained to reach out and touch it. She received a shock: *ice*-cold the thing had become! Angrily ice-cold, colder than anger. Eva drew back her frightened, rejected hand, rolled over and lay on top of it, to console it. (*ET* 43–44)

The "shock" Eva feels can be better understood by examining Steven Connor's remark that "[t]he strangeness of radio comes from the fact that contingency is of its essence" (*Beckett* 65). While Connor uses contingency to mean that one comes upon the radio "by chance, or even surreptitiously," contingency also brings to mind the sense of touch (*Beckett* 66). Eva wishes to be contingent to or touched by her transistor, but, as Connor suggests, the radio's touch is unpredictable. In this instance, the radio is cold, physically and emotionally. Its coldness and lack of bodily contagion underscores its nonorganic state, which contrasts Eva's human feverishness. Yet, as if invested with human agency, the radio fends off Eva's touch, just as a mother might smack away a child's hand.

Through Eva's strange interactions with her transistor, Bowen alludes to the power radio gained throughout the twentieth century and illustrates how radio changed the way we listen to and conceive of sound. By drawing attention to these sensuous changes, Bowen's project aligns with that of Virginia Woolf, her longtime friend and dissensuous literary sister. As discussed in the previous chapter, Woolf reappropriates technological sounds as a means of grappling with modernism's intense aurality. Bowen, however, denies Eva this possibility. Eva's struggles with her transistor reflect, in miniature, those of twentieth-century listeners, who were plagued by "the unsettling omnipresence" of sound (Cohen et al. 5). Connor explains, "The question that a radio aesthetics can never for long set aside is that of location. Where is radio?" (*Beckett* 65). Taking a cue from Marinetti's "La Radia" manifesto, Connor determines that "radio is everywhere. Its power is that of delocalization" (*Beckett* 65). Eva's transistor illustrates this delocalization. The transistor, Eva points out, is unique among other technologies because "*It* can be carried from place to place" (*ET* 126). Its portability signifies radio's progressiveness and pervasiveness in twentieth-century life. Radio, specifically, and sound in general, were so ubiquitous that "listening became an ever more diffuse and involuntary activity" (S. Connor, *Beckett* 68). Eva emblematizes this fatigued listener who, inundated by sound, begins to have aural hallucinations. Bowen illustrates this through various references to disembodied voices. When sick with fever, Eva thinks "She had heard somebody saying, 'How is my darling?'—but when? where? . . . The voice had come in as a door opened—but what door? where?" (*ET* 44). Though this example does not depict radio sound specifically, it does illustrate the effects radio had on listeners. The voice Eva hears, like radio sound, issues from everywhere, yet nowhere, and disorients her. She conceives of sound as an unplaced-place: a door without a location. Eva attempts to place that sound, to give it an origin and a destination. However, like the open door in Eva's dream, sound comes and goes as it pleases.

Bowen draws attention to the lack of control characters exert over soundscapes and against acoustic technologies through Eva's adopted son, Jeremy. Eva does not adopt Jeremy as much as she acquires him, purchasing him on the Chicago black market. Bowen links Jeremy to the auro-visual equipment Eva stockpiles—she first alludes to his arrival while Eva shows Iseult her new technological toys—but with a difference: Jeremy "does not hear and does not speak" (*ET* 168). By subtly associating Jeremy with technology, Bowen persuades us to question the way technology impacts human agency and sensory ability. Jeremy's inability to make or hear sound draws attention to other characters' relationships with sound and sound technologies. In this way, he functions as a "narrative prosthesis": "a mechanism . . . [where] the text uses a character with a disability as a sort of crutch to prop up one or more concerns of the narrative" (Linett, "Modes" 277n6). Mr. Dancey, the vicar of a church and patriarch of a family Eva befriends while at Larkins, best expresses this concern when, pitying Jeremy, he laments, "Crass as sound can be imagine a soundless world?" (*ET* 169). In a seemingly simple question, Mr. Dancey summarizes the complex, conflicted relationship modernist subjects had with sound. Though he proclaims sound is indispensable, he also underscores its harshness, positing it as a necessary evil. Bowen asks us to do just as Mr. Dancey advises. Through Jeremy, she prompts her readers to take note of those senses we value and devalue and to consider how technology enables and impairs the sensuous body. How, she asks, does technology program us, and what happens when we turn off that (radio) programming? What happens when we mute sound?

Bowen answers these questions by proffering a technologically inflected, social understanding of disability. She implicates technology in the disabling process and complicates understandings of both technology and disability. Jeremy's disability, for instance, amplifies Eva's shortcomings—it "shed[s] light on the displacement, the emotional disabilities" with which she grapples—but it also sheds light on other kinds of impairment (Linett, "Modes" 272). Bowen employs "handicap" variously, to describe not only Jeremy's deafness but also other forms of debilitation (*ET* 61). The narrator notes that, in school, Eva was considered "partly handicapped" (61). She is unsure "in what particular or for what reason [Eva] was to be taken to be [handicapped]" though Maud Ellmann suggests that she is "tongue-tied to the point of autism" (*ET* 61; Ellmann, *Elizabeth Bowen* 204). The acoustic technologies to which Eva continually turns may exacerbate her so-called handicap since, as Lewty maintains, "habitual radio listening may enfeeble the refined process of finding words for oneself, as interruptions are more readily absorbed" (160). Lewty's observation helps draw further connections between Bowen's *Eva Trout* and Woolf's *Between the Acts*. Where Woolf describes the damaging effects aural technologies have on listening, Bowen describes the damaging effects such technologies have on speaking, a consequence that would have had particular resonance for Bowen, who grappled with a speech impediment for much of her life.[8] Bowen entangles questions of sensory ability with technological advancement and suggests that the two do not peacefully coexist. Just as technology infiltrates Eva's home, so, too, does it infiltrate her body. She appears increasingly mechanized, akin to the technologies on which she depends. Noting the ways Eva resembles her Jaguar automobile, Céline Magot refers to her as "Bowen's 'mechanical-animal' creation" (136). This creation, Magot continues, "seems to generate a new form of grotesque representation since it draws from archetypal imagery but adds mechanical elements to it. Eva is all at once a mythological and mythical creature, the futuristic Eve, the becoming-machine" (136).

Eva, however, is not the only "becoming-machine" in the novel. Mr. Dancey also appears disturbingly mechanized and, through him, Bowen gives further voice to modernist fears of sensory impairment and technological manipulation. Acoustic technologies, the radio in particular, were primary sources of anxiety and suspicion. Jeffrey Sconce explains, "The uncanny power of [radio] fused with a concern over the power to manipulate the personal and social by external forces" (39). It "evoked anxieties over distant control and loss of self" (Sconce 40).[9] Such anxieties persisted into the late twentieth century, as the character of Mr. Dancey attests. "Occupationally," Bowen writes, "[Mr. Dancey's] anxiety was his voice, which had taken to varying in volume as unaccountably as though a poltergeist were fiddling with the controls, sometimes coming out with a sudden boom or roar, sometimes fading till off the air" (*ET* 23). Bowen equates Mr. Dancey's sensory impairment with failed transmissions, entangling human and technological ability. Mr. Dancey uses his voice to "broadcast" sermons, but he exhibits a frustrating lack of control over said broadcasts—and over his body. Bowen describes his body as a rogue radio, with a powerless operator. Mr. Dancey cannot manipulate his sonic output or soundscape but finds himself subject to it, involuntarily. The radio pervades and invades: it is a "poltergeist" or noisy ghost, an invisible force that possesses Mr. Dancey, just as it haunted modern listeners.[10] Bowen conceives of radio sound as a presence that cannot be exorcised and over which listeners exercised little power.

Bowen emphasizes the inescapable, intrusive qualities of radio through an exaggerated depiction of Mr. Dancey's allergies. Like allergies, Bowen suggests, radio is a daily, embodied disturbance. Bowen describes Mr. Dancey's "handicap"—his uncontrollable sensuous body—in great detail (*ET* 23). She explains that, one day, when Mr. Dancey had run out of Kleenex, he had to repress a sneeze, which cost him an agonizing contortion. At forty-two, he would have been better looking than any of his children were it not for the havoc wrought by his chronic affliction. His alive countenance had seldom a chance to be quite itself; vision, discernment and charity shone from it, but often as though through a blurred pane—inflamed eyelids, sore, swollen nostrils, bloated upper lip. There were few intermissions: when winter relaxed its grip he regularly started to have hay fever. (*ET* 23)

The amount of description Bowen devotes to Mr. Dancey's physiognomy verges on the comical, especially when the narrator announces that his great "affliction" is hay fever. Of all the "convulsive" bodies Bennett and Royle identify in *Eva Trout*, Mr. Dancey's is arguably the most tortured (141). His swollen eyelids nearly blind him, just as his swollen nostrils impair his sense of smell and, one can safely assume, his sense of taste. Interestingly, though Bowen attributes Mr. Dancey's symptoms to "natural" causes, she ends the passage by alluding to a cultural phenomenon, the radio drama. "Intermission" calls to mind the radio dramas with which Bowen was familiar, and she conceives of Mr. Dancey's allergies as a sort of embodied drama from which he has little reprieve.[11] His allergy-induced sensory overload resembles the sonic/radiophonic overload that earlier modernist characters and writers experienced—what Jane Lewty refers to as "the colonization of daily life by radio" ("Virginia Woolf" 150). According to Lewty, with the founding of the BBC (1922), NBC (1926), and CBS (1927), radio became an "insistent presence . . . where unwelcome facts crowd in, irrespective of the mental effort to be selective" ("Virginia Woolf" 159). Certainly, radio might be thought of as a "chronic affliction" from which modern subjects experienced (and continue to experience) "few intermissions" or moments of relief (*ET* 23). Overwhelmed by sensory input, Mr. Dancey fails to dictate his own sensory output: his "countenance" cannot be "quite itself," and he cannot put his best face forward. Like Jeremy, who cannot speak, and Eva, who cannot speak well, Mr. Dancey also fails to transmit. Comparable to a radio gone haywire, Mr. Dancey's hay fever renders him a distorted version of himself.

The radio, however, is not the only technology that damages and distorts: Bowen further emphasizes acoustic technology's disruptive effects through the telephone. After an unexpected phone call from Iseult, for instance, Eva doubts if she had really spoken to her former teacher or "an impersonator" (*ET* 213). She wonders, "Had it all been a trick played by the wire? Alone with a voice, shut up with it, you are fooled by what can be its distortedness" (213). Eva fears not only that her ear is playing tricks on her but that technology does, too. Through the telephone, Bowen asks, can we trust what we hear, or does technology feed us falsehoods and "distortions"? What Debra Rae Cohen says of the radio rings true of the telephone as well: "sound may be and often is 'sound effect'" ("Intermediality" 585–86). The telephone raises questions about the reliability not only of sound technologies but also of human hearing and human being. When Eva ends her call with Iseult, the narrator wonders if "Eva could be an overexcitable ear, so long-lasting having been its desuetude. Might the ear not seem to have registered what it had not?" (*ET* 213). The confusing syntax of the second clause echoes Eva's confusion and exemplifies the sensuous uncertainty that technology creates. The telephone (not to mention the person on the other end) incites a crisis of trust: for Eva, the ear no longer serves as a reliable indicator of truth. Without this reliable, sensuous foundation, the sensory apparatus crumbles and subjectivity, as she knows it, slips. Eva is left contemplating, "What a slippery fish is identity; and what *is* it besides a slippery fish?" (*ET* 213). Such slippage between "the authentic and the counterfeit" is, Pamela L. Caughie asserts, the "special province of sound technology" ("Audible Identities" 106). Sound and subjectivity have a reciprocal relationship so that as the modern soundscape changed, "The very meaning of what it meant to be human changed" (Caughie, "Audible Identities" 105). Eva feels the effects of this change and, after Iseult's phone call, she is left wondering, "What *is* a person?" (*ET* 213).[12]

"Seeing, Seeing, Seeing": Sight and Sensory Deprivation

Eva finds a reprieve from sound and the many questions it provokes through Jeremy. While it is unclear whether Eva was aware of Jeremy's disability before adopting him, Eva appears to, at times, relish and encourage Jeremy's "objection to verbal intercourse" (*ET* 208). Though she "faithfully" takes Jeremy to "ear-and-speech men, or women," and "trie[s] everything, everyone," she quietly celebrates that his "rejections came out the victor each time" (208). Constantine warns Eva that, given her encouragement, Jeremy "may well go on hugging his disability" and that "it's a form of immunity" (192). Insensitive as it may be, Eva seems to envy the immunity Jeremy's deafness offers. Given her anxieties about sound and speech, his disability becomes a unique ability: it enables him to censor the world and to disengage the realms of speech and sound from which Eva shies. With Jeremy, Eva spends several blissful "inaudible years," before she must return to reality and "face the music" (207, 208).

Eva attempts to evade the world of sound by engaging exclusively with sight, the other sensory modality that dominates the novel. By the latter half of the twentieth century, visual media proliferated, and, key to *Eva Trout*, television replaced the radio, "cannibaliz[ing] its genres, forms, and audiences" (Bloom 164). Bowen's audience would have grown accustomed to an ever-changing technological market, where new technologies compete for, and make demands on, the public's time, attention, and energy. In this market economy, mass technologies like the radio and television cannot coexist, or, at least, they cannot coexist equally. One technology dominates another, just as, in the traditional sensory hierarchy, one sense dominates another. We see evidence of this domination and consumption in Eva's and Jeremy's engagement with visual technologies.

For the first eight years of Jeremy's life, he and Eva live a "cinematographic existence, with no sound-track" (*ET* 207). Bowen describes this period as "the at-large American years [when], insulated by her fugue and his ignorance that there could be anything other, [Eva and Jeremy] had lorded it in a visual universe" (208). Bowen fashions Eva and Jeremy as escapees, running from the aural world that others attempt to force upon them. For Eva, this evasion requires a "fugue" state, a sort of selective amnesia, wherein she forgets that sound—or any of the other senses, for that matter—exists. Eva's unisensory practices further emphasize Bennett and Royle's claim that throughout the novel "Eva has been unable to join things—words, thoughts, memories, actions, people—together" (156). Evoking one of the last words of the novel (and the last word Eva speaks), Bennett and Royle remark, "Except during her flowing, phantasmagoric, movie years in America . . . [Eva] is unable to make sense of events because she is unable to 'concatenate'" (156; *ET* 301). We can add the senses to the list of things Eva does not "concatenate," or link together. Safe in her "visual universe," Eva rejects the multisensuous world and opts for a unisensory worldview.

Through Eva's ocularcentrism, Bowen depicts a world where an eyesight-alone mentality fosters disconnection. Bowen's narrator explains that mother and son "came to distinguish little between what went on inside and what went on outside diurnal movies, or what was not contained in the television flickering them to sleep" (*ET* 208). Day to night, visual technologies consume the minds of Jeremy and Eva. Another failed teacher, the screen does not impart knowledge but leaves its pupils (and its pupils' pupils, if you will) ignorant, undiscerning, and overtaxed. Bowen alludes to the repercussions of privileging vision above all other senses by warning that sensory exclusion can lead to social isolation. During this visual period, Eva and Jeremy are dangerously out of touch with the larger world:

> From large or small screens, illusion overspilled on to all beheld. Society revolved at a distance from them like a ferris [*sic*] wheel dangling buckets of people. They were their own. Wasted, civilization extended round them as might acres of cannibalized cars. Only they moved. They were within a story to which they imparted the only sense. (*ET* 208)

"The only sense" Eva and Jeremy "impart" and indulge is vision, and Bowen comments on the danger of this single-sense devotion. Visual technologies slowly eat away at their humanity, insulating and distancing them from reality. Such devoted movie-going promotes what Gilles Deleuze and Félix Guattari refer to as "optic vision." Unlike haptic or "close vision," which fosters a sense of intimacy and "withness," optic vision creates distance (qtd. in Paterson 85). From this distance, Eva and Jeremy perceive larger society as mere spectacle, a visual carnival. The fantastical technology of the Ferris wheel suggests a naïveté and innocence that quickly turns dangerous, and the same can be said of Eva (Smith 228–29). Eva leads Jeremy in precarious sensory practices, just as the two of them perch precariously on the fringes of society, like "a ferris [*sic*] wheel dangling buckets of people" (*ET* 208). The fantastical scene culminates in a dystopic wasteland, where technology self-destructs and consumes itself in the form of "cannibalized cars." If Eva and Jeremy represent just two visual consumers whose actions result in such severe consequences, Bowen asks us to consider the consequences of visual consumption en masse.

Bowen further illustrates the negative impact of the visual through Jeremy. Mr. Dancey, both a father and a Father, pays reverence to the patriarchal sensory hierarchy and Jeremy's seemingly superhuman vision. He proclaims, "Sight to me is the thing—the thing above all things. And more seeing eyes than [Jeremy's] I have seldom seen" (*ET* 169). Though Jeremy has "seeing eyes," Bowen undercuts his visual ability. Instead, she depicts sight as inhibiting and Jeremy as unable to fully process what he sees. Only Iseult recognizes that Jeremy tires of seeing and needs nonvisual stimulation. Iseult meets Jeremy in as mysterious a way as Eva does. Eight years after Eva adopts him, Jeremy returns with her to England, where Eva takes him to Larkins. Upon arriving, they learn that Iseult and Eric have separated (presumably because Eva let Iseult believe she was pregnant with Eric's child) and no longer inhabit the cottage. After learning of Eva's attempted visit, Iseult makes her own visit, picking up Jeremy one day after his art lesson without Eva's knowledge or consent. While Eva frets over her son's kidnapping, Iseult inventories Jeremy's condition. "I cannot tell you what satiated eyes he had," she professes, "or how his weariness of seeing, seeing, seeing without knowing, without knowing, without knowing was borne in on me" (273). By contrasting seeing and knowing, Bowen challenges traditional sensory associations that equate sight with knowledge. Iseult's repetition reads like a chant, illustrating Jeremy's visual enchantment and the damaging, trancelike sensuous state in which he exists.

Eva is forced to confront Jeremy's frustration with "seeing, seeing, seeing" when she encounters one of his sculptures. While Eva house hunts, she sends Jeremy to art class, "where a needy sculptress would teach him to model" (*ET* 199). The narrator relays,

> Jeremy was at work on a head of [Eva . . .] It was a large knob, barely representational—only, he had gouged with his two thumbs deep into the slimed clay, making eye-sockets go, almost, right through the cranium. Out of their dark eyes had exuded such nonhumanity that Eva had not known where to turn. (209–10)

Jeremy fashions Eva's eyes, and their obsession with the visual, as deadly. The sculpture's eye sockets threaten death by practically piercing through the skull, and its lifeless, "black eyes" emphasize an unhuman unseeingness. Like the visual life Jeremy and Eva lead, the rendering of Eva's head is "barely representational," a poor substitute for the real thing. It is a harmful existence against which Jeremy, who violently "gouged" out his mother's clay eyes, rebels.

"To be out of touch does damage": Untouchable Characters and Unsustainable Futures

By drawing attention to the damage that visual fixation can cause, Bowen advocates for other means of knowing and sensing; however, the society that inspires and populates *Eva Trout* is less amenable to the lower senses, touch specifically. Jeremy certainly would benefit from the ability to use his hands, a point that Bowen makes obvious through his sculpture work. Eva sees that Jeremy loves working with clay and "would not be parted from it; he gummed up [their suite at] Paley's by bringing lumps of it home wet" (*ET* 200). During their brief time together, Iseult conceives of Jeremy's hand as an untapped source of power, one that he knowingly cultivates. "Clay was caking on his fingers," she says, "and he watched it, gathering his forces" (273). Though Jeremy finds agency through touch, Bowen creates a society that devalues the hand as a medium of communication and touch as a means of connection. Linett points out that "there is no mention of sign-language in the novel" and explains,

> This absence reflects educational practices at the time Bowen was writing. From the late nineteenth century through the 1970s, the oralist movement dominated educational theory and practice for deaf children; oralism advocated banning signed languages from deaf schools and replacing them with training in lip-reading and speech. (Linett, "Seeing" 480)

Mr. Dancey remarks, "To be out of touch does damage," and this seems especially true for Jeremy (*ET* 171). Because social norms discourage Jeremy from using his hands and touch to communicate, he remains out of touch and isolated from others.

Though the possibility of touch and gesture offer Jeremy a way to connect with others, for the majority of characters, touch disconnects and discombobulates. When touch does appear in the text, Bowen depicts it as selfish: it is emblematic of a society that suffers from self-interest and lack of intimacy. Instead of touching each other, Bowen's characters often narcissistically touch themselves. This habit is most obvious in Constantine, who repeatedly touches his own face. For example, while Constantine and Iseult discuss Eva's care and management, touch features as a distancing device.

Addressing Iseult, Constantine "raised, then touched, a barely-visible eye-brow. 'You would not be entirely single-handed. Not quite unaided [. . .] But you and *I* should, probably, keep in touch? Closer in touch than hith-erto. Er—collaborate'" (*ET* 40). Constantine's awkward invitation to "keep in touch" with Iseult reads ironically. Not only does he guard his touch by keeping his hands to himself, but his question and the qualifying "probably" emphasize his hesitancy to connect with Iseult. The interruptive phrase that ends Constantine's speech underscores his unwillingness to "Er—collabo-rate." Bowen's inclusion of "single-handed" further highlights the disunifying effects of the hand and Constantine's reluctance to reach out, literally and metaphorically, to others. This clumsy moment of touching and not touching is characteristic of Bowen's novel, in which supposedly intimate relationships are largely hands-off.

Though Bowen conceives of touch as a sense that could and should unite people, instead, it provokes suspicion and separation. Iseult ponders the power of touch while writing in her journal one night. She wonders, "What was I once?—who cares. What can I never be again? Intact" (*ET* 98). One who is "intact" is untouched—whole, unimpaired, and not corrupted by contact. Iseult finds the effects of touch irreversible and inescapable, and she laments its power over her. She asserts, "Touch is everything. Touch is a leech. Go up and lie by a cold pillow, hearing nobody breathing? Better keep on at this, these are words at least" (98). As her thoughts show, Iseult both desires and loathes touch. She conceives of it as a parasite that keeps her awake at night for want of intimacy and against which she must protect her-self. Words, "at least," offer some contact and intimacy, but Bowen fashions this form of touch, too, as ersatz and isolating.

Touch is most isolating for Eva, who continually seeks but is denied con-tact with others. During her school years, Eva longs to connect with Iseult, but she feels that "something disembodied Miss Smith," making her intan-gible (*ET* 60). The narrator explains that "neither then nor later did Eva look upon [Miss Smith] as beautiful or in any other way clad in physical being. Miss Smith's *noli me tangere* [touch me not] was unneeded in any physical dealings with Eva—who *could* have touched her?" (60). Bowen's invocation of "*noli me tangere*," Jesus's famous words to Mary Magdalene after his res-urrection, further highlight Iseult's immateriality. But, as the narrator notes, the godlike untouchability Iseult exudes "was unneeded," since Eva, herself unused to touching or being touched, does not turn to the tangible for connection. Instead, Eva reaches out to her teacher in the only way Iseult allows, through words. Exhibiting an uncharacteristic ease with language, Eva memorizes and recites lines from a George Herbert poem that express her desire for contact and further cast Iseult as untouchable. "Yet Thou are not so dark, since I know this," Eva declares, "But that my darkness touch thine / And hope, that may teach it to shine" (65). Though Eva wants only that her disembodied "darkness touch" Iseult's, even the desire for indirect contact drives Iseult away. Iseult's cool response to Eva's recitation prompts Eva to ask, "This will not end Miss Smith?," to which the latter makes no reply (66). Their relationship breaks down after this, thereby reifying Eva's understanding of touch as forbidden sensory territory.

Touch between women, even young girls, seems especially forbidden in the novel, a point that Bowen illustrates through Eva's relationship with her classmate, Elsinore. Corcoran observes that the exchanges between Eva and Elsinore carry "an emotional authenticity which is hardly ever apparent elsewhere" in the novel (128). In these rare moments, Bowen signals the latent, unrealized potential of touch to create intimacy. When Elsinore lies comatose in bed after she "walked into the lake," Eva does not leave her side (*ET* 52). Though the housemaid who tends to Elsinore warns Eva, "*You* must not touch her," Eva does touch Elsinore, and the effect is transformational (53). Bowen writes that "to repose a hand on the blanket covering Elsinore was to know in the palm of the hand a primitive tremor [. . .] This deathly yet living stillness, together, of two beings, this unapartness, came to be the requital of all longing" (54). This scene is similar to those in H.D.'s *HERmione*, where queer touch expands sensory possibility. Like H.D., Bowen locates knowing in "the palm of the hand," suggesting that touch is a productive means of perceiving and understanding others. (She further illustrates this when, years later, Eva and Elsinore run into each other unexpectedly in Chicago, and Elsinore recognizes Eva's hand before seeing her face [140–41].) Touching Elsinore gives Eva a sense of intimacy and belonging that she had not experienced before. Bowen crafts a new word, "unapartness," to signify this new sensation and the unifying power of touch. However, the "tremor"-like, "deathly yet living" qualities of this touch render it inchoate and tenuous and, shortly hereafter, Elsinore's mother arrives to take her daughter away. Eva is, again, denied touch and left wanting the understanding and intimacy it affords. Here H.D.'s and Bowen's depictions of touch diverge. The unifying, queer touch through which H.D.'s characters loosen sensory (and sexual) restraints is not available to Eva and Elsinore. Though Bowen alludes to the generative power of their touch, she creates a society where touch cannot evolve and where touching is, ultimately, an untenable sensuous experience.

The absence of touch enhances the dystopian aura of *Eva Trout* and calls into question the future of the society that populates and inspires the novel. Time and again, Bowen's characters are unwilling or unable to touch one another, and Bowen warns that without touch, especially intimate touch, society will fail to generate life or art. She gestures toward the failure to generate life by highlighting characters who have touchless, sexless, or otherwise unproductive (and unreproductive) relationships. For queer women, in particular, touch is forbidden. We see this when, after the nurse tells Eva not to touch Elsinore, Eva "locked her hands together behind her back, in a token of abstinence" (*ET* 53). Though Eva goes on to have an intimate physical experience with Elsinore, the novel quickly forecloses the possibility of a lasting queer relationship. We see a similar foreclosing when Iseult rejects Eva's touch, a moment Patricia Juliana Smith attributes to Iseult's "lesbian panic" and fear of being outed (238). Unable to touch those she desires, Eva remains abstinent. She explains that she did not try to have a child naturally because she "had disagreeable impressions of love," and "was not anxious to [experiment]" (*ET* 247).[13] Uninterested in having sex with men and not able to intimately touch women, Eva lives a touchless existence. Iseult, too, does not find fulfillment through touch. Though she and Eric were once physically intimate, they are unable to have children, a fact that causes Iseult much suffering. Bowen briefly nods to another couple, Dr. and Mme. Bonnard, who are also unwillingly childless. Bowen's emphasis on these childless couples and the impossibility of intimacy paints a bleak future for society, one where life cannot grow and where art, like the novel Iseult tries to write, is "born dead" (253). Marked by miscarriages and missed opportunities, the sensuous environment Bowen creates stifles touch, leaving little hope for a fertile sensory future.

"Seekers—still seeking"

Bowen depicts this hopeless future, brought about by society's destructive relationship with the senses and technology, through Eva's faux marriage to

Henry Dancey. In the final pages of the novel, Eva begins staging her wedding, an act that replaces the possibility of true contact and intimate touch with empty spectacle. After asking Henry to "act" as her "bridegroom," Eva begins planning their feigned pre-wedding party (*ET* 245). She invites Constantine, the Arbles, and Mr. Denge to Victoria Station for a celebratory send-off. There, Eva and Henry will, ostensibly, embark on their new life together. Unbeknownst to the wedding party, Henry plans to exit the train at some point, leaving Eva to continue alone. Jeremy, Eva decides, will be present for the wedding but will not join her on her journey. He will, instead, indefinitely remain with Dr. and Mme. Bonnard, a couple who have been helping him learn to speak and read lips (238). By this point in the novel, Eva has decided that her time with Jeremy has ended: "The dear game was over, the game was up" (285). However, in one last act of visual imposition, Eva insists to Mme. Bonnard, "I think [Jeremy] should see *I* see he is free of me, and what better way than this to show him?" (289). So begins a final scene that, like the above passage, exhausts itself with references to seeing.

Bowen's description of Victoria Station starts with multiple senses—with "odors [. . .] fanned by a passage of air" and "a dying-down of reverberations"—but this quickly fades from the narrative, which fixates on sight (*ET* 289). Various visual verbs overwhelm the final pages of the novel, to an almost comical effect. As Constantine, Jeremy, and Mr. Denge wait for Eva to arrive at the station, Henry comments, "I haven't *seen* her for rather more than a week," after which he exclaims "I think I see—" before stopping abruptly (291, 292). Constantine similarly remarks, "I have not seen [Eva], one way or another, since her visit to France"; follows up with, "one regretted seeing her go"; and asks after Jeremy, saying, "One sees no signs of him" (292, 292–93, 296). Iseult and Eric Arble, recently reunited, appear on the scene in a notably visual (and laughable) manner by "spotting their spotters simultaneously" (291). When Eva does appear, she, too, is a visual spectacle. She "hove into sight" and "stood tall as a candle, some accident of the light rendering her luminous from top to toe" (294). Eva further draws attention to the eye by asking Constantine, "My father told me my eyes are like my mother's—are they?" (297).

Through repeated references to seeing, Bowen bombards her readers with the visual, just as the modern subject was also bombarded. Vision enthralls the characters in the novel and seeing stupefies them. This is best illustrated via the audience that gathers around Jeremy as he, like his mother, makes a spectacle of himself. While Eva takes center stage, Jeremy performs farther down the platform. Mrs. Caliber, a recently hired nanny, watches him, and her name cheekily alludes to the drama that ensues. Through a series of bizarre plot points, Jeremy finds Iseult's gun, which she left in Eva's hotel suite without her knowledge. This is not the first time Jeremy encounters a gun—Iseult gives him a toy gun earlier in the novel—and it is unclear, after a life spent seeing imitations on screens, if Jeremy knows the difference between the real thing and the toy. The audience Jeremy attracts also appears unable to differentiate between reality and fantasy. They believe the gun, like the boy himself, is "a stage dummy" (*ET* 298). "Audience-minded, as are contemporary crowds," they suspect a "child's ballet enactment of a *crime passionel*? Or a boy model, advertising something: 'Little Lord XXX will shoot up the train, if he isn't given—?'" (299). Inundated by visual culture—from film to advertisements—contemporary crowds are, like Jeremy, always "seeing, seeing, seeing, without knowing" (273). Paradoxically, sight does not provide a clearer picture but obscures understanding. Just as Jeremy's audience is temporarily blind to reality, so, too, are Bowen's readers. We eventually see, however, that the gun Jeremy flourishes is real. Bowen makes one last nod to visual technology's harmful impact when Jeremy, "at sight of Eva, [. . .] sped like a boy on the screen towards the irradiated figure, waving his weapon in salute" (302). Imitating actors he has seen on television and in films, Jeremy fires the revolver, and Eva falls over dead. She dies an "irradiated" or overexposed "figure," a victim of visual excess.

Like the image of Eva's dead body, vision haunts the novel. Bowen depicts this haunting quite literally, through a wandering mass of "seekers" (*ET* 293). These seekers, who go unidentified at first, are members of Eva's extended family, whom she invited to her send-off and had not seen in years. Unsure what Eva looks like, they circle the platform, as if in a trance: "On the return, past, drifted the seekers—still seeking, unflaggingly. Was hope dwindling? Mistlike phantoms, the aunts, uncles and cousins in passing by bent phantom eyes upon Eva" (297). Here again, Bowen emphasizes that seeing does not offer knowledge or certainty. The drifters do not know Eva by sight, just as the onlookers are not convinced the "mistlike phantoms" are real people. Bowen associates seeing not with realism and reality but with Surrealism and fantasy, even absurdism. The habitual back and forth of the ghostlike figures implies that they will continue their fruitless search, ceaselessly. Eva's extended family will go on haunting the station and being haunted by their obsessive see(k)ing. So, too, Bowen suggests, will society. If Eva is akin to Mother Eve, then Bowen implies that we are all her extended family. Through these figures, Bowen gives her readers a glimpse of their future, vacuous selves—spectators turned specters, haunted by the visual.

The final scene in *Eva Trout* does not change as its subtitle, *Changing Scenes*, suggests but stagnates, as does the novel's sensorium. For all its motion, Bowen depicts a society that stalls: *Eva's* train, like the one Eva never boards, does not leave the station. As Sinéad Mooney points out, Bowen's final novel "stops but has no end, not having progressed far beyond Eric Arble's initial verdict on the savagely innocent protagonist: 'Nothing . . . makes sense . . . [Eva] makes sense as much as else'" (32; *ET* 19). Mooney associates *Eva* with a comical "meaninglessness or absurdity" that comes from "the pleasure of no longer having to invest our energies in the labour of making sense" (32). This absurdity stems from a society besieged by seeing and hearing and invested in a limited sensorium that also limits possibility. Bowen acknowledges these limitations. She refers to Eva and Jeremy's "cinematographic existence" as a "sublimated monotony [that] cocooned the two of them" (*ET* 207). Jane Lewty makes a similar observation about the BBC of Woolf's time, calling it a "mass subliminal persuasion—a nullifying blanket of sound" ("Virginia Woolf" 160). This is a statement Bowen herself could have written and with which she likely would agree. Throughout her novel, visual and aural technologies stifle sensation: they "cocoon" and "blanket" characters in a mind-numbing sensory vacuum. The prefix "sub" that appears in the phrase "sublimated monotony" (*ET* 207) positions Eva and Jeremy, along with the society of which Bowen writes, "under": under the influence, under the spell, and caught in the undertow of the "age of speed."

In *Eva Trout*, Bowen and her characters struggle to coexist with technology and adapt to the rapidly "*Changing Scenes*" and sensescapes of modernity. The advent of the age of speed brought intense uncertainty about how technology would impact society and the senses. If, as Maud Ellmann says, Eva is "an intruder from the novel of the future," she brings with her bleak visions, and uninviting sounds, of what is to come (216). Technologies plague Bowen's novel, severing connections among humans and with the larger sensorium. Bowen describes a society whose quest for knowledge—the proverbial apple—cannot be fulfilled by the so-called higher senses of sound and sight alone, nor through aural and visual technologies. Instead, these technologies overpower people, places, and the pages of her book. *Eva Trout* voices a fear of technological takeover that, in many ways, has been realized. The novel exhibits an irony that contemporary readers can appreciate: the more plugged in we are, the less sentient we sometimes feel; the more technologically connected we are, the more disconnected we often become. By portraying the dangers of technological overload, and the aural and visual imposition that accompanies it, Bowen not only captures the angst of an earlier era but also continues to caution readers against technology's insatiable allure and damaging effects.

Afterword

In "Flying Over London," Virginia Woolf describes the experience of flying in an airplane and all the sensuous lushness it evokes. The airplane grants access to a multisensuous space of "fleeciness, substance, and colour," where sensations cannot be easily divided or categorized (Woolf, "Flying" 170). Woolf wonders at "All the colours of pounded plums and dolphins and blankets and seas and rain clouds crushed together, staining—purple, black, steel, all this soft ripeness seethed about us" ("Flying" 170). Though she describes her experience in remarkable detail, at the end of Woolf's essay, we learn that the flight never happened, that the airplane she was supposed to board never made it off the ground.

Woolf's imaginary airplane ride provides a glimpse of the role technology played in modernist re-imaginings of the senses. Woolf's vision illuminates, too, how liberating a sensuous space not controlled by sensory hierarchies and conventions can be. H.D., Loy, Woolf, and Bowen dare to imagine new sensory worlds, where bodies and senses are less constricted. Throughout their novels, technologies and diverse sensing bodies—human and animal—serve as muses for rethinking sensation and perception. Emerging from the uniquely situated modernist period, with its influx of sensory technologies and its ever-moving sensing bodies, their work repositions the senses and reclaims masculine-coded technologies. In instances where the senses and technologies are not so easily shifted, as in Elizabeth Bowen's *Eva Trout*, their work illustrates the stifling creative and social conditions that result.

Together, H.D., Loy, Woolf, and Bowen rewrite narratives not only about the senses but also about modernism. In *Women of the Left Bank*, Shari Benstock notes that women's names do not often appear on the literary manifestos that circulated during the modernist period and that "[t]hose called by Modernist manifestos to rally to the cause were men" (379). This left the impression that modernist women's writing was not politically inflected or that their motivations for writing did not merge. *Dissensuous Modernism* shows otherwise. The pluralistic sensory projects of these women writers, whose approaches differ but whose aims intersect, asks modernist scholars to turn our eyes to the long-overlooked value of the so-called feminine senses and to open our ears to the too-often-unheard voices of female dissent. H.D. and Loy illustrate the danger of a sexist, ocularcentric worldview; Woolf exposes how aural control can lead to sensory habituation and exclusion; and Bowen depicts a world where both of the so-called masculine senses of sight and sound hold too much sway. The disorienting form of each novel is distinct, but the reasons for this disorientation differ in important ways. While *HERmione* reflects a new sensuous consciousness through stream of consciousness prose, *Insel* illustrates the clash between masculine and feminine sensation through a jarring Surrealist narrative. While *Between the Acts* brings together disparate genres, just as it does disparate senses and sensuous beings, *Eva Trout* draws on disembodied prose to illustrate society's sensuous deprivation.

In various and visceral ways, H.D., Loy, Woolf, and Bowen evoke synesthesia, the intersensory, and the multisensuous to challenge divisive, often violent, sensory rhetoric. Such rhetoric, as this study has shown, divides through labels like higher and lower, normal and abnormal, desirable and undesirable. H.D., Loy, Woolf, and Bowen work to expose the damage those divisions cause and to encourage unity, not only among the senses but also among seemingly unlike groups of human and non-human actors. In so doing, they form a dissensual community that, unlike their consensual counterparts, does not establish norms but showcases the value of feminine, queer, and non-normative sensory experiences. By revaluing those sensory experiences, they also revalue the beings behind them. They feature women, queer, nonhuman characters, as well as characters with disabilities, to portray sensory diversity and rewrite limiting sensory narratives. Together, they remind us to smell, taste, and touch modernism anew.

Notes

Introduction

1. Simply put, dissensus is "a conflict between *sense* and *sense*" (Rancière 139). In a shorter definition, Rancière explains that dissensus "aims to produce an effect of strangeness in order to engender an awareness of the underlying reasons of that strangeness, which is tantamount to suppressing it" (143).

2. Hereafter abbreviated *WS*.

3. Paul Victor de Sèze compares the senses of women and animals in his 1786 manuscript, *Recherches Phisiologiques* [sic] *et Philosophiques sur la Sensibilité, ou La Vie animale,* which loosely translates as *A Physiological and Philosophical Enquiry on Sensitivity, or Animal Life.* One compelling example of the perceived link between women's and animals' sensory organs comes from classical philosophy, which conceived of the uterus as "a kind of animal, endowed with powers of movement and its own sense of smell" (*CA* 69). Because of this, when women fainted, physicians would place unpleasant incense near their nose and pleasant incense near their vagina to try to coax the uterus—susceptible to movement and migration, as animals are—back into place.

4. Conor goes on to argue, however, that modernist women also subverted scopic power dynamics, repurposing specular technologies to challenge their status as "woman-object" and remake themselves as spectacular subjects (18).

5. Hereafter abbreviated *CA*.

6. Somerset Maugham echoes this sentiment, declaring, "In the West we are divided from our fellows by our sense of smell. The working man is our master, inclined to rule

us with an iron hand, but it cannot be denied that he stinks. . . . I do not blame the working man because he stinks, but stink he does" (qtd. in Orwell 161). For more on smell's divisiveness and denigration, see Jones, esp. pp. 391–99.

7. Howes and Classen explain that "standard psychological and neuroscientific accounts of [synaesthesia] hold it to be a rare neurological condition that causes an affected individual to experience such 'irrational' sensory associations as tastes being linked to sounds or the letters of the alphabet having colours" (*WS* 11). They hold that "[v]iewing synaesthesia as either a pathology or a gift, misses the key ways in which it is socially elaborated," the ways "cross-modal connections [are] generally shared by all humans" (*WS* 153).

8. Classen attributes the perceived outmoded nature of synesthesia to scientific studies that concluded there were no predictable patterns for sensory confluence. Such studies, she suggests, "seemed to emphasize the idiosyncratic, illusory nature of sensory correspondences" (*CA* 112).

9. For instance, "The tactile tables of the Futurists," Howes and Classen argue, were shorn of touch and "transformed into visual icons" (*WS* 28).

10. Max Nordau, to his credit, maintained that men were just as susceptible to synesthesia and hysteria as women.

11. Each of these technologies were invented in the latter half of the nineteenth century but came into popular use in the early decades of the twentieth century: the telephone was invented in 1854 and popularized in the 1910s; the X-ray was invented in 1895 and in mainstream use by 1925, and the hearing aid was invented 1898 and popularized in the 1920s and 1930s.

12. It is worth noting, too, that not all city-goers were averse to the sounds of technology, which had long been associated with progress. A *New York Times* article from 1920 recounts a Japanese diplomat's visit to New York City and his first impression of the city's sounds. While at first shocked, he later celebrated the city's noisiness, proclaiming that noise "was the thing which announced civilization" (Chenery 13). As if supporting the diplomat's comment, editors placed an advertisement for "The Magic Ear," the "newest aid to hearing," on the same page as the article.

13. Koch himself boasted that "the blackbird and song thrush sang more beautifully" in Britain than in Germany (qtd. in Guida 304).

14. I discuss each of these technologies in more detail in chapters 1 and 2.

15. See "The Classical Version: Making It New through Technology" in the introduction to Scott's *In the Hollow of the Wave*.

16. Seminal studies about Joyce's feminism (or lack thereof) include Suzette A. Henke and Elaine Unkeless, *Women in Joyce* (1982); Bonnie Kime Scott, *Joyce and Feminism* (1984); Sandra M. Gilbert and Susan Gubar, "Sexual Linguistics: Gender, Language, Sexuality" (1985); and Susan Stanford Friedman, *Joyce: The Return of the Repressed* (1993).

17. Susan Stanford Friedman observes a similar phenomenon in Joyce's *Portrait of the*

Artist as a Young Man, where "the move to male modernism coincides with the production of woman as representation—as, that is, a signifier originating in and functioning for the subject who is male" ("(Self)Censorship" 33).

18. H.D.'s half-brother, Eric, was also an astronomist, and H.D. often helped him and her father study and chart the movement of the stars. Adalaide Morris describes H.D.'s father as "an almost pragmatic embodiment of the cultural conflation of the words 'scientific,' 'objective,' and 'masculine,'" qualities that H.D. resists or subverts in her writing (201). For more on the scientific projects of H.D.'s brother, father, and grandfather and an illuminating discussion of how their work influenced hers, see Morris, "Science and the Mythopoetic Mind: The Case of H.D."

19. H.D. went on to star in several cinematic productions created by the POOL Group, the name she, Bryher, and Kenneth Macpherson gave themselves.

20. The camera also influenced Loy's poetry, which she first published in the little magazine *Camera Work*. In *Mina Loy, Twentieth-Century Photography, and Contemporary Women Poets*, Linda A. Kinnahan skillfully traces the camera's influence on Loy's aesthetic.

21. Bowen traveled widely throughout her life and held visiting positions at the University of Wisconsin, Vassar College, Bryn Mawr, and the American University in Rome. For more on Bowen's travels, see Patricia Laurence, *Elizabeth Bowen: A Literary Life*.

22. During and after WW1, scientists publicly criticized the use of poison gas and other technologies of war (Bud 117), while engineers advocated for more socially responsible technologies (Wisnioski 5). In *Engineers for Change: Competing Visions of Technology in 1960s America*, Matthew Wisnioski argues that Americans, in particular, experienced a relatively peaceful relationship with technology from the end of WW2 until the mid-1960s (3). However, engineer Samuel C. Florman asserts that "The Golden Age of Engineering" ended a decade earlier (6, 11). Florman blames novelists, in particular, for helping to spread anti-technological messages. He maintained, "The world of high arts has always had running through it a strain of hostility toward technology. But since 1950, the fastidiousness of the few has become the revulsion of the many" (Florman 17).

23. For example, in Pomona, California, residents' garage doors often opened, unprompted, during missile launches at a nearby test site. This malfunction caused residents to worry that the reverse could also be true and that, by pushing a seemingly innocuous button, they might launch a nuclear missile (Hong 61).

Chapter 1. H.D., Synesthete

An early version of this chapter appeared as "H.D., ~~Imagiste~~ Synesthete," in *Legacy: A Journal of American Women Writers* 35.2 (2018) published by the University of Nebraska Press. Reprinted by permission.

1. Nordau believed that, in the face of twentieth-century technological advancement, "the [d]egenerates must succumb" and that their proclivity to hysteria and neurasthenia would "end their race" (541). In contrast, "healthy . . . more vigorous" individuals, Nordau maintained, "will rapidly and easily adapt themselves to the conditions which new inventions have created in humanity" and will birth "a new generation to whom it will not be injurious to . . . be constantly called to the telephone . . . [or] to live half their time in a railway carriage or in a flying machine" (541).

2. For a more detailed discussion of "common sense" and "dissensus," see the introduction.

3. For French feminist theory on gender and the sensuous body, see Hélène Cixous, "The Laugh of the Medusa"; Luce Irigaray, *An Ethics of Sexual Difference* and *Elemental Passions*; and Julia Kristeva, *Powers of Horror: An Essay on Abjection*. For historical perspectives, see Constance Classen, *The Color of Angels*.

4. The women's suffrage movement, in particular, fueled both social and sensuous change, and the sound of women's voices in the political and public spheres promised further sensory disruption. Such feminism gave birth to subversive figures like the flapper, the quintessential example of the hyper-visible modern woman. For more on the flapper, feminine visibility, and woman as modernist spectacle, see Liz Conor, *The Spectacular Modern Woman: Feminine Visibility in the 1920s*. For more on the sensuous nature of the women's suffrage movement, see Mary Chapman, *Making Noise, Making News: Suffrage, Print Culture, and U.S. Modernism*. For more on the fear of sensory contamination and the regulation of gendered bodies in the modernist period, see Tim Armstrong, *Modernism: A Cultural History*, esp. 65–78 and *Modernism, Technology, and the Body: A Cultural Study*; Tim Edensor, "The Social Life of the Senses: Ordering and Disordering the Modern Sensorium"; and Michael Trask, *Cruising Modernism: Class and Sexuality in American Literature and Social Thought*.

5. See, for instance, Vincent Sherry, *Ezra Pound, Wyndham Lewis, and Radical Modernism* (1993); Daniel Tiffany, *Radio Corpse: Imagism and the Cryptaesthetic of Ezra Pound* (1995); and Rebecca Beasley, *Ezra Pound and the Visual Culture of Modernism* (2010).

6. For more on the relationship between Pound and Gourmont see, Richard Sieburth, *Instigations: Ezra Pound and Remy de Gourmont* (1978) and Scott Hamilton, *Ezra Pound and the Symbolist Inheritance* (2014). See also Pound's tributes to Gourmont in *The Fortnightly Review* (1915) and *Poetry: A Magazine of Verse* (1916), as well as his translation of Gourmont's *Physique de l'Amour*, or *The Natural Philosophy of Love* (1922), which includes Pound's infamous "Translator's Postscript."

7. A survey of titles alone illustrates this impulse: Rachel Ann Connor, *H.D. and the Image*; Christina Walter's *Optical Impersonality: Science, Images, and Literary Modernism*; and Charlotte Mandel, "Magical Lenses: Poet's Vision beyond the Naked Eye" and "The Redirected Image: Cinematic Dynamics in the Style of H.D."

8. Eugenia's experiences mirror those of H.D.'s mother, Helen. William Carlos Wil-

liams, "a frequent guest" at H.D.'s home, said that Helen "led a harassed life and showed it . . . the five children were all over the house . . . When they were at dinner and Mrs. Doolittle noticed that the Professor wished to speak, she would quickly announce: Your father is about to speak! Silence immediately ensued . . . It was a disheartening process" (qtd. in Guest 17).

9. For autobiographical accounts of H.D.'s vexed relationship with Pound, see *End to Torment: A Memoir of Ezra Pound* and *Bid Me to Live: A Madrigal*.

10. As discussed earlier, Pound followed Gourmont, who associated sound and hearing with the uneducated masses. H.D.'s association of Pound with onomatopoeic sounds would have been particularly irksome to the male poet, who saw such noises as symbols of the prosaic.

11. The phrase "eyesight alone" comes from the art critic Clement Greenberg, who proclaimed, in 1958, "The human body is no longer postulated as the agent of space in either pictorial or sculptural art. Now it is eyesight alone . . ." (qtd. in Jones 411). For more on Greenberg's theories on art and sensation, see Caroline Jones, *Eyesight Alone: Clement Greenberg's Modernism and the Bureaucratization of the Senses*.

12. This admonishment appears several times in the novel. Pound often made a similar condemnation when H.D. would "begin to cast her mystic spell and wander into the abstract, the vague" (Guest 24).

13. Posters and newspapers often featured the image of a suffragette strapped to a table or chair while a male doctor loomed over her, forcing a feeding tube down her throat or nose. For more on force-feeding and the suffragette movement, see Carolyn P. Collette, *In the Thick of the Fight: The Writing of Emily Wilding Davison, Militant Suffragette*, esp. chapter 4: "Paying the Price: Militancy, Prison, and Violence."

14. Susan Stanford Friedman calls *HERmione* "a gestational narrative of artistic awakenings that serves vividly as a microcosm of this larger pattern in [H.D.'s] work. The story is really two stories, a birth and a rebirth, in which the second undoes the first to suggest the endlessness of the process of becoming" (101). Likewise, Charlotte Mandel refers to Hermione's "period of illness" as "an incubation that helps her emerge to a fuller sense of herself" (309).

15. Nordau was especially critical of artists who elevated the lower senses, and he seemed to have a particular vendetta against smell. He proclaimed, "Smellers among degenerates represent an atavism going back, not only to the primeval period of man, but infinitely more remote still, to an epoch anterior to man" (503). After years of evolution, he contended, "the sense of smell has scarcely any further share in man's knowledge" and "in order to inspire a man with . . . abstract concepts by scents alone . . . his frontal lobe must be depressed and the olfactory lobe of a dog substituted for it" (503). Nordau identifies Emile Zola, specifically, as one such artist who "shows at times an unhealthy predominance of the sensations of smell in his consciousness" (502). Zola is, in Nordau's terms, "a high-class degenerate" (501).

16. See Brain, *The Pulse of Modernism*, esp. "Sensory Fusion," where he highlights the primitivism that informs this kind of thinking. Brain observes that many modern artists, such as the painter Edvard Munch and the English writer Edward Carpenter, "believed there was a positive correlation between synesthesia and the shaman in so-called primitive societies, as well as between homosexuals and other 'deviant' sexual orientations" (192).

Chapter 2. "choked by a robot!": Technology, Gender, and the Battle of the Senses in Mina Loy's *Insel*

1. Hereafter abbreviated *BM*.

2. Hereafter abbreviated *I*.

3. Elizabeth Arnold discovered the typescript of *Insel* in 1990 in the Beinecke Library (*I* xiii–xix). In 2013, Sarah Hayden discovered an alternate ending to *Insel*, titled "The Visitation of Insel" (*I* xix). This chapter primarily examines the original text and ending.

4. Hayden notes that Loy was familiar with Max Nordau's thoughts on degeneracy as well, which she encountered while drafting what would become *Insel* (*Curious Disciplines*, 189).

5. Hereafter abbreviated *MTB*.

6. See Pound's "Translator's Postscript" in his translation of Remy de Gourmont's *The Natural Philosophy of Love*.

7. While men sometimes sought out the Steinach operation as a way to enhance their masculinity, Steinach was also used in male-to-female gender reassignment surgeries, of which Lili Elbe) was among the earliest recipients. For more on Steinach, see Tim Armstrong, "Making a Woman," in *Modernism, Technology, and the Body: A Cultural Study*, esp. pp 164–76; and Pamela L. Caughie, "The Temporality of Modernist Life Writing in the Era of Transsexualism: Virginia Woolf's *Orlando* and Einar Wegener's *Man Into Woman*."

8. Hereafter abbreviated *CW*. In this essay, Marinetti claims to have invented "tactile art," despite his earlier statements in "Tactilism: A Futurist Manifesto" (1921), where he asserts the opposite. "I have never claimed to have invented tactile sensibility," he writes, "other writers and artists have previously been vaguely aware of Tactilism" (*CW* 375). For more on the controversy surrounding the origin of Tactilism and Marinetti's public disagreements on the topic, see *Critical Writings*, 496–97, note 20.

9. In "Down with the Tango and Parsifal!" which Marinetti addresses to "some cosmopolitan women friends who give tango tea-dances and who Parsifalize themselves," Marinetti renounces the softness of feminine dances, with their "niceties of the skin" (*CW* 132, 133). He warns, "The epidemic of swaying back and forth is gradually spreading worldwide . . . and is threatening to infect all races, turning them into jelly" (*CW* 132). As a remedy, Marinetti advocates for "the brutality of violent possession and the fine fury of

a muscular dance that's uplifting and invigorating . . . *To Hell with the tango*! For the Sake of our Health, our Strength, our Will, and our Virility" (*CW* 133). Marinetti "envisioned a future in which human bodies would merge with machines . . . [in which] a mechanical evolution would refine mankind's bodies and minds" (Parmar 75).

10. Sexologist Thomas Laqueur traces a history that values semen as a source of heat and energy, from the seventeenth century, when "impregnation . . . becomes metaphorically the igniting of women" to the late nineteenth century, when some scientists believed that "'the thriving of girls' after marriage was a result of 'the absorption of semen'" (qtd. in Armstrong, *MTB* 147–48).

11. Miller goes on to say that Insel "literally *embodies* the predicaments of the artist during this time . . . As 'fluoroscope,' [Insel] sees through the bodies he turns to painting, yet what he 'sees through' above all is his own disappearing presence as an artist. In rendering himself as the 'fluoroscope' he has become, Insel at the same time exposes the remains of an avant-garde on the verge of disappearance: a few pale, floating organs rendered luminously visible by the very machinery that has dissolved their organic 'context'" (208).

12. Armstrong identifies a similar trend in Loy's poetry as well. "'The Oil in the Machine,'" he writes, "is typical of Loy's poems on the mechanical in that it resists any simple equation of body and machine. Rather than the machine serving as a desirable replacement for the body, it is a reductive version of the body, while the body is a machine which fails to perform" (*MTB* 115).

13. Interestingly, in the premodern era, the eye was thought to produce seminal fluid, along with the sex organs and brain. Women's organs were thought to produce less potent seminal fluid, which left them with weaker vision and intellect (Classen, *The Deepest Sense* 76).

14. Loy celebrates Curie and her achievements in the poem "Gertrude Stein." For more on Curie in relation to Loy, see Colbey Emmerson Reid, "Glamour and the 'Fashionable Mind.'"

15. Even other modernist women poets, like Amy Lowell, who wrote through and about the female body, found Loy's poetry distasteful. Loy's editor, Alfred Kreymborg, explains, "In an unsophisticated land [like America, Loy's] sophistry, clinical frankness, sardonic conclusions, wedded to a madly elliptical style scornful of the regular grammar, syntax and punctuation . . . horrified our gentry and drove our critics into furious despair" (488). Such radical writing, Kreymborg intonates, was wasted on a "Puritanical" American public that was not ready for the likes of Loy (488).

16. From chapter XLI in "Visitation."

17. For more on the fourth dimension and the influences of Christian Science and New Thought on Loy's work, see Lara Vetter, *Modernist Writings and Religio-scientific Discourse: H.D., Loy, and Toomer.*

18. David Bate identifies the urge to conceal male desire and control the visual in Luis

Buñuel and Salvador Dali's short film *Un Chien Andalou* [An Andalusian Dog] (1929), where Buñuel "sadistically blinds [a] woman with a razor" (Bate 158). Bate describes this scene as "the symbolic castration of the woman's right to see," as well as "a defense on the part of the surrealist against his own desire being *seen*" (Bate 157, 158).

19. Notably, Mrs. Jones's reaction to Insel's X-raying differs from Hans Castorp's reaction to being X-rayed in Thomas Mann's *Magic Mountain.* Sara Danius notes the "noninvasive penetration of Castorp's interior" and stresses that Castorp "had not felt anything at all during the penetration" (80). Castorp's nonreaction illustrates the role gender plays in one's experience of technology.

20. For further discussion of "organoleptic disorganization," see chapter 3, " . . . A zoom severed it": Sensory Interruptions in Virginia Woolf's *Between the Acts.*"

21. For more on Loy's theory of interpretation, see Lucia Re, "Mina Loy and the Quest for a Futurist Feminist Woman."

Chapter 3. " . . . A zoom severed it": Sensory Interruptions in Virginia Woolf's *Between the Acts*

1. Hereafter abbreviated *BA.*

2. Leonard Woolf's note at the beginning of *Between the Acts* verifies that "the MS of this book had been completed, but had not been finally revised for the printer, at the time of Virginia Woolf's death" (2). In the edition from which I work, Leonard Woolf added italics to distinguish the narrative from the play. For an edition of the novel based on the final typescript as Woolf herself left it, see *Between the Acts: The Cambridge Edition of the Works of Virginia Woolf,* edited by Mark Hussey.

3. See Armstrong, *Modernism: A Cultural History* for a discussion of the various ways modernist men arm themselves against the outer world of sensation. For instance, Armstrong references Freud's "protective shield," which serves to "de-amplify" sensation, and Lewis's "disinterested" art, which avoids "attending to its perceptual process" (Armstrong, *Modernism: A Cultural History* 93–94).

4. Not all critics view Woolf's relationship with technology positively. Jane Lewty, for instance, observes that the ceaseless sounds of radio may have exacerbated Woolf's mental distress. Lewty insightfully posits that "Woolf may have felt bombarded by a medley of voices compiled not only from the deepest recesses of her mind, but from the intrusive sounds of radio" (163). Woolf herself made negative comments about technology, though it is important to note that she made many of these comments during the war, about technologies that were particularly destructive.

5. Sensory historian David Howes makes a similar observation about the airplane, suggesting that the sensuous and perceptual change it invites has the power to inspire social and political change: "Looking down on earth from a plane made the geographic bordered dividing countries seem insignificant—there were no borders in the sky. It

was, indeed, hoped by many that 'with the new aerial age will come a new internationalism' as people flew from one country to another, dissolving physical and cultural barriers" (5).

6. For more on the significance of eating in Woolf's works, see Lisa Angelella, "The Meat of the Movement: Food and Feminism in Woolf"; and Vicki Tromanhauser, "Eating Animals and Becoming Meat in Virginia Woolf's *The Waves*."

7. In this way, Mrs. Manresa contrasts with characters like Jane, the kitchen maid, and Mrs. Sands, the cook, whose roles as domestic working-class cooks and caretakers are hidden behind closed doors. Mrs. Sands, in particular, is tied to and limited by her position. Her personal desires and opinions go unnoticed, as when the narrator notes, "What it meant to Mrs. Sands, when people missed their trains, and she, whatever she might want to do, must wait, by the oven, keeping meat hot, no one knew" (*BA* 25).

8. See, for instance, Angela Frattarola, "Recording the Soundscape: Virginia Woolf's Onomatopoeia and the Phonograph," in *Modernist Soundscapes: Auditory Technology and the Novel*; Pamela L. Caughie, "Virginia Woolf: Radio, Gramophone, Broadcasting," in *The Edinburgh Companion to Virginia Woolf*; Caughie, ed., *Virginia Woolf in the Age of Mechanical Reproduction*; Jane Lewty, "Virginia Woolf and the Synapses of Radio," in *Locating Woolf: The Politics of Space and Place*; and Adriana Varga, *Virginia Woolf and Music*. For more on modernism and sound, see Sam Halliday, *Sonic Modernity: Representing Sound in Literature, Culture and the Arts*; Shelley Trower, *Senses of Vibration: A History of the Pleasures and Pain of Sound*.

9. This is not to say, however, that Woolf's opinion of the BBC was entirely negative. Caughie points out that many of Woolf's negative comments about the BBC were made during times of war and that Woolf's feelings about the broadcast company are more nuanced than critics often imply (Caughie 344–45). For more on Woolf and the BBC, see Randi Koppen, "Rambling Round Words: Virginia Woolf and the Politics of Broadcasting."

10. Resa, in Italian, means to "yield" or to "surrender productivity" ("Resa").

11. Adolphi posits, "Though her name can sound like a punishing allusion to her ability to excite a man to erection, it also has additional connotations. The word 'raze,' a near homonym of the final two syllables of 'Manresa,' indicates demolition" (445).

12. See, for instance, Melba Cuddy-Keane, "Virginia Woolf, Sound Technologies, and the New Aurality"; and Bonnie Kime Scott, "The Subversive Mechanics of Woolf's Gramophone in *Between the Acts*," in *Virginia Woolf in the Age of Mechanical Reproduction*, edited by Pamela L. Caughie.

13. Interestingly, in the seventeenth century, some believed that the "elision of the air" created sound. Consider, for instance, these early references to elision, from 1626 and 1660, respectively: "The Cause given of Sound, that it should be an Elision of the Air (whereby, if they mean anything, they mean Cutting or Dividing, or else an Attenuating of the Air) is but a Terme of Ignorance" and "The Production and Modula-

tion of the Voice by the Elision of the Air" ("Elision"). Another obscure definition of elision as "A breaking (so as to make a gap) by mechanical force" seems even more relevant to Woolf's work, though the *OED* notes that this definition is "scarcely recognized in English use" ("Elision").

14. When Woolf was a child, her father, Leslie Stephen—known for his love of mountaineering and botany—took Woolf and her siblings on nature walks, to the Natural History Museum, and to the Regent's Park Zoo. Woolf records many of these outings in her letters and diaries (Scott, *In the Hollow*, 48–53). The Stephen family library reflected the family's interest in plant and animal life and included books on botany, insects, and natural history, as well as an autographed copy of Darwin's *The Origin of Species*, which Woolf valued highly (Scott, *In the Hollow*, 45). Woolf also valued the work of female scientists in the fields of botany and biology, as reflected in her fondness for the agricultural entomologist Eleanor Anne Ormerod (Scott, *In the Hollow*, 62–70).

15. For further discussion of animals in Woolf, see Bonnie Kime Scott, *In the Hollow of the Wave*, especially chapter 5: "Crossing the Species Boundary"; Vicki Tromanhauser, "Animal Life and Human Sacrifice in Virginia Woolf's *Between the Acts*"; and Adriana Varga, "Music, Language, and Moments of Being," in *Virginia Woolf and Music*.

Chapter 4. Sensory Dystopia: Stifling Sounds, Sights, and Technologies in Elizabeth Bowen's *Eva Trout*

1. See Allan Hepburn's introduction to *Listening In: Broadcasts, Speeches, and Interviews*, for an overview of Bowen's radio and film writing. For more on the climate of the BBC's Third Programme during Bowen's tenure there, see Kate Whitehead, *The Third Programme: A Literary History*. For an insightful discussion of how Bowen conceives of radio in her postwar novels, see Emily Bloom, *The Wireless Past: Anglo-Irish Writers and the BBC, 1931–1968*.

2. Bowen attributes these varying attitudes, in part, to age. She says that she retained "an enthusiastic naivety with regard to transport," which she shares with many of her characters, as a result of not being "born into the age of speed" (*Pictures* 41, 42).

3. See, for instance, Elizabeth C. Ingelsby, "'Expressive Objects': Elizabeth Bowen's Narrative Materializes"; Patrick W. Moran, "Elizabeth Bowen's Toys and the Imperatives of Play"; Jacquelyn Rose, "Bizarre Objects: Mary Butts and Elizabeth Bowen"; and Eluned Summers-Bremner, "Dead Letters and Living Things: Historical Ethics in *The House in Paris* and *The Death of the Heart*."

4. Hereafter abbreviated *ET*.

5. Ironically, technologies of transmission may thwart listeners from developing, rather than help them develop, communication skills. For example, Lewty notes that "habitual radio listening may enfeeble the refined process of finding words for oneself, as interruptions are more readily absorbed" ("Virginia Woolf" 160).

6. For a gendered reading of Eva's lack of language, see Harriet S. Chessman, "Women and Language in the Fiction of Elizabeth Bowen." Chessman suggests that Eva and other Bowen characters like her "represent . . . unarticulated and inchoate femaleness" and "hint at the larger silence all women share within culture" (71).

7. As Kate Lacey explains in *Feminine Frequencies*, the radio often served as a friend to women, especially housewives who were isolated from the outside world. A popular German radio slogan read, "If you don't want to be alone, invite the world into your home!" (qtd. in Lacey 32).

8. For more on how Bowen strategically planned speeches to combat her speech impediment during BBC broadcasts, see Hepburn, "Acoustic Modernism," esp. 146. Woolf, too, notes Bowen's speech impediment. See *The Diaries of Virginia Woolf*, vol. 4.

9. Radio also evoked fear through its nearness. According to Stephen Kern, radio (and film) created "a growing sense of unity among people formerly isolated by distance" and this "proximity . . . generated anxiety—apprehension that the neighbours were seen as getting a bit too close" (qtd. in Lewty "Virginia Woolf" 149). Of course, this is not to suggest that radio was viewed only negatively. Cohen et al. note that some modernists (like F. T. Marinetti) thought of radio as liberating, others as productively unifying, and still others as dangerously homogenizing (5).

10. For more on the connection between radio and the occult, see Jeffery Sconce, "Wireless Ego: The Pulp Physics of Psychoanalysis," esp. pp. 33–49.

11. See *Listening In: Broadcasts, Speeches, and Interviews* for four of Bowen's "plays for the air."

12. Elsewhere in Bowen's oeuvre, as David Trotter notes of *To the North*, the telephone is more productive, providing queer or marginalized characters with a sense of community (82). Trotter calls this phenomenon "a foretaste of telephony's Facebook effect" (72).

13. Maren Linett links Eva's perceived asexuality with her "handicap," noting that sexuality is often denied women with disabilities (*ET* 61; "Seeing" 473). For more on disability and sexuality, see Linett, *Bodies of Modernism: Physical Disability in Transatlantic Modernist Literature*, esp. chapter 1, "Mobility and Sexuality," and Rosemarie Garland-Thomson, *Extraordinary Bodies: Figuring Physical Disability in American Culture and Literature*, esp. chapter 2, "Theorizing Disability: Feminist Theory, the Body, and the Disabled Figure."

Works Cited

Adolphi, Andrea. "Luncheon at the 'Leaning Tower': Consumption and Class in Virginia Woolf's *Between the Acts*." *Women's Studies*, vol. 34, 2005, pp. 439–59.

Ahmed, Sara. "Orientations: Toward a Queer Phenomenology." *GLQ: A Journal of Lesbian and Gay Studies*, vol. 12, no. 4, 2006, pp. 543–74.

Angelella, Lisa. "The Meat of the Movement: Food and Feminism in Woolf." *Woolf Studies Annual*, vol. 17, 2011, pp. 173–95.

Armstrong, Tim. *Modernism: A Cultural History*. Polity, 2005.

———. *Modernism, Technology, and the Body: A Cultural Study*. Cambridge UP, 1998.

Arnold, Elizabeth. Afterword. *Insel*. By Mina Loy, Melville House, 2014, pp. 169–76.

Ayers, David. "Mina Loy's *Insel* and Its Contexts." *The Salt Companion to Mina Loy*, edited by Rachel Potter and Suzanne Hobson, Salt, 2010, pp. 221–47.

Bate, David. *Photography and Surrealism: Sexuality, Colonialism, and Social Dissent*. Palgrave Macmillan, 2004.

Beasley, Rebecca. *Ezra Pound and the Visual Culture of Modernism*. Cambridge UP, 2010.

Bennett, Andrew, and Nicholas Royle. *Elizabeth Bowen and the Dissolution of the Novel: Still Lives*. St. Martin's, 1995.

Benstock, Shari. *Women of the Left Bank: Paris 1900–1940*. U of Texas P, 1986.

Bergerson, Andrew Stuart. "Listening to the Radio in Hildesheim, 1923–53." *German Studies Review*, vol. 24, no. 1, February 2001, pp. 83–113.

Bissell, David. "Vibrating Materialities: Mobility-Body-Technology Relations." *Area*, vol. 42, no. 4, 2010, pp. 479–86.

Bloom, Emily. *The Wireless Past: Anglo-Irish Writers and the BBC, 1931–1968*. Oxford UP, 2017.

Bowen, Elizabeth. *Eva Trout, or Changing Scenes*. Anchor, 2003.

———. "Third "Programme." *Listening In: Broadcasts, Speeches, and Interviews*, edited by Allan Hepburn, Edinburgh UP, 2010, pp. 203–8.

———. *Pictures and Conversations*. Alfred A. Knopf, 1974.

Bowler, Rebecca. *Literary Impressionism: Vision and Memory in Dorothy Richardson, Ford Madox Ford, H.D. and May Sinclair*. Bloomsbury, 2016.

Brain, Robert Michael. *The Pulse of Modernism: Physiological Aesthetics in Fin-de-Siècle Europe*. U of Washington P, 2015.

Brown, Spencer Curtis. Foreword. *Pictures and Conversations*. By Elizabeth Bowen, Alfred A. Knopf, 1974.

Bud, Robert. "Modernity and the Ambivalent Significance of Applied Science: Motors, Wireless, Telephones, and Poison Gas." *Being Modern: The Cultural Impact of Science in the Early Twentieth Century*, edited by Robert Bud et al., UC London P, 2018, pp. 95–129.

Burke, Carolyn. *Becoming Modern: The Life of Mina Loy*. Farrar, Straus, Giroux, 1996.

———. "The New Poetry and the New Woman." *Coming to Light: American Women Poets in the Twentieth Century*, edited by Diane Wood Middlebrook and Marilyn Yalom, U of Michigan P, 1985, pp. 37–57.

Butsch, Richard. "Crystal Sets and Scarf-Pin Radios: Gender, Technology, and the Construction of American Radio Listening in the 1920s." *Media, Culture, & Society*, vol. 20, 1998, pp. 557–72.

Cariani, Peter. "To Evolve an Ear: Epistemological Implications of Gordon Pask's Electrochemical Devices." *Systems Research*, vol. 10, no. 3, 1993, pp. 19–33.

Carsen, Rachel. *Silent Spring*. Mariner, 2002.

Caughie, Pamela L. "Audible Identities: Passing and Sound Technologies." *Humanities Research*, vol. 16, no. 1, 2010, pp. 91–109.

———. Introduction. *Virginia Woolf in the Age of Mechanical Reproduction*, edited by Pamela L. Caughie, Garland, 2000, xix–xxxvi.

———. "The Temporality of Modernist Life Writing in the Era of Transsexualism: Virginia Woolf's *Orlando* and Einar Wegener's *Man Into Woman*." *Modern Fiction Studies*, vol. 59, no. 3, 2013, pp. 501–25.

———. "Virginia Woolf: Radio, Gramophone, Broadcasting." *The Edinburgh Companion to Virginia Woolf and the Arts*, edited by Maggie Humm, Edinburgh UP, 2010, pp. 332–48.

Chapman, Mary. *Making Noise, Making News: Suffrage, Print Culture, and U.S. Modernism*. Oxford UP, 2014.

Chenery, William L. "The Noise of Civilization." *New York Times*, February 1, 1920, 13.

Chessman, Harriet. "Women and Language in the Fiction of Elizabeth Bowen." *Twentieth-Century Literature*, vol. 29, no. 1, Spring 1983, pp. 69–85.

Chinn, Sarah E. "Feeling Her Way: Audre Lorde and the Power of Touch." *GLQ: A Journal of Lesbian and Gay Studies*, vol. 9, no. 1–2, 2003, pp. 181–204.

Christensen, Liz. *Elizabeth Bowen: The Later Fiction*. Museum Tusculanum, U of Copenhagen, 2001.

Cixous, Hélène. "The Laugh of the Medusa." *Chicago Journals*, vol. 1, no. 4, Summer 1976, pp. 875–93.

Classen, Constance. "The Witch's Senses: Sensory Ideologies and Transgressive Femininities from the Renaissance to Modernity." *Empire of the Senses: The Sensual Cultural Reader*, edited by David Howes, Berg, 2005, pp. 70–84.

———. *The Color of Angels: Cosmology, Gender and the Aesthetic Imagination*. Routledge, 1998.

———. *The Deepest Sense: A Cultural History of Touch*. U of Illinois P, 2012.

Clements, Elicia. "Virginia Woolf, Ethel Smyth, and Music: Listening as a Productive Mode of Social Interaction." *College Literature*, vol. 32, no. 3, Summer 2005, pp. 51–71.

Cohen, Debra Rae. "Intermediality and the Problem of the *Listener*." *Modernism/modernity*, vol. 19, no. 3, September 2012, 569–92.

Cohen, Debra Rae, et al. "Introduction: Signing On." *Broadcasting Modernism*, UP of Florida, 2009, pp. 1–7.

Collette, Carolyn P. *In the Thick of the Fight: The Writing of Emily Wilding Davison, Militant Suffragette*. U of Michigan P, 2013.

Connolly, Claire. "(Be)Longing: The Strange Place of Elizabeth Bowen's *Eva Trout*." *Borderlands: Negotiating Boundaries in Post-colonial Writing*, edited by Monika Reif-Hüsler, Rodopi, 1999, pp. 135–44.

Connor, Rachel. *H.D. and the Image*. Manchester UP, 2004.

Connor, Steven. *Beckett, Modernism, and the Material Imagination*. Cambridge UP, 2014.

———. "Literature, Technology, and the Senses." *The Cambridge Companion to the Body in Literature*, edited by David Hillman and Urika Maude, Cambridge UP, 2015, pp. 177–96.

Conor, Liz. *The Spectacular Modern Woman: Feminine Visibility in the 1920s*. Indiana UP, 2004.

Corcoran, Neil. *Elizabeth Bowen: The Enforced Return*. Oxford UP, 2004.

Corn, Joseph J. "Making Flying 'Thinkable': Women Pilots and the Selling of Aviation, 1927–1940." *American Quarterly*, vol. 31, no. 4, Autumn 1979, pp. 556–71.

Cuddy-Keane, Melba. "Virginia Woolf, Sound Technologies, and the New Aurality." *Virginia Woolf in the Age of Mechanical Reproduction*, edited by Pamela L. Caughie, Garland, 2000, pp. 69–96.

Cunningham, Anne. "Negative Feminism and Anti-Development in Virginia Woolf's *The Voyage Out*." *Virginia Woolf: Writing the World*, edited by Pamela L. Caughie and Diana L. Swanson, Liverpool UP, 2015, pp. 180–85.

Danius, Sara. *The Senses of Modernism: Technology, Perception, and Aesthetics*. Cornell UP, 2002.

Deleuze, Gilles, and Félix Guattari. *A Thousand Plateaus: Capitalism and Schizophrenia*. Translated by Brian Massumi, U of Minnesota P, 1987.

Des Jardins, Julie. *The Madame Curie Complex: The Hidden History of Women in Science*. Feminist, 2010.

DuPlessis, Rachel Blau. "The Authority of Otherness." *H.D.: The Career of that Struggle*, Indiana UP, 1986, pp. 31–59.

Edensor, Tim. "The Social Life of the Senses: Ordering and Disordering the Modern Sensorium." *A Cultural History of the Senses in the Modern Age*, vol. 6, edited by David Howes, Bloomsbury, 2014, pp. 31–54.

"Elision." Def. 2. *Oxford English Dictionary Online*. Oxford UP, 2016.

Ellmann, Maud. *Elizabeth Bowen: The Shadow Across the Page*. Edinburgh UP, 2003.

———. "Endings." *The Cambridge Companion to Ulysses*, edited by Sean Latham, Cambridge UP, 2014, pp. 95–109.

"Et cetera." Def. 2d. *Oxford English Dictionary Online*. Oxford UP, 2016.

Finnegan, Margaret. *Selling Suffrage: Consumer Culture and Votes for Women*. Columbia UP, 1999.

Fisher, Marc. *Something in the Air: Radio, Rock, and the Revolution That Shaped a Generation*. Random House, 2007.

Flint, Kate. "Sounds of the City: Virginia Woolf and Modern Noise." *Literature, Science, Psychoanalysis, 1830–1970: Essays in Honour of Gillian Beer*, edited by Helen Small and Judy Tate, Oxford UP, 2003, pp. 181–94.

Florman, Samuel C. *The Existential Pleasures of Engineering*. 2nd ed. St. Martin's Griffin, 1996.

Frattarola, Angela. *Modernist Soundscapes: Auditory Technology and the Novel*. UP of Florida, 2018.

Friedman, Susan Sandford, editor. *Joyce: The Return of the Repressed*. Cornell UP, 1993.

Friedman, Susan Stanford. *Penelope's Web: Gender, Modernity, H.D.'s Fiction*. Cambridge UP, 1990.

———. "(Self)Censorship and the Making of Joyce's Modernism." *Joyce: The Return of the Repressed*, edited by Susan Stanford Friedman, Cornell UP, 1993, pp. 21–58.

Gaedtke, Andrew. "From Transmissions of Madness to Machines of Writing: Mina Loy's *Insel* as Clinical Fantasy." *Journal of Modern Literature*, vol. 32, no. 1, Fall 2008, pp. 143–62.

Gallagher, Jean. "H.D.'s Distractions: Cinematic Stasis and Lesbian Desire." *Modernism/modernity*, vol. 9, no. 3, 2002, pp. 407–22.

Garland-Thomson, Rosemarie. *Extraordinary Bodies: Figuring Physical Disability in American Culture and Literature*. Columbia UP, 1997.

Garrington, Abbie. *Haptic Modernism: Touch and the Tactile in Modernist Writing*. Edinburgh UP, 2013.

Gilbert, Sandra M., and Susan Gubar. "Sexual Linguistics: Gender, Language, Sexuality." *New Literary History*, vol. 16, 1985, pp. 515–43.

Gregg, Melissa, and Gregory J. Seigworth, editors. *The Affect Theory Reader*. Duke UP, 2010.

Griffin, Roger. *Modernism and Fascism: The Sense of a Beginning under Mussolini and Hitler*. Palgrave Macmillan, 2007.

Guest, Barbara. *Herself Defined: The Poet H.D. and Her World*. Doubleday, 1984.

Guida, Michael. "Ludwig Koch's Birdsong on Wartime BBC Radio: Knowledge, Citizenship, and Solace." *Being Modern: The Cultural Impact of Science in the Early Twentieth Century*, edited by Robert Bud et al., UC London P, 2018, pp. 293–310.

H.D. *Bid Me to Live*. UP of Florida, 2015.

———. *End to Torment: A Memoir of Ezra Pound*. New Directions, 1979.

———. *HERmione*. New Directions, 1981.

———. "Notes on Thought and Vision." *Notes on Thought and Vision & The Wise Sappho*, City Lights, 1982, pp. 17–53.

Halliday, Sam. *Sonic Modernity: Representing Sound in Literature, Culture and the Arts*. Edinburgh UP, 2013.

Hamilton, Scott. *Ezra Pound and the Symbolist Inheritance*. Princeton UP, 2014.

Hayden, Sarah. *Curious Disciplines: Mina Loy and Avant-Garde Artisthood*. U of New Mexico P, 2018.

———. Introduction. *Insel*. By Mina Loy, Melville House, 2014, pp. ix–xxxii.

Hayles, N. Katherine. "Voices out of Bodies: Audiotape and the Production of Subjectivity." *Sound States: Innovative Poetics and Acoustical Technologies*, edited by Adalaide Morris, U of North Carolina P, 1997, pp. 74–96.

Harris, Laurel. "Hearing Cinematic Modernism in the 1930s: The Audiovisual in British Documentary Cinema and Virginia Woolf's *Between the Acts*." *Literature & History*, vol. 21, no. 1, Spring 2012, pp. 61–75.

Henke, Suzette A., and Elaine Unkeless. *Women in Joyce*. U of Illinois P, 1982.

Henning, Michelle. "Don't Touch Me (I'm Electric): On Gender and Sensation in Modernity." *Women's Bodies: Discipline and Transgression (Sexual Politics)*, edited by Jane Arthurs and Jean Grimshaw, Cassell, 1999, pp. 17–47.

Hepburn, Allan. "Acoustic Modernism: BBC Radio and *The Little Girls*." *Textual Practice*, vol. 21, no. 1, 2013, pp. 143–62.

———. Introduction. *Listening In: Broadcasts, Speeches, and Interviews*, edited by Allan Hepburn, Edinburgh UP, 2010, pp. 1–23.

Hertel, Ralf. "Senses in Literature: From the Modernist Shock of Sensation to Postcolonial and Virtual Voices." *A Cultural History of the Senses in the Modern Age*, vol. 6, edited by David Howes, Bloomsbury, 2014, pp. 173–94.

Holman, Brett. *The Next War in the Air: Britain's Fear of the Bomber, 1908–1941*. Routledge, 2016.

Hong, Sungook. "Man and Machine in the 1960s." *Techne*, vol. 7, no. 3, Spring 2004, pp. 49–77.

hoogland, renée c. *Elizabeth Bowen: A Reputation in Writing*. New York UP, 1994.

Hovanec, Caroline. *Animal Subjects: Literature, Zoology, and British Modernism*. Cambridge UP, 2018.

Howes, David. Introduction: "Make It New!"—Reforming the Sensory World. *A Cultural History of the Senses in the Modern Age*, vol. 6, edited by David Howes, Bloomsbury, 2014, pp. 1–30.

———. "Charting the Sensorial Revolution." *Senses in Society*, vol. 1, no. 1, 2006, pp. 113–28.

———. "Scent, Sound, and Synesthesia: Intersensoriality and Material Culture Theory." *The Handbook of Material Culture*, edited by Christopher Y. Tilley, Sage, 2006, pp. 161–72.

Howes, David, and Constance Classen. *Ways of Sensing: Understanding the Senses in Society*. Routledge, 2015.

Ingelsby, Elizabeth C. "'Expressive Objects': Elizabeth Bowen's Narrative Materializes." *Modern Fiction Studies*, vol. 53, no. 2, Summer 2007, pp. 306–33.

Irigaray, Luce. *An Ethics of Sexual Difference*. Continuum, 1993.

———. *Elemental Passions*. Routledge, 1992.

Jacobs, Karen. *The Eye's Mind: Literary Modernism and Visual Culture*. Cornell UP, 2001.

Jay, Martin. *Downcast Eyes: The Denigration of Vision in Twentieth-Century French Thought*. U of California P, 1994.

Johnston, Georgina. "H.D. and Gender: Queering the Reading." *The Cambridge Companion to H.D.*, edited by Nephie J. Christodoulides and Polina Mackay, Cambridge UP, 2012, pp. 63–75.

Jones, Caroline A. *Eyesight Alone: Clement Greenberg's Modernism and the Bureaucratization of the Senses*. U of Chicago P, 2006.

Jütte, Robert. *A History of the Senses: From Antiquity to Cyberspace*. Translated by James Lynn, Polity Press, 2005.

Kinnahan, Linda A. *Mina Loy, Twentieth-Century Photography, and Contemporary Women Poets*. Routledge, 2017.

Koppen, Randi. "Rambling Round Words: Virginia Woolf and the Politics of Broadcasting." *Broadcasting in the Modernist Era*, edited by Matthew Feldman, Erik Tonning, and Henry Mead, Bloomsbury Academic, 2014, pp. 137–54.

Kreymborg, Alfred. *A History of American Poetry: Our Singing Strength*. Tudor, 1934.

Kristeva, Julia. *Powers of Horror: An Essay on Abjection*. Columbia UP, 1984.

Lacey, Kate. *Feminist Frequencies: Gender, German Radio, and the Public Sphere*. U of Michigan P, 1996.

Laity, Cassandra. *H.D. and the Victorian Fin de Siècle: Gender, Modernism, Decadence.* Cambridge UP, 1996.

Lawrence, Patricia. *Elizabeth Bowen: A Literary Life.* Springer International, 2019.

Lee, Hermione. *Elizabeth Bowen: An Estimation.* Vision, 1981.

———. *The Novels of Virginia Woolf.* Holmes and Meier, 1977.

Lewty, Jane. "Virginia Woolf and the Synapses of Radio." *Locating Woolf: The Politics of Space and Place*, edited by Michael H. Whitworth and Anna Snaith, Palgrave McMillian, 2007, pp. 148–63.

———. "'What They Had Heard Said Written': Joyce, Pound, and the Cross-Correspondence of Radio." *Broadcasting Modernism*, edited by Cohen et al., UP of Florida, 2009, pp. 199–220.

Linett, Maren Tova. *Bodies of Modernism: Physical Disability in Transatlantic Modernist Literature.* U of Michigan P, 2017.

———. "Modes of Dislocation: Jewishness and Deafness in Elizabeth Bowen." *Studies in the Novel*, vol. 45, no. 1, Summer 2013, pp. 259–78.

—-. "'Seeing, Seeing, Seeing': Deafness, Knowledge, and Subjectivity in Elizabeth Bowen." *Twentieth-Century Literature*, vol. 59, no. 3, Fall 2013, pp. 465–93.

Loy, Mina. "Feminist Manifesto." *The Lost Lunar Baedeker*, edited by Roger Conover, Farrar, Strauss, Giroux, 1996, pp. 153–56.

———. "Gertrude Stein." *Modernism: An Anthology*, edited by Lawrence Rainey, Wiley-Blackwell, 2005, pp. 433–37.

———. *Insel.* Melville House, 2014.

———. *The Lost Lunar Baedeker.* Edited by Roger Conover, Farrar, Strauss, Giroux, 1996.

———. "Psycho-Democracy." *Little Review: A Quarterly Journal of Art and Letters*, vol. 8, no. 1, Autumn 1921, pp. 14–19.

Magot, Céline. "Prosthetic Goddesses: Ambiguous Identities in the Age of Speed." *Textual Practice*, vol. 27, no. 1, 2013, pp. 127–42.

Mandel, Charlotte. "Magical Lenses: Poet's Vision beyond the Naked Eye." *H.D. Woman and Poet*, edited by Michael King, National Poetry Foundation, 1986, pp. 301–17.

———. "The Redirected Image: Cinematic Dynamics in the Style of H.D." *Literature/ Film Quarterly*, vol. 11, no. 1, 1983, pp. 36–45.

Marcus, Laura. "Into the Heart of Darkness: *Between the Acts.*" *Virginia Woolf, Writers and Their Work*, 2nd ed., Northcote House in association with the British Council, 2004, pp. 175–86.

Marinetti, F. T. *Critical Writings.* Edited by Günter Berghaus, translated by Doug Thompson, Farrar, Straus, and Giroux, 2006.

———. *The Futurist Cookbook.* Translated by Suzanne Brill, Bedford Arts, 1989.

Massumi, Brian. *Parables for the Virtual: Movement, Affect, Sensation.* Duke UP, 2002.

Merleau-Ponty, Maurice. *Sense and Non-Sense.* Translated by Hubert L. Dreyfus and Patricia Allen Dreyfus, Northwestern UP, 1964.

Miller, Tyrus. *Late Modernism: Politics, Fiction, and the Arts between the World Wars*. U of California P, 1999.

Minow-Pinkney, Makiko. "Virginia Woolf and the Age of Motor Cars." *Virginia Woolf in the Age of Mechanical Reproduction*, edited by Pamela L. Caughie, Garland, 2000, pp. 159–82.

Mitchell, David T., and Sharon L. Snyder. *Narrative Prosthesis: Disability and the Dependencies of Discourse*, U of Michigan P, 2000.

Mooney, Sinéad. "Unstable Compounds: Bowen's Beckettian Affinities." *Elizabeth Bowen: New Critical Perspectives*, edited by Susan Osborn, Cork UP, 2009, pp. 13–33.

Moran, Patrick W. "Elizabeth Bowen's Toys and the Imperatives of Play." *Erie-Ireland*, vol. 46, no. 1–2, Spring/Summer 2011, pp. 152–76.

Morris, Adalaide. "Science and the Mythopoetic Mind: The Case of H.D." *Chaos and Order: Complex Dynamics in Literature and Science*, edited by N. Katherine Hayles, U of Chicago P, 1991, pp. 195–223.

Nordau, Max Simon. *Degeneration*. 5th ed, New York, D. Appleton, 1895.

Orwell, George. *The Road to Wigan Pier*. Camelot, 1937.

Panagia, Davide. *The Political Life of Sensation*. Duke UP, 2009.

Parmar, Sandeep. "Mina Loy's 'Unfinishing' Self: 'The Child and the Parent' and 'Islands in the Air.'" *The Salt Companion to Mina Loy*, edited by Rachel Potter and Suzanne Hobson, Salt, 2010, pp. 71–98.

Paterson, Mark. *The Senses of Touch: Haptics, Affects, and Technologies*, Bloomsbury, 2007.

Pickering, Andrew. "Beyond Design: Cybernetics, Biological Computers, and Hylozoism." *Synthèse* 168, 2009, pp. 469–91.

Pound, Ezra. "Remy de Gourmont." *Fortnightly Review* 104, July–December 1915, pp. 1159–66.

———. "Remy de Gourmont." *Poetry: A Magazine of Verse*, January 1916, pp. 197–202.

———. "Translator's Postscript." *The Natural Philosophy of Love*, by Remy de Gourmont, Collier, 1961, pp. 149–50.

Pridmore-Brown, Michele. "1939–40: Of Virginia Woolf, Gramophones, and Fascism." *PMLA*, vol. 113, no. 3, May 1998, pp. 408–21.

Rancière, Jacques. *Dissensus: On Politics and Aesthetics*. Edited by and translated by Steven Corcoran, Continuum, 2010.

Re, Lucia. "Mina Loy and the Quest for a Futurist Feminist Woman." *The European Legacy: Toward New Paradigms*, vol. 14, no. 7, 2009, pp. 799–819.

Reid, Colbey Emmerson. "Glamour and the 'Fashionable Mind.'" *Soundings: An Interdisciplinary Journal*, vol. 89, no. 3/4, Fall/Winter 2006, pp. 301–19.

"Resa." *Collins Italian Dictionary*. Collins, 2005.

Roberts, Lissa L. "The Death of the Sensuous Chemist: The 'New' Chemistry and the

Transformation of Sensuous Technology." *Empire of the Senses: The Sensual Cultural Reader*, edited by David Howes, Berg, 2006, pp. 106–27.

Rohman, Carrie. *Stalking the Subject: Modernism and the Animal*. Columbia UP, 2008.

Rose, Jacquelyn. "Bizarre Objects: Mary Butts and Elizabeth Bowen." *Critical Quarterly*, vol. 42, no. 1, 2000, pp. 74–85.

Sconce, Jeffery. "Wireless Ego: The Pulp Physics of Psychoanalysis." *Broadcasting Modernism*, edited by Cohen et al., UP of Florida, 2009, pp. 31–50.

Scott, Bonnie Kime. *In the Hollow of the Wave: Virginia Woolf and Modernist Uses of Nature*. U of Virginia P, 2012.

———. *Joyce and Feminism*. Indiana UP, 1984.

———. "The Subversive Mechanics of Woolf's Gramophone in *Between the Acts*." In *Virginia Woolf in the Age of Mechanical Reproduction*, edited by Pamela L. Caughie, Garland, 2000, pp. 97–114.

Serres, Michel. *The Five Senses: A Philosophy of Mingled Bodies*. Continuum, 2008.

Sherry, Vincent. *Ezra Pound, Wyndham Lewis, and Radical Modernism*. Oxford UP, 1993.

Sieburth, Richard. *Instigations: Ezra Pound and Remy de Gourmont*. Harvard UP, 1978.

Smith, Mark M. *Sensing the Past: Seeing, Hearing, Smelling, Tasting, and Touching in History*. U of California P, 2007.

Smith, Patricia Juliana. "'Everything to Dread from the Dispossessed': Changing Scenes and the End of the Modernist Heroine in Elizabeth Bowen's *Eva Trout*." *Hectate*, vol. 35, no. 1, 2009, pp. 228–49.

Summers-Bremner, Eluned. "Dead Letters and Living Things: Historical Ethics in *The House in Paris* and *The Death of the Heart*." *Elizabeth Bowen: New Critical Perspectives*, edited by Susan Osborn, Cork UP, 2008, pp. 61–82.

"synaesthesis, n." *OED*. Oxford UP, 2018, oed.com.

Tazudeen, Rasheed. "Discordant Syllabling: The Language of the Living World in Virginia Woolf's *Between the Acts*." *Studies in the Novel*, vol. 47, no. 4, Winter 2015, pp. 491–513.

Thompson, Trina. "Sounding the Past: The Music in *Between the Acts*." *Virginia Woolf and Music*, edited by Adriana Varga, Indiana UP, 2014, pp. 205–26.

Tiffany, Daniel. *Radio Corpse: Imagism and the Cryptaesthetic of Ezra Pound*. Harvard UP, 1995.

Trask, Michael. *Cruising Modernism: Class and Sexuality in American Literature and Social Thought*. Cornell UP, 2003.

Tratner, Michael. "Why Isn't *Between the Acts* a Movie?" *Virginia Woolf in the Age of Mechanical Reproduction*, edited by Pamela L. Caughie, Garland, 2000, pp. 115–34.

Tromanhauser, Vicki. "Animal Life and Human Sacrifice in Virginia Woolf's *Between the Acts*." *Woolf Studies Annual*, vol. 15, 2009, pp. 67–89.

———. "Eating Animals and Becoming Meat in Virginia Woolf's *The Waves*." *Journal of Modern Literature*, vol. 38, no. 1, Fall 2014, pp. 73–93.

Trotter, David. *Literature in the First Media Age: Britain Between the Wars*. Harvard UP, 2013.

Trower, Shelley. *Senses of Vibration: A History of the Pleasure and Pain of Sound*. Continuum, 2012.

Varga, Adriana, editor. *Virginia Woolf and Music*. Indiana UP, 2014, pp. 74–109.

Vetter, Lara. *Modernist Writings and Religio-scientific Discourse: H.D., Loy, and Toomer*. Palgrave Macmillan, 2010.

Voyce, Stephen. "'Make the World your Salon': Poetry and Community at the Arensberg Apartment." *Modernism/modernity*, vol. 15, no. 4, November 2008, pp. 627–46.

Walsh, Keri. "Elizabeth Bowen and the Futurist Imagination." *Journal of Modern Literature*, vol. 41, no. 1, Fall 2017, pp. 19–39.

Walter, Christina. *Optical Impersonality: Science, Images, and Literary Modernism*. Johns Hopkins UP, 2014.

———. "Getting Impersonal: Mina Loy's Body Politics from 'Feminist Manifesto' to *Insel*." *Modern Fiction Studies*, vol, 55, no. 4, Winter 2009, pp. 663–92.

Whitehead, Kate. *The Third Programme: A Literary History*. Clarendon, 1989.

Wiener, Norbert. "Some Moral and Technical Consequences of Automation." *Science*, vol. 131, no. 3410, May 6, 1960, pp. 1355–58.

Wiesner, Merry E., et al. *Discovering the Western Past: A Look at the Evidence*. Volume II: *Since 1500*. Cengage Learning, 2015.

Wisnioski, Matthew. *Engineers for Change: Competing Visions of Technology in 1960s America*. MIT P, 2012.

Wolfe, Cary. *Animal Rites: American Culture, the Discourse of Species and Posthumanist Theory*. U of Chicago P, 2003.

Woolf, Virginia. *Between the Acts*. Harcourt, 2008.

———. *Between the Acts: The Cambridge Edition of the Works of Virginia Woolf*. Edited by Mark Hussey, Cambridge UP, 2011.

———. *The Common Reader*. Harcourt, 1925.

———. *The Diaries of Virginia Woolf*. Edited by Anne Olivier Bell and Andrew McNeillie, 5 vols., Harcourt Brace Jovanovich, 1984.

———. *Mrs. Dalloway*. Harcourt, 1981.

———. "Flying Over London." *Collected Essays*, vol. 4, Harcourt, Brace and World, 1967, pp. 167–72.

———. "A Letter to a Young Poet." *Collected Essays*, vol. 2, Harcourt, Brace and World, 1967, pp. 182–95.

———. "Oxford Street Tide." *The London Scene: Six Essays on London Life*, edited by Hermione Lee, Daunt, 2013, pp. 17–28.

———. "A Sketch of the Past." *Virginia Woolf: Moments of Being*, edited by Jeanna Schulkind, 2nd ed., Harvest/Harcourt Brace Jovanovich, 1985, pp. 61–159.

Zelazo, Suzanne. "'Altered Observation of Modern Eyes': Mina Loy's Collages and Multisensual Aesthetic." *Senses and Society*, vol. 4, no. 1, 2009, pp. 47–74.

Zizek, Slavoj. *Looking Awry: An Introduction to Jacques Lacan through Popular Culture.* MIT P, 1992.

Index

scholarship, 12; in *HERmione*, 34, 44–47; in *Eva Trout*, 134, 148; in *Insel*, 58, 77–78

H.D. (Hilda Doolittle): *Close Up*, 23; family life of, 23, 163n18, 164–165n8; and film, 19; and optic technology, 23; and the "overmind," 53; *Notes on Thought and Vision*, 53; scholarship on, 33, 165n14

—HERmione: context of, 23, 35; and Frances Josepha Gregg, 34, 41, 48; hapticity in, 34, 44–47; and heteronormativity, 32, 40–41, 52, 54; intersensoriality in, 25, 36, 44–49, 53; and the microscope, 24, 35–36, 38, 50, 52–54; ocularcentrism in, 32, 34, 36–37, 49; and Ezra Pound, 32–34, 39–40; queerness in, 31, 33–34, 43–44; and science, 49, 51, 52; sea life in, 51–53; synesthesia in, 48–51; touch in, 42, 44–48

Harris, Laurel, 103, 115–116

Hayden, Sarah, 57

Hepburn, Alan, 139

Hertel, Ralf, 11, 105

Heteronormativity, 32, 36, 40–41, 52, 54

Higher senses, 3–6, 12, 123, 157. *See also* Distance senses; Masculine senses

Hitler, 24, 26, 58, 114–116. *See also* Fascism; Nazism

Hovanec, Caroline, 27, 121

Howes, David, 3–4, 6, 10, 51, 162n7, 168–169n5

Imagism, 33, 39, 44

Intersensoriality, 8, 10, 12, 34, 159; in works by H.D., 25, 36, 44–49, 53; and in works by Mina Loy, 25, 76; in works by F.T. Marinetti, 61–62; in works by Virginia Woolf, 101, 103, 107, 109, 117, 120. *See also* Sensory integration

Jaensch, E. R., 11

Jellyfish, 50–53

Jones, Caroline A., 8–9, 44

Joyce, James, 20–2, 162–163nn16–17

Jütte, Robert, 4, 6, 36

Kinnahan, Linda A., 57, 67–68, 76–77

Koch, Ludwig, 16

Lewty, Jane, 17, 124, 143, 145, 156, 168n4

Linett, Maren Tova, 139, 143, 153

Logocentrism, 91, 95, 106, 133

Lower senses, 3–6, 109; in artistic works, 10, 22–25, 28, 165n15; in *Between the Acts*, 100, 109; in works by H.D., 30–33, 53; in *Eva Trout*, 150; in

Insel, 55, 68; in the modernist period, 12, 20–25, 28; and technology, 17; and women, 3–6, 72. *See also* Proximate senses

Loy, Mina: and the camera, 20, 57, 68, 77, 163n20; contemporary view of, 72, 167n15; and "electrolife," 88; "Feminist Manifesto," 84; fourth dimension, 73; *Islands in the Air*, 77; "Parturition," 59; "Songs to Joannes," 72; WW2, 67, 92

—Insel: animals in, 81–82, 85–86; electricity in, 57, 63–64, 75, 87; and feminism, 55, 58–59, 67, 88–90; integrationist aesthetics of, 55, 58–59; machines in, 56–57, 62–64, 75–76, 83; and science, 71–75; Surrealist influence on, 24–25, 56–57, 65–66, 71, 83, 159; Surrealist violence in, 67–69, 76–77; touch in, 58, 72, 75–82, 88; X-ray in, 25, 63–64, 77–78

Machines: in *Between the Acts*, 93, 111–112, 124, 127–130; boundaries between humans and, 25, 28, 75–76, 132, 144, 166–167n9; in *Eva Trout*, 119–120; and gender, 35, 56, 62–63, 83; in *Insel*, 56–57, 62–64, 75–76, 83; the threat of, 127–1128, 134–135

Male gaze, 5, 20, 76–77, 83

Marinetti, F. T., 15, 59; "Down with the Tango and Parsifal!," 166–167n9; "Tactilism: A Futurist Manifesto," 166n8; "Tactilism: Toward the Discovery of New Senses," 61. *See also* Futurism: and the senses

Martin, Jay, 11, 68–69, 83

Masculine senses, 2, 4–5, 45, 123, 126, 159. *See also* Distance senses; Higher senses

Megaphone, 25–26, 115–118

Microscope, 17, 20, 23; and H.D., 24–25, 35–36, 38, 50, 52–54

Modernism: and masculine anxiety, 20, 61, 65–66, 168n3; scope of, 13, 29, 130; and sight, 33

Mollusk, 51–52

Mouths, 65, 77, 109–109; as masculine threat, 82–84

Multisensuality, 10; in works by Elizabeth Bowen, 134–135, 147; in works by H.D., 21, 24, 34, 36, 44, 49, 53–54; in works by Mina Loy, 55, 83, 96; in works by Virginia Woolf, 103, 122, 158

Nature: vs. culture, 12, 20, 67, 100; as sensory subversive, 26, 92, 113

Nazism, 11, 67. *See also* Fascism; Hitler

1960s, 35; and modernist scope, 13, 130; fear of technology, 27–28, 127–128, 131, 163n22–23

Smell: animal sense of, 27, 165n15; devaluation of, 7, 9, 30, 32, 51–52, 72; and intersensoriality, 8, 36, 101, 103, 108, 117, 135; lack of, 132–133, 145; in the modernist period, 14, 18; the revaluation of, 2, 16, 22, 25, 46, 54, 56, 73; and social divisions, 7, 99, 161n6; and sensory habits, 104, 118, 124; associations with women, 4, 6, 72, 109, 161n3

Smith, Mark M., 8, 24

Sound: control of, 136–138; distrust of, 146–147; Fascist use of, 26, 114, 116; gendering of, 3, 31–32, 45; as interference, 93–94, 110, 112, 124; and intersensoriality, 9–10, 34, 62, 66, 74–75, 102, 121, 135; and meaning, 84, 95, 105, 109, 111, 115; in modernist scholarship, 2, 11, 17; and nature, 92, 111, 122–123, 134; and new ways of listening, 117, 119–120, 142; privileging of, 130–132, 143, 156–157, 159; and questions of agency, 131, 144; and technology, 14–16, 23 (*see also* Acoustic technology); and touch, 36, 40–41; and transformation, 45–51; early understandings of, 169–170n13; in urban spaces, 14, 99, 162n12; and women, 18, 164n4; and voice, 46, 48–50

Soundscapes, 11, 14, 17, 26, 146; in *Between the Acts*, 103–104, 122, 13; control of, 137–138, 144

Steinach, 61, 63, 166n7

Stream of consciousness, 21, 159

Suffrage, women's, 5, 7, 18, 46, 164n4, 165n13

Surrealists: and the camera, 20, 24–25, 57, 68; and Mina Loy, 24, 56, 65–66, 71, 83, 159; and sight, 69 76–77; and violence against women, 25, 57, 67, 76–78, 167–168n18

Synesthesia: definitions of, 8–9, 162n7; devaluation of, 8–11, 30; in *HERmione*, 48–51; in the modernist period, 10, 17, 162n8, 166n16; revaluation of, 12, 30, 39, 89, 159; and the Symbolists, 9

Taste: devaluation of, 4, 30, 72; and intersensoriality, 53–54, 102, 109, 134; revaluation of, 25, 27, 54, 73, 95; sensory segmentation, 8, 62; and technology, 16; and women, 6, 32, 58, 82, 83–84, 100–101. *See also* Consumption; Eating

Telephone, 164n1; and acoustic interruptions, 93; distrust of, 146; and new ways of listening, 13, 15–16; impact on literary form, 139; and questions of power, 130, 132, 137, 145–146; and women's liberation, 18

Television, 130, 147–148, 155

Touch: absence of, 132, 151–154; aversion to, 79–80; desire for, 141; devaluation of, 4, 6, 30–31, 37, 72, 109; modernist scholarship on, 12; and nonhuman animals, 51, 53; revaluation of, 25, 61, 72, 88; and sensory integration, 42, 44–48, 75, 101–102, 117, 121–122, 134–135; and sight (*see* Hapticity); and technology, 16–17, 132; and violence against women, 40, 76, 78–82 (*see also* Male gaze)

Undine, 50–51

Unisensory worldview. *See* Single-sense paradigm

Vibration, 34, 36, 45, 47–48, 79, 103, 137

Vision. *See* Sight

Visual technology. *See* Optic technology

Wolle, Reverend Francis, 23, 65

Woolf, Virginia: and animals, 26, 99–100, 121–124; and the BBC, 104, 169n9; family life of, 170n14; "Flying Over London," 158; "Letter to a Young Poet," 94; scholarship on, 168n4; on women and domesticity, 169n7; and WW2, 26, 92–95, 115
—Between the Acts: airplanes in, 97–98, 123–124; animals in, 85, 92, 96, 99–100, 115, 121–124, 127; and biopolitics, 92–93, 114; and common sense, 112, 123; context of, 92–95, 168n2; anti-Fascism in, 24, 26, 58, 92–93, 114–117, 126; gramophone in, 93, 97, 110–112, 115, 119–121, 138–139; hybridity in, 93, 102, 121, 140; intersensoriality in, 101, 103, 107, 109, 117, 120, 122; and logocentrism, 91, 95, 106; nature in, 92, 100, 113; and new ways of listening, 115–116, 120, 123–124; and nonsense, 93–94, 96, 105, 115, 123; rural vs urban, 98–99; religion in, 117–119; and sense-making, 93–95, 107–111, 119–120, 125; and sensory habits, 110–111, 113–114, 116, 118–119, 124; sensory performance, 93–95, 108, 110, 114

World War I, 10, 12, 55, 127

World War II, 16; as context for *Between the Acts*, 26, 92–95, 115; as context for *Insel*, 67, 92

X-ray, 17, 20, 23, 162n11; in works by H.D., 38; in works by Mina Loy, 25, 63–64, 77–78

Zelazo, Suzanne, 58, 73–75

Allyson C. DeMaagd is an independent scholar and college success manager at Mid-Shore Scholars.